Imagining India in Modern China

IMAGINING INDIA
IN MODERN CHINA

Literary Decolonization and the
Imperial Unconscious, 1895–1962

GAL GVILI

COLUMBIA UNIVERSITY PRESS   *NEW YORK*

Columbia University Press wishes to express its appreciation for assistance given by the Chiang Ching-kuo Foundation for International Scholarly Exchange and Council for Cultural Affairs in the publication of this book.

Columbia University Press
Publishers Since 1893

New York   Chichester, West Sussex
cup.columbia.edu
Copyright © 2022 Columbia University Press
All rights reserved
Library of Congress Cataloging-in-Publication Data
Names: Gvili, Gal, author.
Title: Imagining India in modern China : literary decolonization and the imperial unconscious, 1895–1962 / Gal Gvili.
Description: New York : Columbia University Press, [2022] | Includes bibliographical references and index.
Identifiers: LCCN 2022000878 (print) | LCCN 2022000879 (ebook) | ISBN 9780231205702 (hardback) | ISBN 9780231205719 (paperback) | ISBN 9780231556125 (ebook)
Subjects: LCSH: Chinese literature—Indian influences. | Chinese literature—19th century—History and criticism. | Chinese literature—20th century—History and criticism. | India—Civilization. | China—Foreign relations—India—History. | India—Foreign relations—China—History.
Classification: LCC PL2274.2.I5 G85 2022 (print) | LCC PL2274.2.I5 (ebook) | DDC 895.109/005—dc23/eng/20220330
LC record available at https://lccn.loc.gov/2022000878
LC ebook record available at https://lccn.loc.gov/2022000879

Columbia University Press books are printed on permanent and durable acid-free paper.
Printed in the United States of America

Cover image: *Autumn in Rajgir.* Copyrights belong to Chang Zheng and Wang Cizhu

For my grandmothers, Ines Gvili and Lea Avrech, who taught
me strength and perseverance

Contents

Acknowledgments

This book represents the end of a long and winding road. I originally had another final destination planned, but then detours presented themselves and I felt compelled to follow them. Sometimes you can't stick to a plan. And I am so happy that I didn't. What began as a dissertation-to-book project slowly crystallized to form a different story. I used two dissertation chapters, and wrote two more, so I could talk about something more important: how Chinese writers turned to India to effect literary decolonization. In this ten-year process, I have had the amazing luck of having the support of many wonderful colleagues, friends, and family members. I am thrilled to thank them here.

I was immensely fortunate to receive graduate training at the Department of East Asian Languages and Cultures at Columbia University. My advisor, Lydia H. Liu, has been a constant source of inspiration. I am grateful to her for having pushed me, since my very first semester, to do new things, to step out of my comfort zone, and to think critically and rigorously about literature. I am also thankful to Shang Wei, Eugenia Lean, and Stathis Gourgouris, my dissertation mentors, for their tireless advice and exemplary scholarship. Gil Anidjar was not only a thoughtful mentor during my years at Columbia but remained a careful and generous reader. We share an obsession with decolonizing Christianity, and it was heartening to discover that I am not alone on this one. I am grateful for Weihong Bao's critical eye and supporting words and letters during and after her stint at Columbia. I also thank

Zvi Ben-Dor Benite, Bob Hymes, Rebecca E. Karl, Dorothy Ko, and David Lurie for their timely advice and encouragement. Haruo Shirane believed in me and made sure I stayed at Columbia to teach after I graduated until I found a tenure-track position. It was a lease on life in the most palpable way and I can't thank him enough. I thank the wonderful friends—now colleagues—I made at Columbia, who made my years there a memorable experience: Sayaka Chatani, Anatoly Detwyler, Yumi Kim, Brian Lander, Liza Lawrence, Myra Sun, Nate Shockey, Brian Tsui, and Sixiang Wang. To Yurou Zhong, my dearest and first friend at Columbia, I owe so much. Thank you dear for years of reading drafts and commiserating.

I consider it a privilege to have joined the faculty of McGill University. I am grateful to my colleagues at the Department of East Asian Studies for their ongoing support and patience, for feedback on my drafts, and for a spirit of collegiality and friendship that keeps our small department strong and forward-facing. I am grateful to Kimberly Chung, Grace Fong, Yuriko Furuhata, Jeehee Hong, Maria Hwang, Rongdao Lai, Tom Lamare, and Robin Yates. At McGill, I also thank Michelle Hartman, Cecily Hilsdale, Poulami Roychowdhury and Jeremy Tai for reading drafts, for coffee and wine, and for taking long walks up Mount Royal with me. I thank my MA students, Hongyang Cai, Weiyu Dang, and Edna Wan, who had contributed research assistantship for the book.

None of this research would have been possible without the help of librarians. I am so very lucky to have had the kind and patient support of Columbia University's CV Starr librarian Chengzhi Wang and McGill East Asian Studies librarian Macy Zheng. I cannot thank them enough for facilitating access to everything I wanted to read. My research has been generously supported by a Columbia University GSAS Travel Grant, as well as research grants from the Fonds de recherche du Québec and the SSHRC. I am thankful for these funds, as they allowed me to research, write, and workshop this book from its initial stages in graduate school to its finalization.

A China-India studies group entered my life in summer 2018. Together with its members I presented at the Association for Asian Studies meeting in New Delhi, and then we took a ten-day trip to Darjeeling to study Chinese-Indian interactions and sites. We have been collaborating ever since and are constantly adding more members, finding more projects to pursue, and writing together. I am grateful to Tansen Sen who first brought us together and always finds ways to fly us out to different parts of the world for meetings even though COVID-19 derailed us for a bit. I also thank my good friend from Columbia, now a collaborator, Arunabh Ghosh, the China-India literature and culture cohort—Adhira Mangalagiri and Krista Van Fliet as well as to Zhang Ke and Cao Yin.

My heartfelt thanks to others who read and commented on this book in parts and in whole, in conferences and otherwise: Yomi Braester, Subho Basu, Harlan Chambers, Tamara Chin, Hyaeweol Choi, Michael Gibbs Hill, Joseph Ho, Stefan Huebener, Melissa Inouye, Clara Iwasaki, Benjamin Kindler, Paul Kreitman, Zhange Ni, Elisheva Perelman, Margaret Tillman, and Ying Qian.

To my dear friends of many years who have kept my spirits up remotely during the months I wrote the larger part of this book, at the height of the COVID-19 pandemic lockdown: Shani Braier-Marcovitch, Reuma Gadassi-Polack, and Shirley Sasson-Ezer—all of you helped more than you will ever know.

I am indebted to my editor, Christine Dunbar, as well as to Christian Winting and Leslie Kriesel for their sound advice and support in the production process of this book. I am grateful to have had Mary Bagg's gentle and masterful copyediting as well. I thank *The Journal of Asian Studies* for allowing me to reprint an earlier version of chapter 2, which appeared in volume 77, no. 1 (2018) as "Pan-Asian Poetics: Tagore and the Interpersonal in May Fourth New Poetry." A section of chapter 3 has previously appeared in *Comparative Literature Studies* volume 58, no. 4 (2021) as "The Woman Question and China-India Horizons in Xu Dishan's *shangren fu*," and I thank the journal for allowing me to use it here.

I dedicate this book to my grandmothers, Ines and Lea—the two strongest women I know, who have created so much under tremendous difficulties. Their life work is my motivation. To my mother and father, Joseph and Esther Gvili, I owe everything. They have supported and made sacrifices their whole lives; the biggest, undoubtably, letting me go and live in another country. I thank them, and I hope and aspire every day to live up to their parenting standard. To my sisters, Michal Gvili and Tal Gvili-Lekner—spending time with you is sheer joy and rejuvenation, and I love you so much.

My husband, Tal Unreich, has been my rock for the past twelve years. Thank you, my love, so much, for coming with me and making all of this possible. Our children, Yoel and Yasmin, make life worth living every day. I thank them for their patience and for all the laughs.

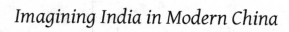

Imagining India in Modern China

Introduction

South-North-South

THE CELEBRATED LITERARY critic Zheng Zhenduo 鄭振鐸 (1898–1958) launched the study of world literature (*Shijie wenxue* 世界文學) in China with his milestone work *An Outline of Literature* (*Wenxue dagang* 文學大綱, 1924– 1927). Zheng modeled his book on popular, contemporaneous English-language textbooks that introduced literary classics hailing from various cultures,[1] but those works dedicated only about ten pages total to Asian literatures, collapsing China, Japan, and India under titles such as "The Mysterious East"[2] and "Sacred Books of the East."[3] Expanding their view, Zheng devoted several substantial chapters to Chinese literary history and wrote at length about Vedic and Buddhist scriptures. He even included an entire chapter on two Sanskrit epics, *Mahabharata* and *Ramayana*—declaring them, for the enlightenment of a new audience of Chinese readers, to be "the oldest literary works in the world."[4]

Essentially, with *An Outline of Literature*, Zheng Zhenduo wrote Asian literature, especially the literatures of China and India, into "world literature."[5] The notion of world literature that informed Zheng's work had been attributed to Johann Wolfgang von Goethe and his famous conversations with Johann Peter Eckermann.[6] Goethe's idea developed a concept pertaining to literatures that form a so-called universal expression of humanity—"by man about man."[7] Its practice in the nineteenth and early twentieth centuries, as seen in the scholarship that Zheng consulted— entailed selecting and anthologizing works in English translation from various cultures and time periods into a new canon known as "literature of the world." Undoing the Eurocentric canonization of world literature, however, was not that easy. Unlike Zheng's chapters on Chinese literature, which rely on primary sources, his engagement with Indian texts was heavily mediated through English-language translations and scholarship. The versions Zheng consulted, along with the English-language studies from which he drew, embedded their discussion of Vedic literature within the parameters of British Orientalism in various ways—from employing terminology such as "The Vedas of the Brahmans"[8] to factual mistakes such as dubbing the *Ramayana* and *Mahabharata* the oldest literary works in the world—mistakes that Zheng then repeated.[9] Thus, despite his effort to defiantly reorient world literature to center what today might be considered literatures from the Global South, Zheng's study is nonetheless marked by the mediation of the Global North and its authority over translation and scholarship.

Zheng Zhenduo's celebration of India as founding Asian world literature is but one example of the story this book tells: how modern Chinese writers imagined India in an ongoing struggle to decolonize literature and undo imperialist knowledge structures. In his seminal *Decolonising the Mind: The Politics of Language in African Literature*, the Kenyan writer and critic Ngũgĩ wa Thiong'o argues that only via a complete abandonment of the colonizer's language—by ceasing to write in English all together—could writers in Africa begin to decolonize the mind. The "fatalistic logic of the unassailable position of English in our literature," Ngũgĩ argued, citing Chinua Achebe here, not only bounds individual minds but also mediates the relationship between colonized peoples, and even their collaborative struggle for anti-imperialist resistance.[10] *Imagining India in Modern China* explores texts that wrestled with their relation to English—an imperial language that could not simply be abandoned as it conditioned and mediated visions of mutual literary horizons.

As a regional ally with long periods of religious and cross-cultural interaction, as well as a shared history of imperialist oppression, India figures prominently in the modern Chinese literary imagination. India's colonization, its struggle for independence, and its leadership in the earliest iteration of Third Worldism inspired Chinese intellectuals and literary figures to develop literary forms that negotiated the legacies of colonialism and charted escape routes from its epistemic brutality. Thus my goal with *Imagining India in Modern China* is twofold.

First, I aim to recuperate a multilayered literary history in which imagining connections to India inspired Chinese writers to envision a new literature in the first half of the twentieth century—an era in which Chinese literary culture was radically reconceptualized. The book begins with the nineteenth-century shared experience of colonial encroachment that facilitated Chinese-Indian camaraderie and moves through the late 1950s, when the motto "India and China are Brothers" became pervasive. It ends on the cusp of the 1962 Sino-Indian War, which abruptly halted a long and fruitful period of collaboration—a rupture that resonates eerily today with waves of ethnonationalism that fuel resurgent border tensions.

This literary history broadens the well-studied trajectory of the formation of modern Chinese literature, a history that traditionally highlights the significance of contacts with Japan. Scholars have demonstrated how interactions with modern Japanese writers, scientists, educators, philosophers, and politicians played a critical role in shaping modern Chinese literature and national cultures.[11] Others have highlighted the significant ways in which intra–East Asian literary contact, focused on the modernized Japanese Empire, contributed to the formation of the region's national literatures.[12] Indebted to and building on these seminal studies, I offer a new perspective by revealing the significance of India for Chinese writers, and by drawing attention to the particular anticolonial characteristics of the Chinese-Indian imagination as it underscores Chinese textual milestones of the first half of the twentieth century.

My second goal with this book is to explore what it means to decolonize literature, by raising the notion of Third World solidarity as a critical problem for comparative literature. With no intention to undermine the foundational studies that frame the birth of modern Chinese literary culture as a project of nation-building,[13] *Imagining India in Modern China* calls attention to anti-imperialist solidarities as fundamentally shaping Chinese literary modernity as well. By showing how China-India connectivity produced new literature and forged regional and transnational networks, this book contributes to the study of South-South allyship, its possibilities and limitations, as ethic and practice.

The regions we now refer to as India and China have shared commercial, religious and cultural exchange beginning as early as the second century CE.[14] The creative renditions of such exchanges in literature, art, and music created a thriving economy of visual art and narrative structures.[15] Cultural exchanges between India and China before the eighteenth century facilitated the spread of Buddhism in China, while the Ming admiral Zheng He's 鄭和 (1371–1433) maritime diplomacy made China a powerful commercial force in the Indian Ocean. But the arrival of the British in the region dramatically redrew the boundaries of interaction between China and India by opening new maritime routes linking Calcutta, Hong Kong, and Shanghai. Through these routes, opium, indentured servants, missionaries, diplomats, and travelers moved between the two countries on an unprecedented scale, often carrying with them textbooks on social sciences, medicine, geography, and literature, printed at newly established printing presses in Malacca and Shanghai. China began to learn about colonial India by reading books and treatises written in English by statesmen and diplomats and disseminated by evangelical missionaries. Prompting a shift in Chinese intellectuals' way of seeing the world as divided into "savage," "half-civilized," and "civilized" states, late nineteenth- and early twentieth-century Chinese-language writings about India adopted from the West a comparative paradigm that aggressively reified a sameness between China and India as "half-civilizations" in dire need of the civilizing mission. This imperialist China-India comparison—presented so often and with such urgency that I call it a "comparative compulsion" (and discuss it in detail in chapter 1)—established an expansive episteme in which to imagine China–India relations. Literature was the realm in which this comparative paradigm flourished—sometimes embraced and sometimes contested—but always bearing the traces of the violent imperial history through which it was created and disseminated. As the chapters of this book will show, spheres of China-India mutual subjugation informed ideals of pan-Asian poetics, studies in comparative religions, folklore and drama, and new theories of socialist realism. From a violent threat of colonial decay grounded in cultural sameness, the comparative paradigm branched out to an investigation of relationality—an imagination of horizons of collaboration that could expose and undo Western imperialism's truth claims and structures of knowledge. Or could it? What, in other words, did it really mean to decolonize literature—or even more broadly, the imagination—and was it even possible?

Decolonization and Literary Studies

Unlike the historical expunging of the agents of Euro-American Empires from the newly founded Republic of India (1947) and the People's Republic of China (1949), untangling the clasp of imperial thought upon the mind remains an ongoing struggle. As recently as early 2021, the Sino-Indian border was still reeling from the resurgence of clashes. Rising ethnonationalist sentiment in both countries was fueled by the respective governments. Imperial-era tropes quickly followed. In China, intellectuals admonished India for stealthily employing British colonial methods in recent skirmishes on the Chinese-Indian border—calling India "a wolf in sheep's skin."[16] The figure of the turban-wearing Sikh-soldier—triggering a collective memory of the Indian sepoys hired to quell the Boxer Uprising (Yihetuan 義和團, 1899–1901)—was invoked in the media time and again.[17]

Studies of national decolonization movements, from the first years of the twentieth century to the decline of the Non-Aligned Movement at the end of the Cold War, often question the movements' transformative value, at times even deeming them a failure. For leaders such as Sun Yat-Sen, Mohandas Gandhi, Mao Zedong, Jawaharlal Nehru, Sukarno, and Gamal Abdel Nasser, it is frequently argued, independence for their countries was only attained by adopting the political model of the nations that formerly colonized them.[18] Yet limiting the definition of decolonization to a struggle for national independence runs the risk of missing out on critical features of anticolonial activities and sentiments, which extend beyond matters of sovereignty to critiques of social and gender equality, cultural transformations, and building alliances with other decolonizing countries.[19]

At the same time, expanding the meaning of decolonization in this way carries certain risks. Since the 2010s, scholars hailing from American history, colonial, and indigenous studies—especially in Australia and North America—have been calling attention to an overuse and abuse of "decolonization." Pioneering this approach, Eve Tuck and K. Wayne Yang have argued that the concept of decolonization is too often used as a catchall that collapses and conflates various projects of social justice and, as such, has the potential to facilitate an erasure of settler responsibility. "When metaphor invades decolonization," they write, "it kills the very possibility of decolonization; it recenters whiteness, it resettles theory, it extends innocence to the settler, it entertains a settler future."[20] Keeping in mind the importance of singling out the violent removal of indigenous populations from their land as distinguishing it from other forms of subjugation—a removal that Patrick Wolfe identifies as colonialism grounded in a "logic of elimination"[21]—particular histories nevertheless compel us to find dynamic frameworks for understanding different colonial projects. Some scholars, like the American historian Nancy Shoemaker, have developed typologies to distinguish between decolonization in the context of settler colonialism and other forms; in Shoemaker's case, between "Extractive Colonialism," "Trade Colonialism" "Imperial Power Colonialism," and "Missionary Colonialism."[22] Writing on contemporary Asian geopolitics, Chen Kuan-hsing demonstrates how, like colonialism, decolonization is subject to shifting historical conditions and redefinitions:

> But in the new context of globalization, the complexity of decolonization goes far beyond the anticolonial, national independence movements of the earlier era. Current decolonization movements must confront the conditions left behind by the cold-war era. It has become impossible to criticize the United States in Taiwan because the decolonization movement, which had to address Taiwan's relation with Japan, was never able to fully emerge from the postwar period; the Chinese communists were successfully constructed as the evil other by the authoritarian Kuomintang regime; and the United States became the only conceivable model of political organization and the telos of progress.[23]

Modern East Asian history, as Chen and others have shown, encompasses various forms of colonialism and settler-colonialism, often simultaneously.[24] For this reason, while *Imagining India in Modern China* fully acknowledges the importance of North American and Australian scholarship on settler-colonialism, I find that the approach to decolonization taken by the Modernity/Coloniality Collective associated with Latin America enables me to engage more productively with the Chinese literary turn to India in the early twentieth century.

Conceptualizing the colonial and decolonial as being not so much juxtaposed as inextricably entangled, recent work by the Modernity/Coloniality Collective expands on some of the pivotal questions that have occupied postcolonial studies since the 1980s.[25] The collective calls our attention to the Peruvian sociologist Aníbal Quijano's framing of the "coloniality of power"[26] as a means to capture the persistence of colonial structures and practices in contemporary culture and geopolitics. The tenacity of "coloniality," to those who seek to pinpoint its explanatory power, emerges from the fact that, unlike colonialism and postcolonialism, which suggest a historical periodization of before and after, coloniality links the past to the present by foregrounding the intersecting power relations and knowledge structures that shape the system of nation-states and global capitalism. Resisting the coloniality of power with decoloniality, write Walter Mignolo and Catherine Walsh, means precisely "the exercise of power within the colonial matrix to undermine the mechanism that keeps it in place requiring obeisance. Such a mechanism is epistemic and so decolonial liberation implies epistemic disobedience."[27] Decoloniality—an exercise of power in epistemic disobedience, is, nonetheless, a work in progress, underscored by the premise that the legacies of imperialism and colonialism continue to define our means of thinking, learning, and writing.[28] Forging fissures and cracks within the colonial matrix of power relies upon knowing that "in decoloniality there is no outside and there is no end to the process."[29]

By examining the ways in which Chinese writers engaged visions of China-India connectivity to chart escape lines from coloniality, this book joins a growing conversation regarding the potential of horizontal solidarity networks from the Global South to pursue the ongoing work of decoloniality—in the past and present. The Global South, a designation used to indicate the position of subjects who hail from formerly colonized areas, recognizes a mutual experience these peoples share, one of suppression transformed to disenfranchisement under global capitalism.[30] As Nour Dados and Raewyn Connell eloquently put it: "The term Global South functions as more than a metaphor for underdevelopment. It references an entire history of colonialism, neo-imperialism, and differential economic and social change through which large inequalities in living standards, life expectancy, and access to resources are maintained."[31]

The world-ordering scheme of North-South dates to the post–World War II era formation of new nation-states; it was solidified with the launching of the Afro-Asian alliance movement at the 1955 Bandung Conference.[32] By the 1980s, the North-South divide had largely replaced the Non-Aligned Movement's term "Third World" in development studies and international relations.[33] The establishment in 1987 of the South Commission, a body consisting of individual representatives from countries of the Global

South, placed a geopolitical emphasis on cooperation between member countries, building on their common experience.[34] In recent years, the analytical lens of the Global South has garnered a particularly powerful position in cultural and literary studies by expanding postcolonial studies' more familiar focus on the dialectics of colonizer and colonized to evaluate the collaboration between subjugated peoples to actively undo the legacies of colonialism and imperialism.[35]

The China-India decolonizing imaginary that I explore in this book contributes to Global South studies in two ways. First, *Imagining India in Modern China* considers the historical period of South-South exchange prior to the 1950s to include earlier anticolonial patterns of solidarity. The anti-imperialist and anticolonial literary imaginary that modern Chinese writers developed by recognizing a mutual experience with India predates the accepted periodization of South-South exchanges and can be traced to the last decades of the Qing dynasty (1644–1912), when literary reform was debated and a thriving print culture in China's port cities facilitated literary experiments at an unprecedented scale. The final years of the Qing also witnessed the rise of a literary sphere that recognized a common history of European imperial violence. This sphere initially developed through encounters between Chinese radical reformers, Philippine exiles, Vietnamese refugees, and Indian freedom fighters, poets, and artists, and took place in Tokyo—then a hub for anarchist, feminist, and anticolonial activism as well as a critical center for Buddhist revivalist work that drew several key late Qing intellectuals.[36] Recognizing this precedent helps us to identify the shifting dynamics with which the China–India connection has been imagined and articulated, variously emphasizing sameness or relationality.

Second, in this book I offer a robust interrogation of the ideals of friendship, solidarity, and brotherhood that remain central to Global South studies today.[37] I do so by shedding light on the contested, yet continued shadow of the North within and upon these interactions, an inescapable mediation built into the history of South-South relations *as* South-South relations. The imperialist knowledge structures that the writers I discuss in this book sought to undo—hailing from British and German philology and Orientalist scholarship and from Anglo American Protestant missionary writings and pedagogy—epistemologically mediated Chinese writers' education and learning about India. In short, while my goal in this book is to explore the project of decolonizing literature, I do not declare that project complete.

Decolonizing literature is not a teleology or a linear narrative that ends with unmediated South-South relationality. Modern Chinese literary texts conjured a horizontal vision of South-South connection, but even at their most optimistic, such texts could never fully disavow the mediating traces of the North—what I call here the "imperial unconscious"—which remained indelibly inscribed within the Chinese literary imagination of China-India connections. The notion of an imperial unconscious is used in different ways in several fields.[38] In my analysis, the imperial denotes the sediments of imperial knowledge structures that can be traced even in anti-imperialist writings.

Consider, for example, the late nineteenth- and early twentieth-century discourse of "Eastern spirituality," arguably an early manifestation of Global South thinking. The idealization of Asia as a source of transcendent redemption arose on the cusp and in the immediate aftermath of World War I, explicitly imagined to counter the devastation wrought by Western materialism's technological prowess. Its tenets—immortalized by "Asia is One," the opening words of the Japanese artist and scholar Okakura Tenshin's 1903 English-language book *Ideals of the East*[39]—claimed a unified sense of cultural identity: shared by the people of the "East" and epitomized in an all-encompassing discourse that collapsed Zen Buddhism, Brahmo Samaj, Japanese minimalist design, Chinese calligraphy, and other religious and artistic forms hailing from East and South Asia. Yet this rejection of Western predatory practices in favor of an Eastern alternative was not created in Asia. Rather, as Peter van der Veer points out, Eastern spirituality was invented in the West before becoming one of the first truly global concepts.[40] The East, as such, was the product of textual and personal exchanges between Chinese, Japanese, and Indian thinkers, artists, and religious revivalists such as Okakura Tenshin, D.T. Suzuki, Swami Vivekananda, Rabindranath Tagore, Feng Youlan, and Taixu, with Anglo-American thinkers and poets like Paul Carus, W. B. Yeats, Walt Whitman, Ezra Pound, and Ernest Fenollosa.[41]

Though the East formed in the West—or, one could argue, an early iteration of the South came into existence in the North—the ideals of an essential Asianness circulated both ways, prompting visions of Pan-Asianism that added new dimensions to Asian spirituality. Rabindranath Tagore (1861–1941), whose exchange with Chinese poets I discuss in chapter 2, is a particularly fascinating figure in this respect. His unprecedented popularity in

Europe and the United States—which climaxed in 1913, when he became the first nonwhite writer to win the Nobel Prize in Literature—hinged upon his being perceived as a representative of Eastern religious traditions. Tagore strategically built on this image, reinforcing it in a Nobel address that proclaimed Asia "the mother of spiritual humanity."[42] What has been too easily forgotten, however, is that Tagore's writings posited Eastern spirituality as a scathing critique not only of Western materialism, but even more so, of the doctrine of nationalism, which he defined as an array of apparatuses used by the modern state to regulate spontaneous interactions within communities. The nation, for Tagore, was an imperialist creation transmitted globally via colonialism and exerting dangerous appeal for Asian reformists and politicians. By contrast, the Eastern spirit, in his writing, spoke not to violent centralization, but to the expressive connections of community structures.[43]

The global discourse on the cultures of Asia as remedy for Western spiritual bankruptcy also informed the China-India imagination of one of China's leading twentieth-century philosophers, Liang Shuming 梁漱溟 (1893–1988). In 1917, Liang taught in the first program of Indian philosophy at Peking University.[44] Four years later, he published a milestone work in the discourse on Asia as essence. Titled *Eastern and Western Cultures and Their Philosophies* (*Dongxi wenhua ji qi zhexue* 東西文化及其哲學, 1921), Liang's work posited three directions of what he defined as human inclination (*luxiang* 路向)—the West, China, and India. The West, Liang wrote, is forward leaning and moved by a desire to dominate nature through science. China, the second direction, works sideways as a will that seeks to be one with nature. And finally, the third direction, India, is a backward movement pointing to Buddhist self-negation. *Eastern and Western Cultures* rejected the Eurocentric developmental model of progress and foretold a leadership position for China and India to save humanity from Western domination. Liang's conceptual framework, however, was not anchored exclusively in China or India but also drew from Henri Bergson's critique of Kantian pure reason. Liang related Bergson's method of intuition—explaining the way humans grasp reality as going *into* an object to become one with it, rather than examining it from a critical distance—to China's tendency to harmonize with nature.[45]

In drawing from Bergson's theory of creative evolution, Liang's work effectively became part of a broader anti-imperialist project taking place across the colonial world in the first half of the twentieth century, spanning the

Americas, Asia, and West Africa. African and Caribbean Francophone communities and Négritude authors and artists adopted Bergson's rebuttal to evolutionary biology and infused their poetry and political proclamation with a "deep conviction of the consanguinity of all forms of life, obliterated in modern consciousness by the positivist classificatory method focused on the empirical differences of things."[46] The renowned poet and leader of the movement for independent Pakistan, Muhammad Iqbal, employed the principles from Bergson's discussion of individuation to frame Sufi metaphysics as a foundation for a revival of Islam.[47] And Egyptian intellectuals in the 1930s, confronted with the new railway system and telegraph brought to colonized Egypt, used Bergson's concepts of *dureé* and intuition to critique technologies of empire and British colonization more broadly as destroying communally based and ethically minded perceptions of time.[48]

Asian spirituality, Sufi revivalism, Négritude's vitalism, and communal temporality—all of these structures of thought and action were premised on a mutual experience of subjugation by the North. Yet, it was also true that these forms of epistemic disobedience emerged and matured in and through conversation with thinkers and texts of the Global North. Oswald Spengler's *The Decline of the West* (1918) was just as important in building the discourse of a redemptive Asia as the pivotal late Qing- and Republican-era thinker Liang Qichao's 梁啟超 (1873–1929) *Impressions of Travels in Europe* (歐游心影錄 *Ouyou xinying lu,* 1920), in which Liang, traveling through the wreckage of World War I, attacks positivism and materialism for robbing human life of all sense of value. The Buddhist thinker D.T. Suzuki and the American Protestant writer Paul Carus coauthored a version of Zen as a "world religion." Infusing "new Buddhism" with evolutionary biology and liberal theology on religious experience, Suzuki then exported a new doctrine back to Japan. There, he helped to launch a reformed version of Buddhism that he declared, simultaneously, a mode of inquiry grounded in religious experience and the national religion of Japan.[49]

All of these intellectual, literary, and cultural projects constituted different means of decolonization, different ways of signaling resistance to imperialist knowledge and technology.[50] They were coauthored by writers and thinkers from Asia, Africa, the Caribbean, Europe, and North and South America, even as they sought to articulate identities that could proudly be proclaimed as exclusively and uniquely Southern. This begs the question: Is it accurate to describe such collective networks of defiance as "Southern theory?"[51] Or rather, what do we lose by framing them that way? The problem with conceptualizing "the Global South" as a geographic, cultural, and political position of enunciation emerges when we examine China–India interactions as imagined in modern Chinese literature.[52] Idealized notions of friendship, bilaterality, or Third Worldism simply collapse. What we find instead are the contested yet indelible traces of Northern/Western mediation. We find the imperial unconscious.

With this concept, I argue for a new way of thinking and talking about decolonization and South-South relations. We need frameworks that equally avoid taking proclaimed solidarity at face value and dismissing it via a Cold War–era rhetoric of "fronts and stooges."[53] We need, furthermore, ways to acknowledge the persistent echo of Northern knowledge and rhetoric, not just as something to rebel against but as a presence that often mediated South-South connections through translation, education, or by providing the literal meeting ground for Southern actors—as in Tokyo, Paris, or New York, where Tagore met with the philosopher Feng Youlan 馮友蘭, (1895–1990) to discuss the meaning of "the East." Epistemically, South-South interaction in the decolonial and even postcolonial eras has never been bilateral, but it is better understood as inevitably, if unevenly, triangulated in various ways— "South-North-South," if you will.

To be clear, recognizing the enduring hold of the imperial unconscious in the minds of those who imagine South-South possibilities does not predetermine or foreclose those possibilities. Instead, it provides a way of acknowledging the undeniable historical realities against which those possibilities were imagined, and which inevitably shaped what could be imagined in ways both subtle and profound. In the Chinese imagination of India in fiction, poetry, translation, and literary criticism, the imperial unconscious worked mainly through the vehicle of the English language, which not only translated Indian literature and thought to Chinese thinkers who more often than not did not read Indian languages, but also furnished the education of those who did.

The Shadow of English

As I begin to investigate the effects of the imperial unconscious on antiimperialist imaginaries, I raise the following question: What happens when one colonial subjectivity willingly links itself in solidarity with another, but can only do so by passing through the language of the colonizer? What, in other words, was the epistemic impact of the English language in mediating and, literally, translating India to China?

These questions underscore the story I tell in this book; they are informed by the sources and texts I am able to consult. The languages I work with, Chinese and English, inevitably shape a narrative that accounts for one side of the China–India literary encounter. Indeed, the study of modern China-India connections would be enhanced by incorporating literary texts in Indian languages. While even a near-native command in one Indian language is hardly enough to cover the extent of Indian writings about China—a sphere that encompasses Hindi, Urdu, Bengali, and Assamese, among other languages—important work on various aspects of these writings has been recently published or is forthcoming, and while writing this book I have benefited tremendously from consulting it.[54] Calling attention to English as a mediator between modern China and India, on the other hand, allows me to investigate the role of translation in what is often imagined as a direct, bilateral, South-South encounter. I aim to shed light on how the English language functioned in the colonial world as what Aamir Mufti termed "a vanishing mediator"—a seemingly neutral imperial and epistemic register through which Asian scriptures and literatures were translated, cementing them as masterpieces of world literature and ushering in literary modernity in Asia. Mufti writes:

> Any critical account of literary relations on a world scale—that is, any account of world literature as such—must thus actively confront and attend to this functioning of English as *vanishing mediator*, rather than treat it passively as neutral or transparent medium, both as a world language of literary expression and as the undisputed language of global capitalism. . . . This is an argument about one distinct line of development from emergent cultural practices in eighteenth-century Europe, a line of development that is embedded in the social life of English as a language of literature, Orientalist scholarship, colonial and postcolonial pedagogy, and imperial administration and power. . . . "World literature" came into being (only) when the cultural system of the modern bourgeois West had appropriated and assimilated—that is, "discovered," absorbed, recalibrated, rearranged, revaluated, reclassified, reconstellated, compared, translated, historicized, standardized, disseminated, and, in short, *fundamentally transformed*—the

widely diverse and diffuse writing practices and traditions of the societies and civilizations of the "East," which extended in the Euro-Occidental imagination from the Atlantic shore of North America to the littoral of the sea of Japan.[55]

Investigating the vanishing mediation of English can help us, for example, to better situate Zheng Zhenduo's attempt to rewrite the canon of world literature by carving a greater space within it for Chinese and Indian classics. As a nonreader/speaker of Indian languages, Zheng Zhenduo indeed had no choice but to consult English scholarship and translations—the mediating role of which on his thinking and writing he did not make apparent in his prose. Yet, by virtue of the desire to be included in a world literature canon as such, Zheng's project, emerging as it did through affinities to Europe's so-called Others, became part of the very translational practice that othered them in the first place.[56]

Studies of translation in colonial contexts have highlighted the ways in which languages are inextricable from the geopolitical power imbalances that set the terms of exchange and transaction.[57] Shaden Tageldin's study of translation in colonial Egypt through what she terms "imperial seduction" sheds important light on a key strategy by which imperialism lodges itself in the mind. For Tageldin, the love that European Orientalist scholars felt for their objects of study—enshrined in arduous learning of languages and scripts of the colonized, robust translation projects from Arabic into European languages, and in their self-designation as custodians of these ancient cultures—seduced the native intelligentsia. Having their culture compared to or, at times, even perceived as superior to European culture, gave the colonized a sense of validation and lured them to love back.[58] The illusion of love on equal terms could render the shackles of cultural imperialism transparent, just as the invention of Eastern spirituality lulled several Asian thinkers by the very imperial logic of cultural supremacy. Republican-era Chinese writers such as Xu Zhimo (徐志摩 1897–1931) and Wang Tongzhao's (王統照 1897–1957) rhetorical framing of India as China's older brother drew from British Orientalists' selective portrayal of Vedic scriptures as embodiments of primordial religion, just as their late Qing predecessors did when they turned to India with the fantasy of finding the hearth of "original" Buddhist culture.[59]

Nineteenth-century Britain was, of course, but one of the countries racing to stake an economic claim to manufacturing and natural resources in

East Asia. France, Belgium, Germany, Russia, the United States, and Japan all became involved in territorial and financial exploits in China. Yet the engagement with the British Empire stands out in modern Chinese history—and not simply because of the brutal nature of the Opium Wars or because Britain pioneered a series of unequal treaties that China was forced to sign, securing privileges therein for European nations, the United States, Russia, and Japan in the early twentieth century.[60] By linking East and South Asia through infrastructure that rendered Calcutta and Canton key sites in imperial itineraries, the British Empire served to mediate India to China and vice versa.[61] During the late Qing, Chinese-language materials about India were almost exclusively translations, often done by missionary-diplomats, from English-language social science textbooks and treatises dedicated to teaching topics such as the European interstate system, the hierarchical stages of civilization theory, and the tenets of evolutionary theory.[62] Missionary journals carried lengthy essays denouncing the superstitious nature, levels of illiteracy, and submissiveness of the people of India. China's reform-minded intellectuals avidly consumed such essays, which warned of a similar fate for China if the latter refused to follow the example of the modernizing Meiji Japan.

In the first decade of the twentieth century—the last years of the Qing dynasty—competing discourses on colonial India permeated Chinese intellectual circles. India was still seen as a cautionary tale by some, but for others, particularly Buddhist revivalists, India began to signify the possibility of a mutual cultural and religious renaissance. For such Chinese intellectuals, like Zhang Taiyan 章太炎 (1868–1936) and Su Manshu 蘇曼殊 (1884–1918), Sanskrit and Pāli studies offered the possibility of approaching Buddhism through the original language of the sutras.[63] But such studies, though often conducted in India or Southeast Asia, still relied on textbooks composed by German and British philologists, and they reflected the prevailing trend of Sanskrit study first envisioned by Sir William Jones (1746–1794), founder of the first institution of Orientalist scholarship, the Asiatic Society, in Calcutta in 1784. Jones pioneered an approach that located grammatical resemblances between Sanskrit and European languages and perceived the latter as the former's descendants. His famed "philologer passage" is credited with launching the discipline of comparative linguistics— with Indo-European studies as its crown jewel.[64] Thanks to Jones and, later, Max Müller's (1823–1900) theory of historical linguistics, an Indo-European language family model that established an evolutionary scheme of language development and grouped Latin, Greek, and Sanskrit within the same family quickly came to dominate all study of Sanskrit and Vedic texts in Britain and Germany. Most importantly, for our purposes, comparative grammar and the Indo-European hypothesis constituted the intellectual framework that Chinese scholars and writers had to work in, work through, and even work against. The language family model, underpinned by the assumed supremacy of Indo-European grammar,[65] deeply informed the fiction and literary criticism of Su Manshu. Yet, as I reveal in chapter 1, even as he subscribed to a Western Orientalist perception of Sanskrit as the most refined language in human history, Su Manshu's fiction actively envisioned a united China–India resistance to the colonial discourse on civilization and progress.

In the late 1920s, as China-India studies were slowly shaping into a new academic pursuit, British and German philological methods continuously informed the field. In 1928, the philologer Alexander von Staël-Holstein, an Estonia-born and University of Halle–trained specialist of Sanskrit and Tibetan, founded the first of its kind Sino-Indian Institute in Beijing. Funded by the Harvard Yenching Institute, and motivated by recent British and German archaeological excavation of ancient manuscripts in Central Asia and Xinjiang, the institute hosted Tibetan, Chinese, American, and European collaborators who employed comparative philology methods to study Sanskrit, Chinese, and Tibetan Buddhist texts[66]—for example, in the reconstruction of ancient Sanskrit texts from later Chinese texts that transliterated Sanskrit with Chinese characters.[67] The formal study of China–India connections thus had its beginnings in Beijing, under the auspices of European archaeology and methods, and American funding.

By the late 1950s, against the backdrop of tightening diplomatic collaboration between the two countries, research into the Tarim Basin–based Tocharian languages by the foremost specialist on China–India connections, Ji Xianlin 季羨林 (1911–2009), compelled him to negotiate the Indo-European paradigm yet again. Defying his teachers, Wilhelm Siegling and Emil Sieg, the two archaeologists who discovered Tocharian scripts and identified these languages as Indo-European, Ji dared to argue that Tocharians are Sino-Indian languages—a hypothesis he spent decades defending. Openly challenging the authority of the Indo-European paradigm through a history of China–India exchange was Ji's way of exposing the far reach of the imperial unconscious and its universalizing of historical linguistics.

Beyond mediating Chinese study of India, English was also the main language from which modern Indian literatures were secondarily translated into Chinese during the first four decades of the twentieth century. While the study of Sanskrit and Pāli slowly gained traction, Chinese students began to study Hindi only in the early 1940s, and Bengali, Urdu, and Tamil were not taught in China before the 1950s,[68] rendering reliance on translations from English a necessity. Xu Dishan 許地山 (1893–1941), a specialist in folklore studies and comparative religion, and Zheng Zhenduo, whose translations of Tagore's poetry took Chinese readerly circles by storm in the early 1920s, both relied on English-language translations to introduce Bengali folktales and publish comparative studies of premodern Chinese and Sanskrit dramas.

Theories of translation tend to focus on only two languages, with the underlying assumption that the translator is versed in the target and source language. Indirect translation, also known as relay translation or mediated translation—that is, "translation of a translated text into a third language"—has received relatively little scholarly engagement, despite its overwhelming pervasiveness across cultures, languages, and histories.[69] The assumption in translation studies that translation happens directly between a source and a target language was established as early as Friedrich Schleiermacher's 1813 widely cited distinction between "domesticating" translations, which draw the source text closer to the target language and culture, and "foreignizing" translations, which pull the reader closer to the source text.[70] Canonical studies in the field continuously focus on a language-to-language trajectory. From Walter Benjamin's celebrated discussion of translation as an act that makes language difference present, to Emily Apter's more recent call to address exchanges involving untranslatability across borders and checkpoints,[71] the historical reality and ubiquity of mediated translation remains a subject that merits further theoretical scrutiny.

Paying closer attention to situations in which translators were not versed in the source language, as was the case for most of the Chinese writers who sought ways to read and disseminate Indian literature and philosophy, raises different types of questions. In a pioneering study of Lin Shu 林紓 (1852–1924)—arguably the most important translator in modern Chinese history, who always relied on assistants in his translation work because he did not read foreign languages—Michael Hill notes: "Rather than frame my readings in terms of a translation's correspondence or fidelity to an original, I

focus on how a translation functions as an intervention in its new context."[72]
Like Hill, I view translation as a historically constitutive process. Moreover,
I find that, unlike contemporary theorists of translation, Chinese translators in the early twentieth century were themselves quite attentive to the
implications of mediated translation (復譯/重譯 fuyi/chongyi), which they dif-
ferentiated from direct translation (直譯 zhiyi). Lu Xun 鲁迅 (1881–1936),
widely considered the father of modern Chinese literature, commented on
the merit of mediated translations in two essays he published in the newspaper Shenbao on June 27 and July 7, 1934. There, Lu Xun argued that mediated translations were simply a necessity. Challenging his interlocutor, the
poet Mu Mutian 穆木天 (1900–1971), who had criticized mediated translations a few days prior and called upon all translators to work with original
languages only,[73] Lu Xun mocked any aspiration for a pristine direct
translation:

> Mu Mutian wants translators who are "self-aware" and commit only their utmost
> strong-suits in producing "definitive" translations; otherwise, [he says], it is bet-
> ter to avoid the work altogether. This is like saying that rather than growing
> thistles and weeds in your garden, it is better if you don't cultivate it at all and
> find an excellent gardener. That way, you could enjoy [only] beautiful flowers for-
> ever. While an idea of the "definitive" exists, "definitive" matters are quite
> rare. . . . What we need to concern ourselves with is to have translators who deal
> with matters by cultivating or by weeding out, and who produce translation
> spheres that are not plagued by disorder and confusion. This is what is called
> [literary] criticism.[74]

Excising uncertainty of any kind from translation was not only impossible,
Lu Xun argued, but stifling, forestalling the very work of discernment and
deciphering at translation's core. Taking my cue from Lu Xun then, rather
than "weeding out" the moments of friction—the thistles and thorns—that
tend to be ignored or devalued in the translation process, I read them as vital
traces of the imperial unconscious left by the mediating language and its
epistemic assumptions. However committed the Chinese writers in this book
were in their efforts to find China–India transcultural connections and thus
make India a point of reference for Chinese literary revival, they could
not help but confront and attempt to negotiate—even through denial—the

looming mediating presence of English and the metanarratives that came with it. Understanding this dynamic reveals one of empire's most enduring, yet unexamined impacts. Far from diminishing the anticolonial critique and fervor with which Chinese writers turned to India, reading Chinese writing during this time for traces of the imperial unconscious only makes clearer the immensely complicated epistemic untangling they undertook.

When Chinese writers imagined connections with India to envision one of the first South-South literary spheres, they did not so much turn away from the North as begin to map out some of its most effective yet invisible forms of domination. Understanding the contours of this dynamic reveals not only the deviousness of imperialism but, no less importantly, makes us aware of the immense task these writers took upon themselves, and appreciative of the cracks they did manage to forge in the knowledge structures that were disseminated to them as axioms.

Structure of the Book

I trace the late Qing rediscovery of India in the context of the Opium Wars and their aftermath in chapter 1, where I highlight the role of Anglo-American Protestant missionaries in mediating knowledge about India to China. Journals essays, study primers, and textbooks in English and Chinese translation compared China to India and declared both to be "half-civilizations" in desperate need of the imperial civilizing mission. Informed by these writings, several key Chinese reformers portrayed India as the ultimate cautionary tale. I focus on one of the most radical voices of late-Qing literary reform, the writer Su Manshu, who challenged the colonial violence of comparison. Associating with Indian and Chinese anarchists in Tokyo, Su Manshu was an ordained Buddhist monk, a translator, and a literary experimentalist. He rejected the comparative logic of "half-civilizations" in favor of anticolonial Buddhist fiction that innovated first-person narration to reflect simultaneously Chinese and Indian voices. My close reading in chapter 1 of the short story "A Record of Seclusion on Sal Beach" (*Suoluo haibin dunji ji* 娑羅海濱遁跡記, 1908) reveals both the potential India offered in imagining resistance to imperialism, as well as the conceptual limits to this imagination, given the role of English in mediating Su's knowledge of India.

Su learned Sanskrit to read Buddhist texts as written, but his training necessarily relied on English-language scholarship that inscribed certain imperialist epistemes within even his discourse of decolonization.

In the second chapter I turn to the 1920s, when Chinese writers began to view India as an essential fount of "Asianness," which at the time they viewed positively as spiritual and inclusive, in comparison with "Western" divisiveness and war-mongering. Poets and literary critics such as Wang Tongzhao, Zheng Zhenduo, Bing Xin 冰心 (1900–1999), and Xu Zhimo drew upon the religious poetry of Rabindranath Tagore to develop new ideas about the function of poetry. I focus on Tagore's 1924 visit to China and the debates regarding "Eastern Spirituality" that his presence and writing prompted. Inspired by partial translations of Tagore from English, which often edited out Tagore's scathing critique of nationalism, Xu Zhimo and Bing Xin delineated an Asian spiritual sensibility that, they argued, manifested in connections between man and the universe. Poetic expression, they wrote, could model itself on such connections and extend them to society via emotional stimulation. Close readings in the chapter include such poetics of emotional stimulation in an unfamiliar poem about Tagore by Xu Zhimo, as well as new readings of Bing Xin's canonical short poems (xiaoshi 小詩). Through these readings, I underscore the selective way in which Chinese poets embraced Tagore's Pan-Asianism, leaving out its more radical critique of nationalism and capitalism.

I examine the fiction and scholarship of the May Fourth writer Xu Dishan in chapter 3. Xu, a teacher of Sanskrit and a scholar of Buddhism, Daoism, and folklore studies, researched Chinese and Indian folklore and drama exchange. Being unversed in modern Indian languages, he translated several books of Indian folktales from English. Although his translations from English could not completely disavow the premises of colonial folklore studies that informed the texts he worked with, Xu's research of Indian folktales radically challenged the fundamentals of folklore studies as they were practiced in China in the 1920s. Rather than anchoring his studies, translations, and short fiction in the then popular understanding of folklore studies as means to extract primordial national characteristics, Xu investigated folklore as a transregional and omnipresent social practice, and as a token of cultural exchange between China and India. In his fiction, where the plots were often located in South China, South and Southeast Asia, Xu developed a narrative form I call "cyclical realism," which rejected European realism's linear developmentalism in favor of a cyclical logic of Buddhist and Hindu reincarnations. Through close readings of two short stories, *The Merchant's Wife* (1922) and *Chun Tao* (1934), I argue that Xu Dishan's cyclical realism not only provides a framework for analyzing the China–India literary sphere in Chinese literature, but also adds new layers to our understanding of realism, the most revered literary genre in twentieth-century China.

In chapter 4 I trace the Chinese translation and performance of one of the first global bestsellers of world literature, the Sanskrit Drama *Śakuntalā and the Ring of Recollection* by the fifth-century poet Kālidāsa. I focus on the celebrated 1956 translation by China's pioneering Indolog, Ji Xianlin, as well as the massively successful Beijing-based theater production in 1957 that was adapted from his translation. I describe the shifting dynamics of the Chinese reception of the drama, at first, through translations based on French and German versions that were informed by European romanticist interpretation of Sanskrit dramaturgy, and then, in Ji Xianlin's erudite translation from the original Sanskrit. Ji's translation came at a time when India was high on China's diplomatic agenda and Chinese Indology was at a historical peak. Ji's translation did not deny the European clout of the play. He cited, for example, Goethe's expressed admiration of Kālidāsa to assert *Śakuntalā*'s position as a milestone of world literature. This, however, did not hinder Ji from grounding his translation in rigorous comparative research into traditions of literary and dramatic mimesis that India and China share. Employing a Chinese-Indian shared mimesis of resonance, Ji made a critical intervention in the literary paradigms of the Mao era. My close readings of Ji's editorial translation choices, and of related essays he wrote on *Śakuntalā*, underscore his effort to contribute to China's revolutionary culture and expand the meaning of socialist realism. Ji posited Kālidāsa's portrayal of reality as the epitome of truthfulness (*zhenshi* 真實). This central tenet of Chinese socialist aesthetics aimed to create a realism that offers an idealized version of reality and thus propels the creation of a socialist society.

In the epilogue I briefly depict the collapse of the 1950s visions of China-India brotherhood in the wake of the 1959 Tibetan Uprising and the Dalai Lama's subsequent asylum in India. The 1962 border conflict, seen very much as a continuation of the 1959 crisis, drastically reshuffled regional geopolitics. The 1962 Sino-Indian War also revealed the difficulties nation-states encountered in maintaining boundaries established under imperialism—difficulties that continue to echo to this day as periodic border skirmishes. Importantly, writers and translators continued to engage India in their work. While India after 1962 no longer inspired multiple visions of an Asian resistance front in Chinese literature as it did from the late Qing and until the late 1950s, individual voices today continue the work of decolonizing literature by mourning, in their writing, the connections that were lost in the colonial past, and the enduring legacy of colonialism in structuring contemporary understandings of each other.

ONE

Unsettling the Violence of Comparison

We need scarcely remark, that what is said regarding India, is for the greater part equally applicable to China.

—"NOTICES OF RECENT PUBLICATIONS," *THE CHINESE RECORDER*, 1875

IN SUMMER 1908, the Tokyo-based Chinese revolutionary journal *People's News* (*Minbao* 民報, 1905–1910) published a story, in two installments, titled "A Record of Seclusion on Sal Beach" (Suoluo haibin dunji ji 娑羅海濱遁跡記).[1] Set in India, the story follows a young melancholic male protagonist who journeys to an idyllic, otherworldly land laced with beaches and dense forests of the evergreen Sal trees sacred to both Hinduism and Buddhism. He joins a group of Indian revolutionaries seeking to strike against the British colonizers, as the narrative combines a plot driven by anticolonial revolutionary ardor with layers of Buddhist allusions and verses drawn from classical Chinese poetry and English Romanticism. "A Record of Seclusion on Sal Beach" was never completed, and its provenance remains dubious. In the preface, the text is presented as a retranslation—more specifically, a Chinese-language translation of an English-language translation of an original Indian work—by the well-known late Qing and early Republican-era writer and translator Su Manshu. Studies have never been able to confirm the source text from which the story was allegedly translated, and this fact, along with other clues in the text itself, have led scholars to conclude that Su was the actual author.[2]

A polyglot, poet, and painter, Su Manshu is nevertheless remembered primarily as China's pioneer of sentimental fiction and the first translator of English Romantic poetry into Chinese (he favored Shelley and Byron). Su Manshu's depiction of characters tormented by unfulfilled love and suffering the vicissitudes of displacement have received much more attention than the unfinished, unidentified "A Record of Seclusion on Sal Beach." But I argue that the story deserves closer consideration because it opens a window onto a critical dynamic shaping early modern Chinese literary reform in the last decades of the Qing dynasty (1644–1912). Calls for literary reform during this period saw new literature in modern vernacular as the crown jewel of civilizational progress—an idea advanced by both Western colonial discourse and Chinese intellectuals and writers seeking to modernize Chinese literature. Their calls for reform intersected temporally and thematically with a burgeoning interest in and engagement with colonial India, a neighbor whose meaning for China was the subject of extensive deliberation. Crucially, Chinese engagement with India at this time was inescapably mediated through an imperial lens, literally and epistemically filtered through English-language translations. Colonial discourse and writing continually framed the two countries as comparable, even as the terms and conclusions of comparison remained contested. Was India a cautionary tale from which China could learn or a grim reminder of a shared backwardness from which neither society would ever escape?

I trace these processes of colonial mediation and comparison in this chapter to show how they shaped—but could not fully determine—Chinese writing about India. Examining both Western and Chinese authors and texts engaged in this comparative compulsion reveals how interaction between China and India was indelibly influenced by, and yet could not be defined by, the colonial relations that facilitated it. As I will show, Western powers may have set the initial terms of comparison, but they did not control them, nor could they control the ways in which Chinese intellectuals would work *within* those terms and wrest from them new meanings—albeit meanings that still bore traces of an imperial unconscious. In this way, I highlight how the violence of comparison, but also its unpredictability, enabled Chinese thinkers to reimagine their relationship with India in ways that both reinscribed and unsettled imperial assumptions.

I begin by establishing the multilayered and intersecting colonial relations connecting China and India during this period, from the increasing circulation of treatises and texts comparing the two, to the tensions and aftermath of the Opium Wars. Throughout, I highlight the pivotal role played by Anglo-American missionaries in forging epistemological links between the two cultures. I then show how the processes of translation and comparison initially driven by what Christian imperialists referred to as "diffusive benevolence" were taken up by Chinese writers, whose literary practices eventually offered new understandings of what China and India might mean to each other. Finally, through a close reading of "A Record of Seclusion on Sal Beach," I show how Su Manshu's employment of the literary form of pseudotranslation sheds new light on the ways Chinese writers grappled with the potentials and pitfalls of their inevitably mediated relationship with India.

Reencountering India in a Century of Imperialism

The nineteenth century was a period of consistent turmoil in China. The first half of the century was unsettled by the government's unsuccessful efforts to regulate its rapidly growing population, factionalism, and the corruption within the imperial court, as well as by a series of natural disasters—droughts, floods, earthquakes, and epidemics. Such conditions were then only exacerbated by the intensifying, increasingly violent exchanges with the British Empire in its relentless attempts to force the Qing into opening ports of free trade along the Chinese coast. By the early years of the nineteenth century, the British Empire's massive opium industry had completely remade the region. The Bay of Bengal became the center of the imperial economy with opium growth centered in the jurisdiction known as the Bengal Presidency and distribution carried out in China. Soldiers and weaponry were mobilized throughout the region. By transporting goods and trading, regulating the movements of laborers, and policing and securing the borders of its zones of control, the opium trade secured a network of British links between East and South Asia, including India, China, and Japan.[3] China's urban centers, already grappling with the aforementioned pressures, were now severely burdened with opium addiction. Culminating in the First and Second Opium Wars (1839–1842; 1856–1860), the opium trade exacted a devastating human cost on Qing China along with significant economic losses in war expenses and reparations. In the aftermath the struggling dynasty was forced into signing a series of unequal trade treaties granting extensive extraterritorial rights, first, to the British Empire and then to the United States, France, Russia, the United Kingdoms of Sweden and Norway, and Portugal.

James Hevia has convincingly shown that unlike India, China never became a formal British colony for several reasons—namely, that colonizing India proved such a costly endeavor that the British lost interest in governing the second most populated region on earth. Yet Britain unofficially incorporated China into the empire's fold during the period known as Pax Britannica by manipulating China's political institutions for Britain's own economic advantage. This was done through various strategies from gunboat warfare to unequal treaties, and from garnering extraterritorial privileges to establishing new institutions for the regulation of trade, such as the China Maritime Customs Service.[4] New institutions of colonial modernity such as hospitals, naval academies, missionary schools, and courthouses mushroomed. Their establishment was justified by new knowledge paradigms, in particular, the European interstate system and the doctrine of international law, which forced China to recognize its new position as one among multiple powers. The terms, norms, and distribution of power of the nineteenth-century interstate system not only solidified late Qing China's position as part of an imperial itinerary of expansion, but also redefined the stakes for China's interactions with and writing about India, both of which increased exponentially during the nineteenth century.[5]

Significantly, maritime China and South Asia exchange routes were in place long before the British expansion into Asia. When Portuguese forces inaugurated the European colonization of the Indian Ocean region in Kerala in the early sixteenth century, they made use of existing commercial networks that linked China and India by way of Malacca and the Bay of Bengal, and were originally established by the Ming admiral Zheng He's expeditions in the fifteenth century.[6] Cementing their dominance in South and Southeast Asia by gradually pushing the Portuguese out of the picture in the late sixteenth and early seventeenth century, the subsequent entry of the Dutch expanded these maritime routes under the imperialist imperative of harvesting natural resources and exploiting labor for economic growth. Yet it was the British colonizing entity, the East India Company, and its trading hegemony in the second half of the eighteenth century that dramatically developed communication and travel networks between the regions constituting China and India. From 1800 onward, trade in opium and cotton in the routes linking Bombay to Calcutta, Guangzhou, and Macau thrived, despite the Qing's consistent attempts to curb the opium trade.[7] These distribution pathways redrew the map of travel between China and South Asia, with increasing flows of people, goods, and information moving between South China, Singapore, Malaysia, and India, as traders, missionaries, refugees, indentured servants, and laborers traveled between China and India, either as final destinations or en route to build railroads and mines in Cuba, Peru, and the United States.[8]

The Opium Wars and their aftermath crystallized the contacts that were already increasing between Qing China and British India and prompted an urgency among Qing statesmen and intellectuals to learn about and analyze the colonization of India by Britain. Matthew Mosca has shown that the Qing's attention to the British colonization of India in the eighteenth and nineteenth centuries completely recast China's ideology of external relations—from a regionally specific and flexible "frontier policy" to a unified "foreign policy" by which China became keenly aware of and positioned itself in relation to competing global powers.[9] The nineteenth-century production of materials about India by the Qing was staggering in relation to earlier periods. Qing officials commissioned geographical surveys of the British territories, and many of them produced eyewitness accounts of the colonial situation of India. These accounts often reflected a growing anxiety for the future of China.[10] Late Qing newspapers and journals brimmed with commentaries and short stories attempting to explain the reasons for India's colonization and draw conclusions in light of the British Empire's increasing encroachment upon Chinese independence.[11] These late Qing writings were preceded by a flow of treatises and textbooks that compared China and India in terms of multiple variables: population numbers, geographic conditions, agriculture, religions, and customs. Circulating in China mostly through Protestant missionary print presses, journals, and schools, these texts—which ranged from geography school textbooks to reform proposals and evangelical tracts—established a comparative lens that sought to identify the Chinese and Indian national character, respectively, and rank each among the nations of the world, on a scale between savage and civilized.

The Comparative Language of Civilization

The China-India comparisons that circulated in China over the course of the second half of the nineteenth century were the products of a broader

comparative framework that served to justify the Western empires' colonization and expansion schemes. This framework compared between nations
of the world in order to locate them within an imagined hierarchy of civilizational progress, at the top end of which "civilized" and "enlightened"
countries alone enjoyed sovereignty.[12] Nineteenth-century imperialism
embedded itself in a logic of deferrals—underscored by an allusive promise
of autonomy once the civilizing mission is completed and the natives have
reached a desired level (never completely defined) of enlightenment.[13]

Lydia Liu writes that an epistemic separation between civilized and non-
civilized peoples fundamentally shaped schemes of world order from as far
back as the 1494 Treaty of Tordesillas's division of the New World into spheres
of influence belonging to Spain and Portugal. By the nineteenth century, the
discourse of stages of civilization matured, producing various iterations of
the idea that human societies in the world develop through three to five
stages of society, from savage to barbarian/half-civilized, to civilized/
enlightened. This developmental logic provided justification for the unequal
treaties forced upon China, as sovereignty was only granted to civilized
countries and was rightfully lost by nations who did not pass through the
stages of civilization already embodied by countries in Europe and the
United States. This globalized schema ranking countries and their peoples
as savage, half-civilized, and civilized quickly permeated various disciplines
and fields of knowledge, including economics, geography, evolutionary biology, anthropology, history, and literary studies.[14]

China and India were both deemed "half-civilized" based on perceived
commonalities such as low levels of literacy among the population, centuries-
old governance structures, resistance to global trade and, significantly,
what was defined in Victorian society as "the woman question," which posited that a society's level of civilization was reflected by the condition of its
women. Bodily practices such as Chinese foot-binding and Indian widow
immolation were cited as evidence that the two countries were utterly
underdeveloped and thus prime candidates for the civilizing mission that
underscored the Victorian tenet of imperial benevolence.[15] Indians and Chinese, in short, needed to be saved from themselves.

In various writings in political philosophy and economy that engaged
with the paradigms of civilization and world order—including works, for
example, by paragons such as Herbert Spencer—China and India were often
placed alongside Turkey, Egypt, and at times Russia and "the other feudal

states of Europe" in terms of systems of governance and family structures.[16] But one distinct cluster of writings—which, as it happened, were also the most widely circulated texts in China—focused on drawing similarities between China and India in particular. The producers of these writings were British and American Protestant missionaries, who were often also specialists in Sanskrit and classical Chinese, scholars, translators, and diplomats.[17]

Christian proselytization rights were sanctioned under a special clause of the unequal treaties. These privileges were justified under the principle of freedom of religious worship, which was perceived as part and parcel of all civilized countries. Imported to Asia, under the auspices of the doctrine of international law and along with free trade, the idea of freedom of belief served as a criterion for assessing the civilizational level of the different Asian states. In practice, however, freedom of belief was interpreted and imposed in ways that promoted Christianity.[18] Colonizing entities could not officially force populations to accept Christianity, but their right to attempt to proselytize was guaranteed and protected.[19] The principle of freedom of religious belief cleverly leveraged the language of religious pluralism within the discourse of civilizational stages to locate and promote Christianity, and Protestantism more specifically, as the religion characterizing the apex of human civilization. Societies that lacked institutionalized Christianity were considered half-civilized at best. This association of Christianity with civilization also informed the European interstate system and the doctrine of international law in ways that extended far beyond legal provisions for imperialist pursuits and evangelization. European orientalist scholars of India and China were almost always avid Christians, such as Max Müller and William Jones in India, who often, like the China-posted James Legge, Karl Gützlaff, Walter Medhurst, and Thomas Wade, served as missionaries themselves.[20]

Christian missionaries formed a significant part of colonizing and imperial projects from their inception. Catholic and Protestant evangelists were among the first nonmilitary or trade-related personnel to travel the maritime imperial routes linking East and South Asia. Fifteenth-century Portuguese Jesuits made frequent use of the maritime networks sanctioned by the Portuguese state and paired with private traders en route to the Ming court in attempts to spread Christianity in China.[21] By the late eighteenth century, Protestant British missionaries also began to operate in Asia, and by the 1810s, American missionaries began to join them in massive numbers. The latter sought the British missionaries' support by providing infrastructure and sharing information about evangelization success rates, as well as strategies that seemed to work, and texts and materials that proved captivating for the heathen mind. Calling this British–American cooperation "Christian Imperialism," Emily Conroy-Krutz writes that this was an imperialism that was not as interested in nation-states or in territorial expansion as it was in spreading the Protestant religion while making use of existing infrastructure and networks established by Britain and the United States. The frequent focus of Anglo-American conversations, maintained through letter exchanges and journal articles in missionary-sponsored newspapers, were the two most populated countries of the world: China and India.[22]

Importantly, Christian imperialism was a mode of cultural circulation that was logistically dependent upon state-built infrastructures but operated autonomously in terms of the content and collaborations deployed for evangelization. Recognizing this compels us to pay close attention to the particularly Christian inflection that characterized the China–India comparisons so popular among missionary apparatuses. Protected by the Great Empires, missionaries established robust printing and text circulation mechanisms that spanned South and East Asia as early as the first years of the nineteenth century. In Dutch Malacca, the arrival of British Protestant missionaries transformed the region into a major print center. The London Missionary Society was particularly eager to erect printing presses there; they hoped that the large Chinese-speaking communities already established in Malacca as a result of centuries of commercial exchange in the Indian Ocean would work for the printing presses, assist in translation and proselytizing, and help pave the way to evangelize China proper.[23] The printing houses in Malacca preceded print presses in Hong-Kong, Shanghai, and Calcutta that transmitted Bibles and evangelical tracts, but also reading and geography primers, translation of science treatises, works on anatomy, international law, and (at times) major works of fiction popular in the English-speaking world. The utopian novel *Looking Backwards* by Edward Bellamy (1888), for example, translated to Chinese by the missionary Timothy Richard in 1891, became the first modern science fiction work to be translated into Chinese.[24]

In their capacity as translators and circulators of information at a time when late Qing Chinese statesmen and intellectuals were eager to learn about colonial India, missionaries played an important mediating role, solidifying the sense that cultural affinities between China and India would be the former's downfall, unless it implemented vast reforms to its governance, education, and economy.

Comparison—of languages, scripts, religions, racial features, national characteristics—was a critical technology of modern empires, for which, the production of taxonomies based on comparative methods formed indispensable governance tools.[25] Enabling and bolstered by the nineteenth-century booming of comparative disciplines (comparative linguistics, religion, folklore),[26] the study of perceived commonalities and differences and the ensuing establishment of hierarchies between ethnic groups, religions, and societies shaped an imperial discourse on China and India as cultural doubles, that particularly engaged the missionary mind.

British and American missionaries incessantly compared between China and India's approaches to science, trade, and literati culture as well as the respective condition of women in essays published in missionary journals, such as the *Calcutta Review*, *The Chinese Repository*, and *A Review of the Times* (*Wanguo gongbao* 萬國公報). Examples abound. The medical missionary Benjamin Hobson (1816–1873), who pioneered the translation of scientific terms from English into Chinese, for example, remarked on one occasion: "Medical science in China is at a low ebb. The knowledge of anatomy and surgery in ancient Greece and Rome was much superior to anything now in India and China."[27] The sentiment Hobson expressed here—of two cultures that stopped developing and became stagnant—was a staple in many of these comparative works. In 1856, the missionary and renowned scholar-translator James Legge translated into Chinese a geography textbook titled *Graduated Reading: Comprising a Circle of Knowledge in 200 Lessons*. The book, printed by the London Missionary Society Publishing House in Hong Kong, was reprinted and circulated widely among late Qing intellectual circles. Consisting of two hundred one-paragraph "lessons," *Graduated Reading* divided the world into savage, half-civilized, and civilized nations and coupled China and India together in the second category.[28]

Beyond producing comparative texts, missionaries also fashioned institutional connections based on their comparisons. One of the foremost proponents of this approach was John Murdoch (1819–1904). Murdoch was a Scottish missionary in India and Sri Lanka who, in 1858, established the Christian Vernacular Education Society, an organization dedicated to printing and publishing Christian textbooks in all major vernacular languages in Madras. Murdoch's writings on education and Christian literature were enthusiastically received by his colleagues in China, and two visits he conducted there led to the founding of a Christian Literary Society branch in Shanghai.[29] Teaching materials for use in missionary schools and for distribution among the population, such as geography textbooks and English language primers that proved successful in India, were translated into vernacular Chinese for the purpose of education. Advertisements for such teaching materials in missionary journals would include wording that emphasized China-India connections, such as: "Specially reprinted and carefully revised with full translations in Chinese from the series of school-books published by the Christian Literature Society for India," or "this series of useful school books, which was originally prepared for the schools in India, has been found equally adapted to the Chinese, but has hitherto lacked the Chinese translation which each pupil had to copy."[30]

Diffusive Benevolence

Institutionally robust and pertaining to disciplines from anatomy to geography and beyond, missionary writings obsessively highlighted China and India as similar cultures, in which similar pedagogies were argued to work precisely because of the countries' imagined resemblances. In missionary journals that were distributed in China, and which were avidly consumed by China's foremost late Qing reformers, the comparative tone was urgent, insisting on the need for China to reject this purportedly shared cultural heritage and embrace instead the growth offered by the civilizing mission. Journals such as *The Chinese Repository* (1832–1851) made numerous references tying China and India together in a shared economy of stagnation, and they prophesied a similar fate of India to China: a march of the current empires to take it under control and civilize it by force. *The Chinese Repository*'s 1834 issue, for example, offered this harrowing prediction:

> Europe, since the sun of the Reformation arose, has been agitated and shaken to her very center: a spirit of noble origin has gone abroad, and as it has gathered strength, it has elevated and blessed the nations. The freedom of thought was boldly arrested; and men began to feel that each had a right, and that each was bound to think for himself. But not so in the East. The kingdoms and tribes of

India, like the members of a once rich and prosperous family, which have become dissipated and reduced, have been content to slumber. For centuries, the inhabitants of Hindostan were all wrapped in the thickest darkness; superstitious rites, the most appalling and degrading, pressed down the people with a mountain's weight: and in this condition, had no influence come in to relieve them, they must have continued as long as the generations of men endure. Armies could march through the land in every direction; they could conquer and subdue its inhabitants—could even change some of their external form; but they could never effectually reach the more permanent and important features of intellectual, moral and religious character. China has been conquered again and again, and changes of a certain character—as in costume and the like, have taken place; but the principle usages, manners, customs, laws and religions of this nation remain unchanged. On these, military power acts in vain—or else only to degrade and to destroy. To correct, to improve, and to elevate the intellectual and moral power of this nation, another influence must be employed—an influence which though silent in its operations, like the light and the heat of the sun, is equally powerful.

An influence of this description is felt in some parts of India, and the slumbering intellect of the inhabitants is beginning to show signs of life. A crisis has come. But if the present favorable opportunities of giving a right direction to the waking and expanding energies be neglected, they will surely take a wrong direction, and political, mental and religious anarchy will be the inevitable consequence. The present condition of India is, therefore, justly viewed with deep interest and anxiety. But the inhabitants have been awakened out of their slumbering, and brought to their present interesting attitude, not by the thunders of heavy artillery; "*but by the noiseless operation of wide and diffusive benevolence, on the part of strangers situated at a distance equal to half the globe's circumference.*" Letters have been the means, or rather they have been made the channel, through which treasures, richer than all of the merchandise of India, have been conveyed to its inhabitants. A Roman emperor could march his armies through the British Isles; but it was left to other men in a far different capacity to lay the broad and deep foundations of that nation's greatness. Again, in their turn, British armies could march over the plains of Hindostan, but they could never turn the mind of a Hindoo from his vain and wicked superstitions to intellectual and moral improvement.

What *was* true of all India is now in its fullest extent true of China. This whole nation is in a profound sleep and while she is dreaming of greatness and of glory, she is borne backward by a strong and rapid tide of influence; and if the nation be not speedily roused, who can tell where her retrogression will end?[31]

Written by Elijah Coleman Bridgman, then editor of the journal, this editorial encapsulates all the components of missionaries' compulsive China-India comparison. For Bridgman and his peers, the main axis of comparison was "the more permanent and important features of intellectual, moral and religious character," which Bridgman starkly contrasted with Europe post-Reformation, using a beloved Protestant trope of awakening. Whereas in Europe, nations awakened to struggle for freedom of thought and elevated themselves, "not so in the East": China and India remained half-civilized, in deep slumber, sunken in their heathen ways to the point of oblivion.

Crucially, no foreign conquerors or strong armies could instill a deep change in these cultures, to render them free of superstitions. A different kind of power was needed "to correct, to improve, and to elevate the intellectual and moral power of this nation." This power—the power that Christian missions brought to these countries—was silent, but effective. It worked not through military might "but by the noiseless operation of wide and diffusive benevolence, on the part of strangers situated at a distance equal to half the globe's circumference." These exact words appeared two years earlier in *The Calcutta Christian Observer*[32] and had been reprinted in other Asia-based missionary journals, including *The Siam Repository* (1870).[33] They are also found in other writings, such as in letters collected by the founder of the Bengali Renaissance, Rahmon Roy.[34] Popularizing a discourse of "diffusive benevolence," Bridgman and others were completely unabashed about the imperial mission's deadly impact on "heathen" cultures. Like the diffusion of gaseous particles gradually reforming air or water, Christian imperial benevolence noiselessly but inexorably expanded its global reach. Its diffusive force would enlighten China, as it had in "some parts of India"—namely, the colonial capital of Calcutta, where intellectuals had been "awakened out of their slumber."

But what exact form was this diffusive benevolence to take? Through what mechanisms could the civilizing power of Christian salvation be conveyed most effectively to those who needed it? The answer for a vast number of missionaries was literature: "Letters [literature] have been the means, or rather they have been made the channel, through which treasures, richer than all of the merchandise of India, have been conveyed to its inhabitants," wrote Bridgman. Alongside the missionary hospital and the literacy programs in missionary schools, one of the main conduits for diffusing benevolence across the colonial world was literature in local vernacular languages. The translation and dissemination in colonies and semi-colonies of novels such as *The Pilgrim's Progress, Robinson Crusoe,* and *Uncle Tom's Cabin* established fiction as a form of pedagogy aimed at creating local communities of readers who would reform their own societies. Frequently cited was the elite Bhadralok class, whose so-called slumbering intellect, once awoken, began to clamor for social reform. Gauri Viswanathan notes that the colonial government quickly seized the opportunity to use the popularity of novels that missionaries introduced not directly for conversion, but rather, as part of an agenda of turning natives into willing subjects of the empire because the English text was seen as an extension of the Englishman himself—whose progress, wealth, and power was to be desired.[35]

Often more effective than sermons or evangelical tracts, the idea of literature as a medium of moral progress deeply informed missionary movements across the globe.[36] Fruma Zachs has shown that missionaries in the 1880s funded many publications of local fiction in Egypt, and in the Greater Syria area including Lebanon and Palestine. In 1856, William Woodbridge Eddy, head of a large American missionary family stationed in Aleppo, wrote that his mission aimed to educate locals by "reviving the spirit of literature among themselves, nourishing a sympathy for each other and creating love for their own country and language and race."[37] In India, missionary publishing presses in Bengali, Tamil, Marathi, and Malayalam were the first to distribute contemporary fiction works.[38] Along with composing and translating fiction, missionaries solicited among the local populations—inside and outside the circles of Christian converts—literary portrayals in vernacular languages of contemporary social reality. The primary mechanism missionaries used for encouraging modern vernacular writing in their various posts was organizing prize essay competitions through which missionaries would post advertisements in newspapers and journals that solicited writings in various forms from fiction to essays.

In 1895, adding to the aforementioned list of causes leading to the decline of the Qing dynasty, China suffered a crushing defeat by Japan in the First Sino-Japanese War. Missionaries were quick to blame China's loss on what they viewed as social backwardness, a trait Young J. Allen (1836–1907), editor of the widely disseminated journal *A Review of the Times*, epitomized as the Three Evils of Chinese Society (*san bi* 三弊): opium, foot-binding, and formulaic writing. The writing referred specifically to the *shiwen* (時文) style used in the composition of the much maligned Eight-Legged Essay, a part of the civil service examination system that for centuries, served a singular process to select Chinese literati for careers in public service.[39] In the aftermath of war, John Fryer (1839–1928), a missionary serving as director of the translation bureau at the Jiangnan Arsenal in Shanghai, organized a competition in which participants were asked to send works of "new fiction" (*shixin xiaoshuo* 時新小說) addressing the ruinous effects within China of the three evils. This competition was the first call for socially engaged literature in Chinese history.[40]

Fryer's competition built on decades of previous missionary experience of such competitions in India, Egypt, and Syria. In her study of the colonial government's attempts to contain female infanticide in western India, Padma Anagol examines how prize essay competitions held as early as 1844 were employed by the British government to recruit reform-minded intellectuals to denounce infanticide culture. The winner of the 1844 essay competition, Bhau Daji Lad, is known today as the "founding father of Bombay" for his involvement in establishing the Bombay Association, which later became the Indian National Congress.[41] In Gujarat, around the same time, high-caste Hindu literati who were trained in colleges newly established by the colonial state clamored against the polylingualism of Gujarat and established the Gujarat Vernacular Society, which sought to standardize a Guajarati vernacular to serve as the "language of the people." They implemented the missionary prize competition scheme on many occasions, calling for literature to be written in "pure Gujarati."[42] Sometimes, missionaries extended their comparative compulsion to the essays they solicited. In a 1904 issue of *Gleaner* (figure 1.1), authors were even invited to contrast and compare the superstitions—and thus the civilizing efforts necessary—across sites, in this case: China, India, and Africa.

Fryer's 1895 competition had a significant afterlife in the late Qing. John Fryer became a household name among the Chinese intellectual milieu, and even featured as a literary character in several milestone late Qing novels.[43] From that moment on, calls for writings about opium, foot-binding, and formulaic writing were regular features in journals of the period and became a meaningful discursive construct for Chinese reformers. Solicitations for

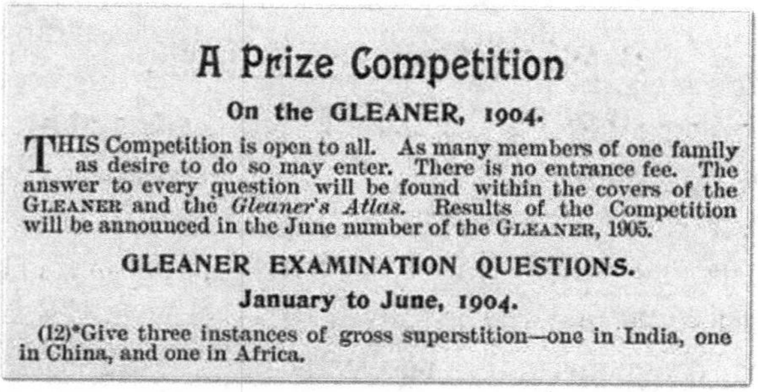

A Prize Competition
On the GLEANER, 1904.

THIS Competition is open to all. As many members of one family as desire to do so may enter. There is no entrance fee. The answer to every question will be found within the covers of the GLEANER and the *Gleaner's Atlas*. Results of the Competition will be announced in the June number of the GLEANER, 1905.

GLEANER EXAMINATION QUESTIONS.
January to June, 1904.

(12)*Give three instances of gross superstition—one in India, one in China, and one in Africa.

FIGURE 1.1 *The Church Missionary Gleaner,* June 1, 1904, 94.

writing with subject headings such as "Call for Papers by the Heavenly Feet Society" (a society for the abolition of foot-binding launched by Reverend John MacGowan in 1875 in Xiamen[44]), "Present Health Conditions in China and How They May Be Improved," "The Opium Curse," and "The Evils of the Lottery System" were frequent between 1895 and the late 1920s.[45] Liang Qichao, who arguably launched the modern Chinese literary reform of the twentieth century in 1902, specifically listed opium, foot-binding, and formulaic writing as desirable subject matters for new fiction as early as 1897.[46]

In the years after the first missionary-organized new fiction competition, debates ensued over the power of new fiction as an agent of social reform; concerns about its ability to mold the national character through engaging plots and characters who struggle with contemporary challenges permeated journals dedicated to overthrowing the Qing and revolutionizing the structures of family, education, and social interaction in China. This idea of new vernacular literature as a medium of social transformation was inseparable from the burgeoning practice of China-India comparison, which, by the last decade of the nineteenth century and the first decade of the twentieth, inspired literary theory as well as literary practice.

Fomenting local literatures was a crucial tool in the arsenal of diffusive benevolence. As a channel, in Bridgman's words, for awakening the dormant population of China and India, new literature was understood as capable of pushing nations away from superstition and closer to (Christian) civilization. Reflecting upon current events in new vernacular literature was perceived as the highest form of enlightenment. This idea animated canonical nineteenth-century pedagogical texts on nations of the world, such as

Conrade Malte-Brun's *Universal Geography: Or A Description of All Parts of the World*, which notes: "A civilized nation is that which has arranged its knowledge in the fine arts; which, to express the various sentiments of the human heart, has created the 'Belles Letters.' "[47] The two volumes *A Compendium of Geography* (*Dili quanzhi* 地理全志), a widely circulating geography book composed in Chinese by the missionary William Muirhead, similarly noted: "The state of affairs in the nations of the world is understood in four stages: first, savage tribes, second, the beginning of ceremony and etiquette, three, fully developed ceremony and etiquette, and four, literature and artistry."[48] In other words, on one end of the spectrum was civilization, complete with belles-lettres; on the other end was savagery. In the middle, China and India stood side by side, locked in a comparison by which a purportedly shared but ossified culture, ridden with superstition, predestined them for a similar fate of colonization. The comparative paradigm with India also helped shape the writings of several of China's leading reformers. While some sounded the warning that China must not become India, others pushed forward the boundaries of comparison, by invoking a China-India shared history as a source of strength.

India in Late Qing Visions of Reform

In 1898, under ever increasing unequal treaties buttressing imperial encroachment into China proper, a group of reform advocates managed to convince Emperor Guangxu to enact wide-ranging reforms pertaining to every aspect of Chinese society: abolition of the imperial examination system in favor of establishing modern universities; industrialization with a focus on trade training, manufacturing and commerce; changes to the military and the legal systems, and conversion of the government to a constitutional monarchy.[49] The new imperial edicts enacting these reforms were executed for 103 days, until a coup d'état by Empress Dowager Cixi and her supporters led to the imprisonment of the emperor and the expulsion of the reformers outside China. From their places of exile, the reformers continued to write and publish plans for transforming China's governmental and social structures and formed societies and journals to proclaim their ideas. In their writings, India featured prominently as a point of reference.

The leader of the 1898 reformers, Kang Youwei 康有為 (1858–1927), arrived in 1901 to Darjeeling and stayed there for two years. En route to and in Darjeeling, Kang meticulously depicted his experiences and everyday life in India, including detailed accounts of religions, politics, and arts. In his travelogue *Notes of the Journey to India* (*Yindu youji* 印度遊記), as well as in his other India-related writings, Kang employed the comparative urgency that described India in relation to China's current condition and future, and he expressed a very critical stance to contemporary India's customs, its food, and especially to the decline of Buddhism in India—a disappointment Kang felt as he failed to locate Buddhist monuments and relics. In his portrayal, Kang echoed the civilizational paradigm, which related India's colonization not to the Western empires' aggression, but to Indian internal causes, namely India's caste system, which, he argued, rendered the lower castes unfit to fight and resist the British.[50] His writing distinctly manifests the comparative compulsion, which situated the two half-civilizations as one and blamed both for their own demise, culminating in the taking over by "foreign conquerors." Kang defined India as China's mirror: he criticized the Muslim Mughal Empire, which he compared to the Manchu Qing dynasty, explaining that India became a colony because the Mughal rule ignored the importance of national unity and allowed multiple independent domains to coexist under their rule. Kang Youwei's India essays, writes Adhira Mangalagiri, fundamentally shaped debates over ways to reform the Qing state to move in the direction of Meiji Japan, which had successfully implemented reforms that rendered it rich and powerful. If Japan—especially after its victory in the Russo-Japanese War in 1905—was, in the eyes of late Qing revolutionaries, a progressive beacon and an ideal, India was a warning sign. China and India were described by them as moving in the same dire direction toward Western subjugation. China had but a slight advantage over the now fully colonized India, and it would avoid the same fate only by learning from the comparison and moving in the opposite direction.[51]

In the first decade of the twentieth century, as the Qing continued to descend further into economic and military chaos, and as Western nations tightened their grip over territories and resources in the aftermath of the Boxer Uprising, essays about colonial India filled Chinese journals and newspapers across the political spectrum, from the commercial *Shenbao* (申報) to the anti-Manchu revolutionary *Minbao* (民報) to the anarchist *Tianyi bao* (天義報). The content varied from news coverage of

India-Britain interactions and India's struggle for independence to analyses of India as a "lost nation" (wangguo 亡國) and discussion of the lessons China had to learn if it were to avoid the same path.[52]

Residing in Japan after the failure of the 1898 reforms, Liang Qichao 梁啟超 (1873–1929), Kang Youwei's former student and partner in the 1898 reformers group, also published several essays that viewed China and India as equally ossified and reluctant in the face of progress. In 1899, in an essay titled "Distinctions Between Three Groups of People from Civilized to Savage" (Wen ye san jie zhi bie 文野三界之別), Liang declared both China and India resistant to civilization—unlike Japan, which had successfully embraced the process.[53]

Alongside the views of colonial India as a deterrent example, a new discourse on Indian culture began to emerge among late Qing intellectuals, in response to an Asia-wide Buddhist revival, particularly, a surging interest in the Yogacara school of Mahayana. Yogacara practice focuses on raising awareness and understanding of processes of cognition and consciousness in order to achieve enlightenment and thus overcome the karmic cycle of rebirth. These qualities made Yogacara especially popular among Japanese and Chinese literati—many of whom began to practice Buddhism in Japan and in conversations with Japanese Buddhists. Within the late Qing reform discourse, Yogacara was fundamentally reshaped from a practice aiming at individual release from the suffering inherent in life to a vision of social redemption through practice and learning. Buddhist learning offered knowledge and praxis to which intellectuals turned during a chaotic time of the Qing's disintegration. From Buddhist revolutionaries and spiritual leaders such as Zhang Taiyan to literary writers and critics such as Lu Xun and Zhou Zuoren 周作人 (1885–1967), late Qing Chinese intellectuals actively read, interpreted, collected, and anthologized Buddhist sutras and treatises.[54]

Spanning China, Japan, Sri Lanka, Myanmar, and Thailand, the revival of Buddhism occurred in response to nineteenth-century imperialism. It offered a critique of Western hegemony by actively resisting the developmental paradigm of civilization and the domination of positivist thought.[55] Its emergence coincided with and influenced the direction of Qing debates over modern India. Liang Qichao was an emblematic transitional figure in this respect. Already in China during the 1898 reform movement, Liang helped form a new branch of learning along with other reformers such as

Tan Sitong 譚嗣同 (1865–1898), Xia Zengyou 夏曾佑 (1863–1924), and Di Baoxian 狄葆賢 (1873–1939), who, together, helped to found the new branch of Buddhist Learning (*foxue* 佛學). Upon his arrival to Japan in October 1898, Liang was introduced to Japanese intellectual circles as a Buddhist revivalist by the leading newspaper *Ōsaka mainichi shinbun*, which depicted him as one who "has devoted himself to Buddhism, and willingly sought to save the masses."[56] He read current Japanese scholarship on Buddhism's role in the modern era, and immersed himself in the Japanese milieu of the budding discipline of religion studies, which included such adepts as Anezaki Masaharu.[57] In an essay he published in Japan in 1902, titled "On the Relationship Between Buddhism and the Government of the People" (Lun fojiao yu qunzhi zhi guanxi 論佛教與群治之關係), Liang argued that Buddhism offered China a much-needed source of resilience to sustain itself within the flux of the modern era. Buddhism, in actuality, Liang argued, does not teach to renounce the world but to rather enter into it and engage (*nai rushi er fei yanshi* 乃入世而非厭世); in this age, he said, we must turn to Buddhism as it teaches self-sustenance (*nai zili er fei tali* 乃自立而非他力), rather than reliance on Buddha or bodhisattvas.[58]

"On the Relationship Between Buddhism and the Government of the People" forms an integral part of Liang Qichao's reform-era proposals for China's national salvation. Yet the timing of its publication—just a couple weeks after the publication of his more well-known essay, bearing almost the same title, "On the Relationship Between Fiction and the Government of the People" (Lun xiaoshuo yu qunzhi zhi guanxi 論小說與群治之關係), raises attention to its significance, not only for Liang's own intellectual path, but also for the shaping of modern Chinese literature in conversation with the Buddhist revivalist thought that imagined India as its origin.

"On the Relationship Between Fiction and the Government of the People" was a clarion call for China's writers to become aware of the power of fiction to renew a nation if used to promote beneficial causes—or, conversely, to doom a nation to decline if left in the hands of those who failed to understand fiction's immense power. The essay opened with the memorable plea: "If one intends to renovate the people of a nation, one must first renovate its fiction." The essay, published in the flagship literary journal *New Fiction* (*Xin xiaoshuo* 新小說) founded by Liang, drew from his studies of Buddhism to propose a theory of literary function. Discussing the functional mechanism of fiction, Liang identified four powers that work to gradually intensify the effect of fiction on the mind: fumigation (*xun* 熏), immersion (*jin* 浸), stimulation (*ci* 刺), and lifting (*ti* 提). When describing the way fiction works on the reader, Liang relied heavily on Buddhist concepts of delivering a believer from ignorance to enlightenment. Fiction's fumigating function, Liang explained, resembles entering a cloud of smoke and becoming thurified by it. It is the necessary first step of enlightenment. While fumigation, immersion, and stimulation work on the reader's mind from the outside, the function of lifting "originates from within and works outward. This in fact is the highest attainment in Buddhism," he wrote.[59] Borrowing from Buddhist epistemology, Liang Qichao thus phrased a first-of-its-kind theory of literary efficacy in modern Chinese history—a theory that further shaped Republican-era literary criticism, as seen in the writings of critics such as Chen Duxiu 陳獨秀 (1879–1942) and Zhou Zuoren (to state just two examples).

Through his study of Buddhism, Liang began to discuss India within a different conceptual framework—not as a cautionary tale but as the origin place of Buddhism. This culminated in 1923, with Liang's invitation to Rabindranath Tagore to visit China. Referring to Tagore's homeland as "China's elder brother," Liang Qichao and his peers in Tokyo studied Indian history not via a paradigm of sameness, but by beginning to delineate how, during more than two thousand years of Buddhism—through "unification and disintegration, prosperity and decline, there must have been relationships and interdependence" between China and India.[60] The reciprocation Liang Qichao identified between Buddhism and literary function—specifically, drawing from Buddhism to theorize how literature stimulates the reader—sheds new light on the critical role twentieth century Buddhism played in shaping the rise of modern Chinese literature.[61]

Liang and his contemporaries' attraction to Buddhist thought compels us to consider anew Liang's aforementioned statement, "If one intends to renovate the people of a nation, one must first renovate its fiction." This formative moment in new Chinese literature also speaks to how the imagination of India, perceived as the primordial origin of Buddhism, pivoted in literary modernity a reevaluation of sameness-based comparison and an investigation of contact and exchange. Liang's journal *New Fiction*, popular among late Qing, Tokyo-based circles of Chinese reformers who both read and wrote for the publication, became the main stage for debates and discussion over the need for (and ways of) reinventing Chinese fiction in order to transform and modernize China. Su Manshu, whose work we turn to now, was an avid reader and contributor to the journal.

Born in 1884 in Yokohama to a Chinese father and a Japanese mother, Su Manshu received tonsure at age 14 and became a Buddhist monk, traveling in 1904 to Bangkok, where he studied Sanskrit at Wat Mangkon Kamalawat, the foremost Chinese Buddhist temple in Thailand.[62] Su spent the first decade of the twentieth century residing in Japan and traveling to South and Southeast Asia often. He visited Sri Lanka as well, and vistas he remembered from his trip abound in the poetry and the illustrations he published. In 1899, Su enrolled in the Datong School System (Datong xuexiao 大同學校)—a network of educational institutions established by Chinese sojourners in Japan such as Kang Youwei and Liang Qichao, among others. These Chinese reformers collaborated with Japanese educators to form the Datong schools with the distinct purpose of inculcating newly arriving overseas Chinese students to a reform-minded curriculum based on the Meiji model which combined modern citizenship training with what was termed national learning (guoxue 國學).[63] Su Manshu graduated from the Yokohama Datong School in 1902, and it is very likely that he met and interacted with Liang Qichao through this network. In 1904, Su contributed a piece that became part of the longest and most sustained literary theory debate within New Fiction, regarding the relationship between the novel form and society.[64]

During this period, Su Manshu closely associated with Chinese anarchists and Buddhist activists, including such late Qing paragons as Zhang Taiyan, Liu Shipei 劉師培 (1884–1919), He-Yin Zhen 何殷震 (1884–1920), and Zhang Ji 張繼 (1882–1957).[65] In 1907, Su became a founding member of the Asia Solidarity Society (Yazhou heqin hui 亞洲和親會), a short-lived yet influential alliance of exiles and activists from across Asia who sought refuge in Tokyo. Members of the society included Chinese anarchists, Japanese socialists, Indian anticolonial activists, and refugees from the US-occupied Philippines, Vietnam, and Myanmar. They gathered under an emergent idea of "Asia" defined as an alliance of peoples of different countries collectively suffering under the yoke of Euro-American imperialism and vying to support each other's struggle for independence. Importantly, they conceived of "Asia" as a space unified by an imagined precolonial past, which they portrayed in their writings as an idealized era of thriving connections and cultural affinities.[66]

Buddhist culture featured centrally in the rhetoric of anti-imperialist activism, especially in the writings of the Chinese members of the Asia

Solidarity Society, such as Zhang Taiyan, Su Manshu, and Liu Shipei. These writers were interested in Buddhism as a historical construct tying India to China and other Asian countries such as Japan, Thailand, Sri Lanka, and Myanmar. The society's discussions focused on India as the origin of Buddhism and revealed a growing interest in Sanskrit language and its study; within the society Su Manshu formed a Sanskrit Study Society for the purpose of collecting and preserving Sanskrit texts and promoting the study of Sanskrit language among Chinese intellectuals. Encouraged by Zhang Taiyan, Su planned and began to compose an eight-volume study titled *Sanskrit Grammar* (*Fanwen dian* 梵文典), for which he received praise by Liu Shipei, Zhang Taiyan, and Chen Duxiu.[67] Although *Sanskrit Grammar*, published under the auspices of the Asia Solidarity Society, is no longer extant, the surviving preface and table of contents demonstrate Su's conviction that knowledge of Sanskrit provides access to core scriptures, thus enabling the Buddhist practitioner immediate access to the root of all knowledge (*zhu jiao zhi genben* 諸教之根本). The table of contents situates *Sanskrit Grammar* as a broad-strokes study of linguistic principles, including chapters on the Sanskrit script, the function of vowels (*muyin* 母音) and consonants (*ziyin* 子音), and numerals. Su translated extensively from the English texts of the top contemporaneous Sanskrit philologists: Max Müller (*A Sanskrit Grammar for Beginners*, 1866) and Monier Monier-Williams (*An Elementary Grammar of the Sanskrit Language*, 1846; *A Practical Grammar for the Sanskrit Language*, 1857).[68] Su's original contributions included chapters on phonetic transcription between Sanskrit and Chinese and a translation he completed from Sanskrit of the *Heart Sutra* (*Xinjing* 心經), placed next to Max Müller's celebrated English translation of the same sutra. The table of contents of *Sanskrit Grammar* bespeaks the wide support for the study of Sanskrit, with prefaces by Zhang Taiyan, He-Yin Zhen, as well as by an Indian independence activist and member of the society, the Indian lawyer Borohan.[69]

The growing consensus on the importance of Sanskrit among the late Qing, Tokyo-based intellectual milieu added new layers to debates about colonial India at the time. As the birthplace of Buddhism, India was glorified as the cradle of the culture that made its way across Asia and linked peoples by a common belief and practice. India's colonization by the British began to occupy the minds of thinkers and essayists as more than a foreboding cautionary tale. Chinese activists, as evident, for example, in numerous essays supporting the Indian resistance against British colonialism,[70] began to rethink their engagement with India so as to make sense of imperialism as a systemic mechanism of oppression. Through his literary practice, Su Manshu pioneered a critique of imperialism through effecting China-India connections via innovations in narrative voice.

Translation as "Literary Relations"

Su Manshu is celebrated not only as an inventor of the modern male subjectivity in Chinese literature, but also for his pioneering use of first-person voice.[71] Less attention has been paid to his identity as a translator,[72] or to the role played by Hinduism, the study of Sanskrit, and the history of India's anticolonial resistance in shaping Su Manshu's fiction.

Versed in Chinese, Japanese, English, and Sanskrit, Su was one of the first translators of European and Indian literatures to Chinese. He translated from Sanskrit the drama *Śakuntalā and the Ring of Recollection* and the long poem *Cloud Messenger* by the fifth-century poet Kālidāsa (*Śakuntalā* and its reception in China are the subject of chapter 4). From English, Su translated the poem "Baugmaree" by the Bengali poetess Turo Dutt (1856–1877), who wrote in English and French, as well as works by the Indian philosopher and independence activist Sri Aurobindo Ghose (1872–1950). He also translated and published a volume of English Romantic poetry.

Su's thinking about the act of translation and its meaning was never gathered in a comprehensive treatise, but reading through his translations, his fiction, and his poetry along with some of his editorial work, such as *Sanskrit Grammar*, reveals his frequent engagement with translation as a critical force in literary practice. His fiction and poetry present a tapestry of languages, with Sanskrit, Chinese, and English words appearing together in different scripts or in transcription. Translated works are a consistent theme in his fiction; Su would often cite from his own poetry translations, transforming translated poems to parts of dialog given in the character's voice.[73] Far from a cosmopolitanism approach of a globe-trotting romanticist, as Su has often been studied, the multilingualism of his writing bespeaks a view of translation work as a practice that shines a light on power imbalances and contemporary geopolitics. His study of Sanskrit, underscoring a deep interest in India's anticolonial struggle and in Buddhist revivalism, informed a theory of translation that pushed new literary practice to recognize and undo the Christian imperialist comparative compulsion.

In his critical writing, Su took care to note if a translation he was producing was direct (*zhiyi* 直譯) or a retranslation (*fuyi* 復譯 or *chongyi* 重譯), which in the latter case would mean adding another layer of mediation. His editing work and fiction writing highlighted the problem of mediated translation as a central query for new literature: How does a third mediating language complicate the idea of translation and the relationship between cultures?

In 1908, the same year in which he published *Seclusion on Sal Beach*, Su edited and published an anthology, titled *Literary Relations* (*Wenxue yinyuan* 文學因緣), with a press in Fujian. This anthology put together English translations of Chinese classics, done by British and American missionaries and diplomats such as James Legge, Herbert A. Giles, and George T. Candlin, with translations to Chinese of poems (by Byron and others English poets) made by Su Manshu and colleagues. To these, Su Manshu added his own translation to Chinese, from English, of a well-known epigram Goethe wrote to celebrate *Śakuntalā*, the fifth-century classic that during the nineteenth century became one of the first global bestsellers across Europe. The pairing of English language translations of Chinese classical poetry with Chinese translations of English poetry invokes a particular type of literary relation between the crown jewels of Chinese literature—Tang poetry and the Book of Odes (*Shijing* 詩經) with milestone English Romanticism. The inclusion in *Literary Relations* of Goethe's epigram, however, is curious. What is a retranslation, from English, of a German text, about an Indian drama, doing in this anthology?

One could make the case that Goethe meshes well with the Romantic inclination of the Chinese translation section of the anthology. Yet, by retranslating an epigram written to commemorate a Sanskrit drama—which Su himself translated from the original into Chinese, and which, as Su Manshu knew well, spoke to German nineteenth-century fascination with India in general and Sanskrit theater in particular—Su did more than showcase Romantic literature. With this editorial choice, Su Manshu opened up *Literary Relations*—not just the anthology but literary relations themselves—to include, along with the Qing and the British Empires, India, represented by the celebrated Sanskrit drama, in retranslation.

The preface to the anthology makes this move apparent as it veers, without transition, from elaborating the contents and providing biographic information about the various translators to discussing at length the superiority of Sanskrit language and Indian culture. For example: sentences of sweeping scope such as, "Of all the languages of the world, none matches Sanskrit in beauty, second is Chinese, and third are European languages," are followed by unrelated editorial asides, such as "James Legge translated the *Book of Odes* in full, and one notices the differences between his translations and those included in 'The Middle Kingdom,'"[74] which then move toward blanket statements based on the editor's judgment, such as "India is the origin of all philosophy and culture. It far surpasses Greece, who is its junior." Without any perceived relation to the content of the anthology, Su discusses the classical epics the *Ramayana* and the *Mahabharata* and elaborates upon the plot of *Śakuntalā*. The preface concludes with a vignette recollecting a boat trip at sunset after visiting the ruins of an ancient pagoda, in which Su cites from one of his own poems: "The setting sun on the River Ganges/A thousand jade green peaks/The crying wind in Bihar/Ten thousand misty trees."[75]

The logic behind the narrative disconnects that Su embeds in the preface—thus repeatedly inserting India and Sanskrit into a debate over Chinese-English and English-Chinese translation—reveals an understanding of translation as something much broader than the transmission of information between two languages. Su's collection situates "literary relations" between not two but three partners—Chinese, English, and Sanskrit, bound together through Western imperialism. Relations—*yinyuan*—is a Buddhist term that in its foundation denotes the idea of causes (*yin* 因) and conditions (*yuan* 緣) of a certain outcome, and indexes as such the Buddhist central idea of *karma*—a chain of events where one impacts the creation of another. "Literary relations," and thus the book's eponymous title, invokes a particular understanding of translation as a chain of events connected by cause and effect; the appearance of Sanskrit and Indian scenery in the preface implicitly asserts India's connection to China, England, and the United States. Literary relations between Chinese and English literatures are bound to extend to India because of the latter's colonization by England, which in turn helped shape China's encounter with the empires. Translation is a way of understanding literary relations—such as those that led Goethe to compose a poem about *Śakuntalā* and later led Su Manshu to translate that poem to Chinese, from an English translation. Follow the translingual translational path of such works as *Śakuntalā*, Su seems to be saying, because translation is enabled by and creates literary relations in a broad sense—a chain of causes and results that shape what gets translated and how. Committed to the Asian Solidarity Society's vision of China-India connections grounded in a shared past of religious exchange, Su was nevertheless acutely aware of the limitations of this imaginary. His work as a translator, directly, or through an existing translation of an original, made him notice and highlight the inescapable role of English in mediating the modern China-India encounter; it led him to include India and Sanskrit as part of a modern English translation of Chinese classics and vice versa. "A Record of Seclusion on Sal Beach," to which I turn next, opens up the problem of translation and linguistic mediation to phrase an anticolonial literary expression that repurposes the colonial comparative compulsion.

Pseudotranslation as Device

"A Record of Seclusion on Sal Beach" follows the journey of a young protagonist named Buhui (不慧). Aspiring to seclude himself from his immediate environment, Buhui wanders off and ends up on a beach lush with Sal trees during monsoon season in the southern part of Bihar. The story is deeply rooted in Buddhist language and tropology. In Buddhist terminology, the name Buhui literally means "lacking wisdom," particularly, lacking the wisdom to discern life's true underlying principles. Naming the protagonist Buhui immediately frames him in need of an awakening, which in the story takes shape in two forms: the religious and the revolutionary.

As Buhui walks along the beach and into the adjacent forest, he hears two lovers singing to each other inside a cave. Their songs—cited in the text in English and in Chinese translation, and featuring excerpts from Byron's book-length narrative poem *The Island* (Su Manshu's translation) and from *Śakuntalā* (Monier Monier-Williams's translation)—serve as a device to connect natural scenery to human sentiment by referencing how the beauties of nature compete with the qualities of the beloved. Byron's "Are the dropping caves without a feeling in their silent tears?"[76] transitions to Kālidāsa's "Her ruddy lip vies with the opening bud."[77] When Buhui hears the lovers singing, his loneliness and distress surge, and he attempts to drown himself. The singing couple—a husband named Zhuangzhe and a wife who remains unnamed—rescue Buhui and affirm that he has arrived at the heavenly realm of Sal (*suoluo tian xiang* 娑羅天鄉) where they have been hiding out. As

Buhui and the reader quickly discover, their seclusion is not based on the religious practice of austerity. Rather, the couple are leaders of a guerilla anticolonial resistance network, led by an old Buddhist monk. Buhui joins the couple and their comrades as they emerge from the cave to launch an attack on British colonizers. Through lengthy sermons on cosmogony given by Zhuangzhe, Buhui comes to experience his two intersecting awakenings—first to the fundamental truth of Buddhahood, that life is suffering and the way to end that suffering is the Noble Eightfold Path, and second to the reality of revolution, a result of historical oppression by colonial powers who took India by force and decimated the freedom of its population.

In the two-line preface he appends to the story, Su Manshu tersely notes that "A Record of Seclusion on Sal Beach" was composed by an Indian man, and Su has simply translated the story from an English translation. The original writer, Su adds, uses divine speech[78] to convey the tragedy of a lost nation (*wangguo* 亡國). The original writer, however, in both my reading and that of other scholars, is likely Su Manshu himself. This fact can be gleaned not only from the lack of evidence about the writer (Su Manshu mentions that his name is *Qusha* 瞿沙/Ghōncha, but no one has managed to track down this individual), but also from the writing, which resembles Su's style in other fictional works, as well as the similarity of the protagonist Buhui to other melancholic and tormented characters in the more well-known novellas Su wrote, such as Sanlang in *The Lone Swan* or Zhuang Shi in *The Broken Hairpin* (*Sui zan ji* 碎簪記, 1916).[79] Moreover, the proverbs used throughout the text consistently draw from Chinese traditional sources, including poems by Qu Yuan, Tao Yuanming, and Li Bai, and citations from the Confucian classics the *Zuo Tradition* (*Zuozhuan* 左傳) and the *Book of Rites* (*Liji* 禮記), among others. It seems unlikely that a contemporary Indian writer would be that familiar with them. And yet, Su Manshu goes to a great deal of trouble to hide his own deception. All the characters in the narrative are Indian and there is no mention of China. In the depictions of scenery, the text introduces many Sanskrit terms for flowers, trees, natural phenomenon, Buddhist deities, and Hindu gods—all transcribed into Chinese and given in English with a definition—such as "Varsna" (*fasa* 伐薩) for the rainy season, "Asok-Tree" (*alunjia* 阿輪迦) for the Saraca asoca plant, and "Sirishw" (*shilishahua* 室利沙花) for the Acadia flower with which women in Sanskrit poetry, as well as in *Seclusion on Sal Beach*, decorate their ears.[80] Su goes as far as inserting comments where the translator is "correcting" factual mistakes made by "the writer."[81]

Pseudotranslation—a translation without a source text—has existed in many literary cultures across time and space.[82] Often, writers opt to present their works as translations of a more highly valued source text so as to render authority to their own voice, allowing them to introduce new ideas and new literary inventions into the literary sphere in which they operate.[83] Moreover, depicting the translation process within a work of fiction (as Su Manshu does here) blurs the boundaries between "source" and "target" texts, and raises broader questions about the function of translation at large.[84] Pseudotranslation thus gains a particular explanatory power as a literary form that pushes the reader to ponder metafictional issues—namely, the idea that the boundary between reality and fiction is in fact, porous.[85] It is very likely that Su Manshu pretended to be translating an Indian original story so as to redeem the position of India in the eyes of many late Qing intellectuals—to present an alternative to the popular late Qing depiction of India as stagnant and at fault for its own demise. Replacing this narrative with a tale of anticolonial resistance, delivered by a (supposedly) authentic Indian voice, exposes the evils of colonialism to Chinese readers as the singular cause for India's subjugation and fosters in those readers a sense of solidarity.

Yet this explanation does not account for Su Manshu's claim that "A Record of Seclusion on Sal Beach" is doubly translated from the English (*chongyi* 重譯). By positing the provenance of the text in this way, Su Manshu in effect reveals, through the notion of translation, a sense of literary relations that establishes English as mediating between India and China. Translating India as a hub of resistance begins to forge a new comparative narrative—not of lost-nation sameness, but of inspiration and the yearning of both countries for a different future. It is important here to remember that for Su Manshu, translation, real or fake, illuminates literary connections that are inseparable from the historical reality in which literature functions. Within the China-India-Britain triangulation, translation as a theme and strategy reveals the shadow of imperialism looming over the imagination of solidarity.

Heteroglossia as Anticolonialism

Along with the heightened presence of the act of translation and the persona of the translator in the text, the employment of "divine speech"—as

Su Manshu refers to the text that is rife with Buddhist allusions and rhetoric—detaches Buddhist tropology away from the more familiar contexts of allegory, hagiography, or poetry. In this modernist tale of revolution and resistance, Buddhist speech structures two types of reality in the narrative—a mimetic reality that is nevertheless illusory, and a higher reality that is the realm of truth. As Buhui discovers that he is in the territory of Sal, he asks Zhuangzhe: "I have heard of Sal beach. Immortals reside here. Is this a dreamworld, or not?" Zhuangzhe responds: "We are not immortals, but hermits. And yet, in comparison with the evil world [eshi 惡世], this place is no different from a realm of immortals."[86] In a Buddhist-informed text, this hesitation between reality and dream does not undermine the narrative's authenticity but rather strengthens it: in Buddhist thought the world of sentient beings, the evil world of suffering and attachments, is an illusion. By entering the otherworldly realm of Sal beach, Buhui enters the realm of ultimate truth, which Zhuangzhe and his wife further relate to him as they begin to narrate a revisionist history of the world and of India. Throughout the narrative, Buhui documents these speeches on palm tree leaves, thus elevating them to Buddhist sutras, which were preserved on palm leaves in India.

Zhuangzhe opens with a cosmogony of the world's creation of the four forms of birth—the four ways by which living beings are born into the three realms and six destinies: from moisture, from eggs, from a womb, and through metamorphosis. The world undergoes cycles of destruction and rebirth, wars are rampant, and suffering increases. Yet India experiences glorious days, such as those described in the *Ramayana*, which Zhuangzhe discusses as a historical source. With the arrival of great robbers, India is destroyed and its people humiliated. In the aforementioned two-line preface to the story, Su explains that in the story, "great robbers" (*da dao* 大盗) means "white people," and indeed the term is repeated throughout the story to refer to British colonial powers.

Unlike many of the late Qing writings about India, whether in fiction, geographic treatises, or essays, the loss of the nation is not depicted here as a result of faulty Indian characteristics, particularly a lack of desire to civilize. Zhuangzhe's wife emotes: "We, the descendants of Rama, how did we stoop so low? We have lost the land of our fathers; our brothers and sisters are humiliated. If the former Kings would still be alive, the great robbers would not tear across our land!" Zhuangzhe adds: "It is said since time immemorial 'when dark clouds amass, it is a time to kill.' Though I had been living [here, in seclusion], outside the ordinary world, I have not for a day forgotten the fear, the hatred. That is why we are now planning to go back into the world."[87] Immediately after, forty people, including the couple and Buhui, emerge out of the cave in search of vengeance. In defiance of the colonial designation of half-civilization, and of the late Qing common depictions of Indians as debilitatingly stagnant, Su Manshu depicts them as a group of Indian Buddhists who are determined to climb mountains and cross rivers to regain their independence. When they stop in one of the villages to radicalize the local population, the most dramatic encounter in the story materializes as the revolutionaries clash with colonial forces that are not soldiers, but Christian missionaries:

> Suddenly, four great robbers appeared, embracing a woman, beautiful and lavishly dressed, as if playing a role in a play. Everyone looked at her, wondering if she is playing the role of a demon bee (*fengyao* 蜂妖). Dressed in black clothing, [the four men] had something shiny dangling from their neck, a shape consisting of two intersecting lines, shimmering bright like a butcher's knife. Buhui shouted: "Stop! I ask you: is it your type who tramples the land of my fellow Indians, who eats the flesh and drinks the blood of my Indian brothers?" The oldest one answered him: "Why, brother? We are not of that type! We have come here to bring you the truth of God, to proclaim the Great Dao of God's love for humanity!"[88]

The encounter with the missionaries is a confrontational climax in this text because it reveals something beyond the atrocities of land seizure and blood shedding: the epistemic brutality of diffusive benevolence. The devious violence exhibited when missionaries refer to the colonized as "brothers" while assisting their oppressors is laid bare as Buhui immediately retorts to the missionary: "Who do you call brother?! A messenger of God, you say you are? You are the vilest of all evil!" In lengthy monologues, Zhuangzhe, his wife, and an elderly leader all elaborate upon the evils of colonialism, enshrined in their words by missionary invasion. They call for the return of India to Indians, who have no need for a foreign God. Finally, Buhui and his group decide to spare the missionaries' lives. In return, the missionaries agree to betray their own people and direct the revolutionaries to a nearby foreign settlement that they plan to attack. As the revolutionaries head in that direction, Buhui overhears a conversation between the missionaries and the young lady who came with them:

> The long-bearded one said to the young woman: "At lunch today, I spilled some salt, how dangerous!" (according to the customs of some countries, one should avoid spilling salt on the table. If that happens, one must dispose of the salt by throwing it behind his left shoulder to reverse the bad luck). The young woman responded: "how perilous! And I sneezed three times!" (according to the custom of some countries . . . three sneezes are perceived as a bad omen). Another missionary then said: "And I saw a white rabbit on a side-street, we must be vigilant!" Having said their piece, the mob of robbers clasped their chests and knelt down, rolling their eyes up to the sky and feeling the presence of God.[89]

Leaving the missionaries in this position, the group continues on, and upon reaching the village, plans and executes an attack that results in a hard-won battle. The brief passage that concludes the encounter with the missionaries seems at first out of context. Why after an indictment of responsibility for stealing, murdering and occupying the fatherland, would the narrative shift with no transition to a conversation about folk beliefs? We could argue that this dialog shows that the missionaries are struck by the vengeful fervor and passion of the revolutionaries and are linking events happening earlier (the salt spilling, the sneeze), in light of this encounter, to portend the future and try and reverse its course. But to someone familiar with the work of missionaries in the colonial world, such as Su's contemporary readers, a different reading likely emerged, one that shone a light on the hypocrisy of Christian diffusive benevolence. One of the most written-about topics in missionary journals, the most extensively attacked in missionary schools, and the most frequent prompt in a missionary essay competition was the problem of "superstitions"—the term missionaries used to describe local customs and folk religious practices. Missionaries wrote and preached that clinging to superstitions, instead of embracing Christianity, was the most dramatic hindrance for Chinese and Indian half-civilized peoples, preventing them from becoming fully civilized. By adding a passage that not only depicts the missionary's blind faith in so-called superstitions of salt spilling and sneezing, but also includes clarifications of these customs in brackets, the translator/writer assumes the ethnographic voice that missionaries have adopted in their depictions of China and India. Missionary ethnographers thus become ethnographed subjects, as the colonized voice themselves from inside the missionary's voice and ridicule it.

This narrative strategy, by which the voice of the implied author/translator joins that of the narrator or a character in the text, is the main structural element Su Manshu uses to expose the duplicitous nature of imperialist discursive constructs, such as "superstition" and "Christian brotherhood." In another notable passage, the use of heteroglossia[90] undoes the conceptual pillars of international law as they were introduced in China during the late Qing. As Buhui addresses one of the villagers he meets and tries to convince him to join them, he analyzes, with razor-sharp precision, the sinister mechanisms of Western imperialism: "These great robbers turn to laws, rights, and the drawing of boundary-lines in their beloved treaties. So sure are they that my brothers and I would not one day rise against them! The crooks! Just look at Rousseau's unfounded theory that all people have the natural rights of freedom and equality. Today, these ideas are used to seize people's property and their land!"[91]

Jean-Jacques Rousseau was one of the most popular European thinkers among late Qing reformists and revolutionaries since 1899, when a partial translation in classical Chinese of *Du Contract Social; ou Principle du Droit Politique* (1762) was published in Shanghai, followed with commentaries by luminaries such as Yan Fu 嚴復 (1854–1921), Liang Qichao, Zou Rong 鄒容 (1885–1905) and others. Many intellectuals received Rousseau enthusiastically and adopted his ideas in order to promote various political agendas. Some embraced Rousseau's portrayal of state sovereignty as protecting natural individual rights, while others, such as Su Manshu's close ally, the anarchist Liu Shipei, drew from Rousseau's views on equality to promote the abolishment of all governments.[92] Su Manshu, however, exposes in these words spoken by Buhui how Euro-American empires savvily dangle the trophies of international law—rights, freedom, and equality to justify colonization. As I mentioned earlier, the discourse on stages of civilization profoundly shaped these terms and their employment in drawing the unequal treaties signed with China—perceived as a half-civilization whose right of sovereignty had yet to arrive. On a narratological level, by using Buhui's voice to unmask the epistemic violence of Western imperialism, Su Manshu ruptures the suspension of disbelief imperative for the fictional act. For how would the Indian character Buhui know about Rousseau's theories and their utilization in drawing treaties, considering that he has only recently become aware of the plight outside his personal melancholy? And why would an Indian revolutionary agitating among his population to resist the colonial occupation of India, highlight the unequal treaties—the treaties China was forced into signing in the aftermath of the Opium Wars? In this crucial moment, the "translator"—who already appears in bracketed comments in the text—joins his voice to the voice of his protagonist to create a mutual expression of struggle. As the voice of the Chinese implied author and the Indian character fuse, the sameness-based comparative compulsion breaks down: India is, to the Chinese reader as Su imagines him, not a warning sign, but an ally.

The Imperial Unconscious

Although considered incomplete, *Seclusion on Sal Beach* ends as Buhui, injured by a bullet after a battle with British colonialists, tries to find out whether the group's elder spiritual leader, Zhanglao, survived the attack. The abrupt ending, in medias res, leaves the reader in a state of uncertainty. On the one hand, the group of revolutionaries seems destined to failure—their heroic resistance will end in calamity. On the other hand, leaving the story open-ended retains a shade of hope for their future and for the possibilities of local armed resistance against the colonizers.

Through themes, narrative voice, and the generic frame of pseudo-translation, Su Manshu's work exposes multiple layers of the imperial project, epitomized in the ferocious might of diffusive benevolence, which under the guise of God's eternal love not only cemented the colonization of India but also made India into China's terrifying double. Su Manshu knew, we read in this story, how sameness-based comparison kept China and India at odds, denying them the negotiation of a subject position by the very language of rights and freedom. Su defined translation as the backbone of modern literary expression—lodging "literary relations" within world order and rupturing the narrative of his story with the voice of the implied author/translator. Shedding light on the triangulation of China, India, and Anglo-America, by which English mediated the modern China-India encounter, Su was finally able to imagine, through literary expression, not a precolonial nostalgia but a decolonizing horizon, underscored by a China-India connection in which two voices are joined in resisting and undoing the civilizing paradigm of the great empires.

At the same time, however, Su's decolonizing imagination had its own conceptual limitations. Conscious as he was of the false promises of civilization, an imperial unconscious nevertheless haunted his narrative. Examining the residues of imperial structure and knowledge in United States history, Ann Laura Stoler writes: "To be haunted is to reckon with such tactile powers and their intangibilities. To be haunted is to know that such forces are no less effective because of disagreement about their appropriate names. . . . To be haunted is to be frequented by and possessed by a force that does not always bare a proper name."[93] Stoler's capturing of how empire lodges itself persistently into the modus operandi of a society or a culture, even when its taxonomies are openly refuted, is the crux here. To my mind, this critical insight could be expanded: empire often haunts not as an outside force—a specter that can be known and reckoned with—but from within, as acts of epistemic disobedience within the colonial matrix of power are almost always, inevitably, marred by traces of hegemonic logic on the mind. It would behoove us, I argue, to read decolonizing narratives as palimpsests that evince both anticolonial imperatives and the marks of the imperial unconscious. In Su's work, the English-language mediation of knowledge about India was so powerful and so pervasive that, at the same time as it inadvertently facilitated his resistance strategies, it also left traces of imperial knowledge in the resistance itself.

Woven into the story of Buhui's revolutionary awakening is a narrative of the history of India from prehistoric times until today. *Seclusion on Sal Beach* repeats a late Qing, Buddhist precolonial idealism, by which the decline of Buddhism in India ultimately led to India's demise. At the same time, Zhuangzhe, his wife, and the old leader Zhanglao reiterate, in the portrayal of Indian history, some of the most enduring premises of British colonial historiography. According to this historiography, which was translated from English to Chinese during the Qing, Sanskrit was introduced to India by Aryans—groups of peoples who migrated from eastern Europe to central north India and brought about the Vedic renaissance, perceived as India's highest point of Sanskrit culture:

> One day, by a streaming brook, Zhuangzhe's wife told Buhui: "Once upon a time, Lord Rama was exiled by his father and traveled south where he resided with his wife Sita. Once, they passed through Lanka (Lanka is the Land of Monkeys, in present day Ceylon), where the Rakshasa King Ravana lusted over Sita and

kidnapped her. Indignant, Rama commanded a massive army to overcome his foe, retrieved Sita, executed Ravana, and erected his brother as king instead. Rama's bravery remains unparalleled. After that, in succession, Aryans [*Alian-ren* 阿利安人] came from Central North India, inhabited the south, and erected their glorious culture which we follow today."[94]

Su Manshu's use of "Aryans" here is key. In Buddhist or Hindu texts, the Sanskrit term Arya denotes a meaning close to "precious" or "noble." Su, however, refers here to a nineteenth-century European construct. British Sanskrit philology, under Max Müller's leadership, recast "Aryans" to denote the first populations who spoke languages of the Indo-European language family. The theory of Aryan migration, which derived from the study of the Indo-European language family, attempted to account for the origins of Vedic culture and the composition of the first inhabitants of the Indian sub-continent. This theory posited the migration of peoples of "light-colored skin" from eastern Europe and central Asia to the Indus valley, where they mixed with the indigenous, "dark skinned" population. The Aryan migration changed the cultural makeup of the region, most notably by introducing the Sanskrit language and the Vedas. And as Thomas Trautmann shows in his seminal genealogy of the term "Aryans," the Indo-European hypothesis, which posited that different languages such as Sanskrit, Latin, Greek, Gothic, Celtic, and Old Persian all stem from the same ancestral language, was first raised in 1786 by the eighteenth-century Sanskritist William Jones. An avid Christian, Jones hypothesized that Sanskrit was originally spoken by the ancestors of the three sons of the biblical Noah who spread across the world. By the nineteenth century, the Indo-European language family model shaped ethnological studies conducted at Madras, Bombay, and Calcutta. These studies solidified the notion that indigenous Indian populations mixed with Aryan Sanskrit-speaking populations.[95]

In highlighting the Aryan paradigm in the history of Sanskrit culture, Su Manshu's narrative reflects the intellectual prowess of the Indo-European language family model from which the Aryan migration theory emerged. The ostensible discovery of the Indo-European model by Sanskrit Orientalists swept the European intellectual world, revolutionized the study of linguistics, and launched new disciplines such as comparative philology and historical linguistics.[96] These were the foundation of Su Manshu's Sanskrit training. As we have seen, he drew from two of Max Müller's textbooks in his *Sanskrit Grammar* and showcased Müller's translation of the *Heart Sutra*. Considering the hegemony of British Sanskrit scholarship, epitomized in having access to printing and disseminating textbooks, this should come as no surprise. Su's approach to the Sanskrit language and to Indian thought, as we see in this narrative and in his other writings, was necessarily mediated by European Orientalist scholarship and its imperatives. And how could it not be? The British hegemony of Sanskrit study was unmatched as was the axiomatic position of the Indo-European language model and the Aryan migration theory.[97]

British scholars learned the basic principles of Sanskrit analysis from Indian pundits who taught them the key texts of Vyakarana, the classic discipline of Sanskrit analysis dating to treatises of the revered philologist and grammarian Panini, from the Indian subcontinent (sixth century BCE). Highly ideological in its promotion of Vedic culture, Vyakarana defines Sanskrit not as a product of history but as a sacred, eternal, and incorruptible language. British Orientalists passed the techniques of Vyakarana that they learned in India to German scholars, whose studies of Sanskrit fundamentally shaped German Romanticism, particularly Herder and Schlegel's definition of Sanskrit as the original Ursprache—the perfect language, belonging to a higher spiritual order. India, in the writings of Sanskrit Romanticists, came to be seen as the origin place of all human languages and philosophy.[98] Su Manshu often repeated the idea that Sanskrit was the mother of all languages and India the cradle of all human culture. Similarly phrased sentences testifying to India being the source of all culture repeat in *Literary Relations* and *Seclusion on Sal Beach*, which came out in the same year, and in his most well-known novella, *The Lone Swan*.[99] Recounting one of Buhui's conversations in *Seclusion on Sal Beach*, Su repeats almost verbatim the statement he made in *Literary Relations*: "Sleepless and agitated, Buhui shed tears, and the spiritual leader of the group, Zhanglao, addressed him, his voice billowing like the sea: 'My dear boy, our country is lost, what do you say? You must know that our country is a vast and profound ocean of philosophy, that it even looks down on Greece, who is its junior.'"[100]

Su Manshu's elevation of Sanskrit in his writing has been understood as rejecting Western culture in favor of a Pan-Asian cultural horizon.[101] A closer look reveals a more nuanced and multidimensional engagement with the hegemony of the Indo-European model. Touting Sanskrit as the most beautiful language in human history, Su's assertion in *Literary Relations* echoes

Vyakarana pundits and British and German orientalists. Yet right after this statement he notes that "second is Chinese, and third are European languages,"[102] and thus introduces a renegade line of thinking into the heart of the Indo-European paradigm. If historical linguistics placed Sanskrit on a pedestal because of its comparability to Greek and Latin, Su Manshu drew Sanskrit closer to Chinese. His claim, though distinctively marked by the imperial logic of comparative grammar, simultaneously envisioned its undoing—a proposal that would be taken seriously in the next few decades by a budding field of China-India historical and cultural interactions that focused on the study of Chinese-Sanskrit loanwords to establish a different family tree linking the two languages via a history of contact and exchange.[103]

Conclusion

By admonishing the discursive constructs of sovereignty and civilization while retaining certain facets of orientalism, Su Manshu's writing exhibits the duality endemic to colonial conditions. Think of Franz Fanon's objection to the Négritude movement's essentializing of black identity as grounds for a full-fledged resistance to colonialism.[104] Or Homi Bhabha's coinage of "mimicry," which denotes a process by which colonized people gain an agentic position to enact anticolonial politics counterintuitively, by imitating colonial culture in ways that distort an assumed original essence.[105] Or Elleke Boehmer's idea of colonial disobedience as a "double process of cleaving," by which the cleaving *from* colonial discourse through acts of transgression hinges upon cleaving *to*.[106] By borrowing or appropriating the language of colonial power, these examples reveal the particular means by which the colonial encounter creates liminal spaces in which shadows often loom over (or haunt, to cite Stoler again) resistance. In the case of late Qing writers, that liminal pace was brought into existence through mediated comparison—a search for commonalities between China and India that was inherently mediated by the English language and its representatives. Fundamentally shaping a new encounter between Chinese reformers and the idea of colonial India, imperial diffusive benevolence unleashed the epistemic violence of the comparative compulsion, but also, certainly unintentionally, its potential to be distorted and cracked. The horror of replication—the idea of China-India cultural sameness and mutual fate—intermingled with an investigation of interaction and collaboration in anti-imperialist resistance. China-India comparison was polyphonic: its writers voiced these two possibilities, at times simultaneously. While the late Qing literary encounter with India inaugurated an aesthetic of decolonization, effected by redefining translation and innovating narrative voice, in no way was literary decolonization a linear story by which India was first a cautionary tale and then came to embody an unscathed vista of brotherhood. As late Qing writers and activists cracked open the imperial logic of comparison, they opened their writings to variegated imaginations of China-India spheres. The imperial unconscious, the specter of empire that looms over Su Manshu's stories and essays, remained a presence to be grappled with in future interactions, real and imagined.

TWO

What Is Rising There in the East?

In the meanwhile, I go to China, in what capacity I do not know. Is it as a poet, or as a bearer of good advice and sound common sense?

—RABINDRANATH TAGORE, LETTER TO ROMAIN ROLLAND, 1924

BY THE EARLY 1920s, the global Tagore fad had swept through Chinese literary circles. Rabindranath Tagore's (1861–1941) poems were first translated into Chinese from English by Chen Duxiu—a close friend and collaborator of Su Manshu, who quite possibly recommended Tagore's work for translation in the first volume of the journal *New Youth* (*Xin qingnian* 新青年 1915–1926)—arguably the most important publication to come out of China's modern literary and cultural reform movements. Many have studied the embrace of European modernism and literary realism by the New Culture and May Fourth movements (*Xin wenhua yundong* 新文化運動; *Wusi yundong*; 五四運動).[1] But it was actually an Indian literary superstar, Tagore, who became one of the most widely distributed writers in the modern Chinese publication world. Tagore's 1924 tour in China has attracted numerous critical analyses throughout the years and continues to pique scholars' curiosity. The literary luminary's attempt to raise support for his vision of an Asia-wide spiritual front in a rapidly materializing world remains a particularly fraught topic.[2]

In this chapter I take the 1924 visit as a point of departure to unpack the historical significance of "the East" in an imagination of China-India connectivity created in Chinese poetry of the 1920s. By promoting the possibility of a China-India spiritual alliance against so-called Western values, Tagore inspired prominent May Fourth poets to develop new ideas about the function of poetry. The two poets I examine in this chapter, Xu Zhimo and Bing

Xin, envisioned, in verse, what I call Pan-Asian poetics: the idea that there exists an Asian religious sensibility connecting man to the universe around him, and that poetry could model itself on this particular sensibility to fashion similar interpersonal connections within members of society.

Importantly, the relationship Chinese writers formed with Tagore and with his writing—much like the discourse on Eastern spirituality that underscored that relationship—was, at no point, merely a China-India story. To understand the role Tagore's writings had in shaping new poetry in 1920s China, we need to situate Tagore's experience in China and the Chinese experience of Tagore in its proper historical context—a global moment of intensive engagement with Asia as an imagined alternative to Western materialism between the two world wars. This moment was discursively grounded in an essentialized understanding of a singular Asian moral sensibility, which many believed could usher Asia into modernity on its own terms.[3]

Perceptions of an all-Asian identity shared a fascination with an imagined Eastern mentality—a cultural identity epitomized in local traditions, craftsmanship, and artwork, in contrast to Western "materialist" achievements in statecraft, science, and technology.[4] Yet significant differences between ideals of Asianness arose across regions for various reasons. According to Cemil Aydin, cohesive distinctions between a materialist West and a mystical East emerged simultaneously in the last two decades of the nineteenth century to defy an imperialist view of Asian civilizations as inferior. In the aftermath of World War I, these ideas expanded to various critiques of the existing world order in larger East Asia and the Middle East. After 1930, a starker division solidified between various promotions of Asian cultural and spiritual unity and the implementation of these ideals in official regional leadership schemes.[5] For example, the Japanese Empire's employment of the concept of the Greater East Asia Co-Prosperity Sphere to justify and propagate its colonization projects across the Asia-Pacific prompted several Chinese and Indian politicians to reject the Japanese notion of Asianness as imperialist and uphold national strengthening in its stead. As Brian Tsui shows, these were the grounds for forming a political alliance between the Chinese Guomindang Party (GMD) and the Indian National Congress Party, amounting to a Nationalist Pan-Asian formation which rejected Japanese imperialism and Soviet internationalism.[6] Here I am less interested in how Pan-Asian notions of Asian essence facilitated policy, but rather, I focus on how ideals of Eastern spirituality impacted a cultural realm of literary production in China.

Recent scholarship on early twentieth-century Pan-Asianism calls attention to the role played by religious thought in envisioning an Asian way of life.[7] Writing on the impact of Quran translations on Japanese Pan-Asianism before and after 1930, for example, Hans Martin Krämer reminds us that deliberations over defining an Asian spirit were couched in religious terminology, which always—whether discussing Islam or Buddhism—bore the distinctive marks of Christianity, especially as disseminated by Protestant missionaries.[8] Sanctioned by trade treatises that their nation-states forced China, Japan, and Korea to sign, evangelizers also played a key role in introducing the concept of "religion" to East Asia during the nineteenth century, often identifying rising conversion rates to Christianity with higher levels of civilization.[9] As a result, Christian notions of worship not only mediated different definitions of religion, but also had a role in shaping an ideal of Eastern spirituality and its ability to serve both national and transregional identities. Scholarship on China's response to the Eastern spirituality ideal has generally focused on Chinese Marxists' scathing critiques of Tagore's lectures in China as counter-modernist, apolitical, and abstract, while paying less attention to the ways in which a discourse on religion informed both these critiques *and* an array of enthusiastic responses that emerged from May Fourth Movement poets.[10]

The self-reflective question Tagore asks in his letter to Romain Rolland— *Would he travel to China as a poet or a politician?*—was, in fact, rhetorical.[11] Tagore's own career testifies to the impossibility of separating these two roles. By situating the development of Tagore's politics of the East within a global discourse on religion and spirituality, and examining the reception of this idea in China, we can link Tagore's presence to ideals of interpersonal communication manifested in writings by May Fourth writers, specifically the poets Xu Zhimo and Bing Xin and the essayist/literary critic Wang Tongzhao. Investigating the exchange with Tagore and his work as an event that deeply informed Chinese poetry enables a new understanding of the Eastern spirituality project not as a failure, but as a vehicle for the Chinese envisioning of modern literature's role in society. As many studies have established, modern Chinese literature was formed, from its inception, as a national salvation project: writers and readers of the New Culture and May Fourth generations pinned their hopes on the possibilities of literature to "renovate the people of a nation," in the widely cited words of Liang Qichao.[12] The critical thinking on how literature was to achieve this feat, however, extended beyond the boundaries of the Chinese nation-state, and much further than India as well.

The Global Tagore

Tagore's development of an Eastern spirituality agenda dates back to his experience in the Swadeshi Movement's resistance to the 1905 partition of Bengal. The violent outcomes of that struggle and its failure had left the poet disillusioned with nationalism as an ideology capable of uniting a religiously and culturally diverse India.[13] By 1913, in his Nobel speech, Tagore had completely abandoned his previous patriotic stance. In its stead, he presented a full-fledged ideal of a spiritual Asia rising to counter a morally bankrupt, materialist West that was consumed by industrial greed and blind to the dehumanizing effect of "the machine." For Tagore, the terminology of "the machine" carried a literal meaning, as the oppressive means of capitalist production, as well as a figurative meaning, referencing the array of apparatuses used by the modern state to control the spontaneous day-to-day interactions of communities.[14] "It is the East in me which gave to the West," Tagore declared upon receiving the Nobel Prize. "For is not the East the mother of spiritual Humanity and does not the West, do not the children of the West amidst their games and plays when they get hurt, when they get famished and hungry, turn their face to that serene mother, the East?"[15] Broadcast on the eve of World War I, Tagore's speech sparked a hugely popular discourse worldwide in that war's aftermath. Between 1913 and 1930, he became one of the most popular and widely read authors in the world, the "first international literary celebrity,"[16] with followers from Europe to the United States and Latin America, and from East Asia to Africa and the Middle East: his poems were read, his plays performed, and his presence desired all over the world.

Tagore's popularity spread in Europe and the United States, where he epitomized an Indian religious and cultural renaissance that would spark a revival of the spirit in an industrializing world. Peter van der Veer demonstrates that the concept "spirituality" emerged in the West during the second half of the nineteenth century to provide a distinctively modern alternative to institutional religion, one that promised to mitigate the drastic changes wrought by industrial production. This new emphasis on religious sensibilities rather than a formal church per se—augmented by the simultaneous rise of the study of world religions—enabled the envisioning of Asia as the source of an original, uncontaminated religious essence.[17] Indeed, one of the most attended speeches at the Parliament of World Religions at the 1893 World's Columbian Exposition was given by the delegate who represented Hinduism: the revivalist Swami Vivekananda (1863–1902), father of "Hindu spirituality" and a major influence on Tagore. Identifying as the son of India, which he proclaimed, just like Tagore would two decades later, to be the "mother of spiritual humanity," Vivekananda predicted a global religious revival, an awakening to "the great central truth in every religion, to evolve God out of man."[18]

Much has been written on the ways in which Protestant evangelical theology and practice informed the Bengali Renaissance, in particular, Brahmo Samaj—a movement to reform Hinduism via monotheistic attributes, that was established by Tagore's father, Debendranath Tagore (1817–1905), and embraced by Vivekananda.[19] But it is important to keep in mind that the channels transmitting information between Protestantism and Hindu scriptural traditions worked both ways. Vivekananda's emphasis on the mutuality between God and man—perceived as the ubiquitous presence of the divine in every aspect of life—meshed well with American Protestants' integration of religion and social reform, inspiring not a few American thinkers to develop a more general sense of "religion." Vivekananda's popularity contributed greatly to the profound success of Tagore in the United States in the early twentieth century.

The pervasiveness of religious imagery in Tagore's poems and lectures— from the direct and extensive use of "God" to a tropology of deliverance grounded in light and music—was buttressed by his physical appearance. With his long hair, beard, turban, and white robes, Tagore's appearance invoked associations of biblical prophets and the Christian savior. Several Christian revival movements in Britain and the United States were openly inspired by Tagore's works. Kathi Kern notes that the suffragist Clara Colby (1846–1916) saw Tagore as representing a mystical East capable of assuaging a spiritually impoverished West. With this perception, Kern writes, "Colby took her place in a long line of Americans—from Transcendentalists to Martin Luther King Jr.—who, in conversation with Indian writers, philosophers, and spiritual leaders, collaborated on essentializing a powerful, persistent idea of Indian Spirituality and its potential to transform the West."[20] More often than not, "transforming the West" actually meant augmenting and improving upon Christian thought. One typical essay on Tagore's poetry published in 1914 in the *Methodist Review*, for example, marveled that "this singer whose religious life has been built upon the Vedas and the Upanishads . . . speaks with manifest authority and immediate appeal to the Christian mind."[21] Another gushed: "There are no preachers nor writers upon spiritual topics, whether in Europe or America, that have the depth of insight, the quickness of religious appreciation, combined with the intellectual honesty, and scientific clearness of Tagore. . . . He writes, of course, from the standpoint of the Hindu. But, strange to say, his spirit and teaching come nearer to Jesus, as we find him in the Gospels, than any modern Christian writer I know."[22]

In England, W. B. Yeats, Tagore's co-translator and composer of the first English translation of his work *Gitanjali* in 1912, attributed to Tagore the capacity to bring English-speaking readers back from their modern secular existence to a connection with God. "We had not known that we loved God," Yeats asserts, "until we read Tagore. India has discovered the spontaneous soul, the divine that we lost touch with and is offering it to us here, through its literature."[23] The first introduction of Tagore to a Chinese audience, written by Chen Duxiu for the second issue of *New Youth*, echoed this Anglo-American emphasis on the author's abundance of religious sensibilities: "Tagore, contemporary Indian poet, proponent of the Eastern Spiritual Civilization (*dong yang zhi jingshen wenming* 東洋之精神文明), Nobel Prize laureate, renowned in Europe, viewed by Indian youth as an advanced thinker. His poetry abounds in ideals of religious philosophy (*zongjiao zhexue zhi lixiang* 宗教哲學之理想)."[24]

In the years between Chen Duxiu's 1915 *New Youth* introduction and 1929, more than ninety Chinese writers and critics translated and wrote about Tagore in over 350 essays published in various newspapers and journals, with five different publishing houses publishing eighteen of his books in over thirty-one editions before 1929.[25] These translations, done from English, often followed the Anglo-American habit of celebrating the universal sense of religion Tagore was seen to convey, while editing out his critique of nationalism and profit-driven imperialism.[26] The irony of his reception in Asia via Western Christian appropriations of his work did not escape Tagore. In 1920, a young PhD student at Columbia University, Feng Youlan, who would, a decade later, introduce premodern Chinese thought worldwide as philosophy, interviewed Tagore in New York.[27] The topic of their conversation, which took place in English and was rendered in Chinese by Feng Youlan, was "A Comparative View of East and West." As they were conversing, Feng asked Tagore how the poet could maintain that we must aspire to achieve spiritual completeness in this life, when Buddha himself had proclaimed the world an illusion and relinquished life. To this, Tagore responded with a warning to his younger interlocutor to refrain from understanding the East via the West:

> Here you are simply buying into a mistaken Western preaching of Buddhism. Westerns don't understand Buddhism, and you can take Mrs. Rhys Davids as an example of that.[28] One must go to India and spend a few years there before they could try to explain these things. Buddha's saying that we must relinquish this world means that men are fettered by their corporeality, which is why everything is an illusion. If you want the truth in its entirety, you must first rid yourself of negative desires. Then the true mind (*zhenxin* 真心) realizes its full potential and a true and complete love emerges. Love (*ai* 愛) is the truth. Buddhism consists of two branches: Hinayana—"the smaller vehicle," which teaches negative passivity (*xiaoji* 消極), and Mahayana—"the great vehicle," which teaches positive activity (*jiji* 積極). Buddhism prioritizes love. We should like to ask, how could love be brought into effect with no activity? In days of antiquity many Buddhist monks sacrificed everything to preach. Could they do this without being active? Could they do this without love?[29]

The lesson Tagore imparted to Feng Youlan amounts to an exercise in reading: we should never read texts, even scriptures—a most prescriptive literary form—too literally. The paradox of very active monks reciting sutras that preach inactivity underscores the core of Buddhist epistemology. Telling Feng not to learn Buddhism from Westerners, Tagore used this provocation not to pit an "East" and "West" essence that renders one side a better Buddhist, but to invite Feng to expand his methods of reading beyond the hermeneutics he is learning at the philosophy department of Columbia. Feng, however, like many of Tagore's readers, encountered his own conceptual limits as he analyzed Tagore's message, after the meeting was over: "Tagore argues that though there is only one truth, it has two aspects. This can be observed in the Eastern emphasis on passivity and Western emphasis on activity. In other words, Tagore is a monist and China's old doctrine is dualist."[30]

Feng's relentless attempts to box Tagore into an "ism" was common in the English-language media that Feng was reading, which consistently depoliticized Tagore's multifaceted notion of spirituality, especially its critique of nationalism. Chinese readers in the 1910s and 1920s read Tagore in translations done from the English. In these versions, Eastern spirituality suspiciously resembled ideas promoted by the recent Chinese Self-Strengthening Movement (*Zi qiang yundong*, 1861–1895), which advocated employing a framework of "Chinese essence, Western function" (*Zhong ti xi yong*) to reform the government and meet diplomatic and military challenges. The movement's stark failure to install a constitutional monarchy, escalating in the bloody aftermath of its proposed reforms of 1898, made Tagore's message of Eastern exceptionalism particularly volatile for several Chinese intellectual circles, especially, the Marxists.[31]

Being as cognizant of the Euro-American reductive understanding of his work as he was of one-way readings of Buddhism, Tagore nevertheless relentlessly used the vast exposure he received as a prophet of new connections to God to voice his criticism of the modern idea of the nation-state as fundamentally immoral and to form Asian-based alliances to stand in its place. Tagore articulated his earliest vision of a Sino-Indian Pan-Asianism in 1916, during his lecture tour to Japan. The poet located China and India as contrasting with Japan's embrace of Western science and materialism:

> The lamp of ancient Greece is extinct in the land where it was first lighted, the power of Rome lies dead and buried under the ruin of its vast empire. But the civilization, whose basis is society and the spiritual ideal of man, is still a living thing in China and in India. Though it may look feeble and small, judged by the standard of the mechanical power of modern days, yet like small seeds it still contains life and will sprout and grow, and spread its beneficent branches, producing flowers and fruits when its time comes and showers of grace descend upon it from heaven.[32]

Such were the beginnings of Tagore's idea of a Pan-Asian spiritual front that pivoted China and India. Eight years would pass before Tagore would arrive to test the ground for Sino-Indian collaboration.

The Visitor

On April 12, 1924, the date Tagore disembarked in Shanghai, large crowds waited to greet him. For a brief moment this enthusiastic welcome overshadowed crucial concerns that several leading Chinese intellectuals raised regarding the visit, particularly its timing. One year prior, on February 14, 1923, Zhang Junmai 張君勱 (1886–1969), a philosopher specializing in German New Idealism and French vitalism, delivered a talk at Tsinghua University titled "Life Philosophy" (Renshengguan 人生觀). In that talk, Zhang resisted what he saw as his country's adoption of a wholesale materialist view to understand the human condition. The particular nature of human life, he declared, is subjective and anchored in free will and intuition. For these reasons, scientific rationale could not account for the fullness of life. This provoked an immediate response from Ding Wenjiang 丁文江 (1887–1936), founder of the Chinese Geological Society. Ding described the scientific method (kexue fangfa 科學方法)—defined as "the classification of all the facts in the world and the search for order among them"[33]—as the only valid means to understand human life. The exchange between the two intellectuals grew into a heated controversy, in which many of the major thinkers and cultural reformers in Republican China voiced their opinions on the fundamental question: Can science explain the truth of human life? The responses, in the form of journal and newspaper essays, were later collected and published in a volume titled Science and the Philosophy of Life (Kexue yu renshengguan 科學與人生觀, 1924), edited by the luminary literary critic Hu Shi 胡適 (1891–1962).

Far from a narrow scholarly squabble, the debate touched upon fundamental questions, namely: Should people's changing circumstances of life in the new Republic of China—reflected in every aspect from health to subsistence to education and family—be defined in strictly objective, biological and quantifiable terms, or should spiritual and subjective concerns be incorporated? Tagore's China tour, concurring with the publication of the first volume of essays pertaining to the debate, constituted a critical extension of the science and life deliberations. In his writings, Tagore persistently brought "life" to bear upon the problems of the modern era and regarded the scientific method, as Ding explained it, as an epistemological weapon of the national machine. By historicizing the introduction of positivist science to Asia, Tagore unveiled the nation—which he always wrote as "Nation," with a capital N—as an instrument of imperialist pursuits. In 1917, he wrote in *Nationalism in the West*, which was translated into Chinese in 1923:

> This government by the Nation is neither British nor anything else; it is an applied science and therefore more or less similar in its principles wherever it is used. It is like the hydraulic press, whose pressure is impersonal, and on that account completely effective. . . . . Its one wish is to trade on the feebleness of the rest of the world, like some insects that are bred in the paralyzed flesh of victims kept just enough alive to make them toothsome and nutritious. Therefore it is ready to send its poisonous fluids into the vitals of the other living peoples, who, not being Nations, are harmless. For this the Nation has had and still has her richest pasture in Asia. Great China, rich with her ancient wisdom and social ethics, her discipline of industry and self-control is like a whale awakening the lust of spoil in the heart of the Nation. She is already carrying in her quivering flesh harpoons sent by the unerring aim of the Nation, the creature of science and selfishness.[34]

If the science and life debates began as a domestic controversy, the arrival of Tagore—whose writings were already in circulation—redefined the stakes of the argument by locating the distinction between a positivist developmental understanding of life and a vitalist, spontaneous one as a distinction between "West" and "East," respectively. Liang Qichao, who was responsible for inviting and facilitating Tagore's tour in China, was one of the more outspoken critics of materialism, and he exhibited this new framing of the debate in a speech welcoming Tagore. Liang returned in 1920 from a tour in Europe which was reeling from the atrocities of World War I. Deeply affected by the sights in war-stricken Europe, Liang, who twenty years prior had advocated a Western-Japanese model for China's modernization, now embraced Tagore's vision of a China-India unity:

> During the period of 700 or 800 years, we [China and India] have lived like affectionate brothers, loving and respecting one another. And now we are told that, within recent years, we have at last come into contact with the civilized (!) races. Why have they come to us? They have come coveting our land and our wealth; they have offered us as presents cannon balls dyed in human blood; their factories have manufactured goods and machines which daily deprive our people of their crafts. . . . . If we can avail this occasion to renew the

intimate relationship which we had in India and to establish a really con-structive scheme of co-operation, then our welcome to Rabindranath Tagore will have real significance.[35]

Immersed in nostalgia for an imagined precolonial past, Liang echoed many of the issues Tagore raised throughout his lectures in China, particularly the devastation wreaked on human life by modern warfare technology and imperialist capitalism.[36] But Liang's faith in the potential of such a Sino-Indian brotherhood was not shared by many.

Particularly resentful toward Tagore's message were the Marxist think-ers, who raged when Tagore would turn to his audience and proclaim him-self a revolutionary: "If you want to reject me, you are free to do so. But I have my right as a revolutionary to carry the flag of freedom of spirit into the shrine of your idols—material power and accumulation."[37] Chen Duxiu, one of the die-hard materialists publishing within the science and life debates, blamed Tagore for deluding China's youth with Eastern spiritual-ity, which threatened to reinstate the very institutions that the May Fourth Movement sought to leave behind. We already have enough confusion and meaningless discussions of "spirituality," Chen admonished, exclaiming: "Go back to India! We have enough freaks here in China as it is!"[38]

Qu Qiubai 瞿秋白 (1899–1935)—a leading figure in the Chinese Communist Party, and also a poet and prolific literary critic—was a bit more restrained in his wording, though no less critical. As Qu saw it, Tagore objected to the idea of the nation-state and raised India as an exemplary country—a non-nation—that preserved its own inheritance in the face of Western material-ism. But India was a British colony, Qu pointed out, and Indian troops were actively assisting British colonialism by maintaining order in the Shang-hai foreign concessions. The "nation-state," Qu insisted, is thus an abstract concept to Tagore. If one wants to object the nation-state, one must fight its foundation: the class system. In Qu's view, Tagore offered no plan to organize resistance to the British rule among the Indian peasants, and his "harmony of East and West" would never come true without class strug-gle. "Thanks, Tagore," Qu concluded in a similar, only slightly more subtle manner than his comrade Chen, "We have enough Confuciuses and Men-ciuses here in China as it is."[39] Before long, Liang Qichao was openly accused of conspiring with Zhang Junmai to bring Tagore to China so that the sci-ence opponents could have the last word in the debate.[40]

Taking Tagore to task for his "abstract resistance" to modern progress was a widespread phenomenon outside China as well. Tagore's scathing critique of the colonial project was obscured in Euro-American media and also went unacknowledged by his Chinese critics. Neither mentioned Tagore's involvement in the resistance to the 1905 partition of Bengal, or his renouncement of the knighthood granted to him by the British Crown in 1919, in response to the Jallianwala Bagh massacre in Punjab, in which British army troops fired at unarmed Indian civilians, killing 379 people. The fact that Tagore pointed to the nation-state as mother of all imperialist evils earned his particular anticolonialism a cold reception in places such as England and the United States, and heated protest in Japan and China.

In China, Tagore's failure to engage with his audience on a meaningful level disappointed him. On several occasions, a pamphlet denouncing Tagore was distributed at his lecture venues, making his final departure from China a bitter one. He commented upon leaving: "Some of your patriots were afraid that, carrying from India spiritual contagion, I might weaken your vigorous faith in money and materialism. I assure those who feel thus nervous that I am entirely inoffensive; I am powerless to impair their career of progress, to hold them back from rushing to the market place to sell the soul in which they do not believe."[41]

These parting words reveal the poet's understanding that his message had been unheeded because it was perceived as an abstract, "spiritual" hindrance to a "career of progress." Indeed, neither Tagore nor his avid Chinese supporters such as Liang Qichao provided a concrete plan of action. This lack of a political prescription, Partha Chatterjee argues, was another reason Tagore's anticolonial critique generally failed to arouse a substantial political movement.[42] Although the idea of a Chinese-Indian spiritual alliance failed in the realm of realpolitik,[43] Chinese poetry became a particularly productive site where the potential for Chinese-Indian collaboration was not just debated but actualized.

The Emotional Giant

Escorting Tagore during his visit and serving as his translator was Xu Zhimo, one of the leading poets of the May Fourth period. Upon returning from his studies at Cambridge University in 1923, Xu became one of the founders of the Crescent Moon Society (Xinyuepai 新月派, 1923–1933)—a literary society whose name was drawn from Tagore's collection of poems with that title.[44] In addition to interpreting for Tagore, Xu contributed several pieces to a special volume on Tagore's work published in preparation for the visit by the most important literary magazine of the era, *Fiction Monthly* (*Xiaoshuo yuebao* 小說月報). His prose poem, titled "Sunrise Over Mount Tai" (Tai shan richu 泰山日出), illustrates the importance of Tagore's ideas for a Chinese envisioning of a Chinese-Indian literary horizon. In the poem, during the experience of watching the sunrise atop the Chinese historical landmark of Mount Tai, the speaker suddenly has a vision of being joined by Tagore, who, while not referenced directly in the text, is identified by Xu Zhimo in his introduction to the poem. At the very moment when light penetrates darkness, the imagined encounter dramatically commences:

Then, inside the vast sea of clouds,
Alone I stood on that small island, enveloped in dim mist
As suddenly, a strange dream was taking shape:
My body spread boundlessly,
The mountain peak below me was nothing but a pebble
There stood a giant, draped in flowing hair
His beard billowing in the wind like a black flag,
Flapping and floating

Erect stood the giant on the tip of the earth
Facing upward, towards the East,
His long arms open wide—
Hoping, greeting, urging,
Quietly calling out,
Worshipping, praying, crying
Shedding warm tears of joy and sorrow that I have admired for so long

These tears are not trickling down for nothing
This silent prayer will not go unanswered
The giant's finger is pointing eastwards—
What is there, what is rising there, in the East?
The East is filled with splendid beautiful colors

The East is a light infinitely bright
It has shined; it has arrived here at last

Sing, praise, this is the revival of the East!
It is the victory of light![45]

The peak of Mount Tai, one of the most sacred mountains in Chinese history, served as the location for the offering of the Feng and Shan sacrifices by the emperor. It is a quintessentially Chinese location, imbued with cultural and historical significance. By invoking Mount Tai as the location for a poetic encounter, Xu establishes the ideal scenario for a fantasy of resonance and growth. At the moment that the giant appears, the speaker's body becomes boundless; his being is transformed into something higher and vaster. Here, the giant's presence, in effect, enlarges the presence of the lyrical speaker. This description of the bearded, long-haired Tagore as a mysterious giant joins a plethora of similar references to the poet's so-called mystical appearance. The cover photo on the special Tagore issue in which this poem was published reinforces this aura; the viewer is drawn immediately to his eyes, which suggest a trancelike intensity (see figure 2.1).

Intensity is the key to understanding the greatness of the giant in this poem. Hoping, praying, waving his hands, and crying, the giant is motivated by an emotional outpouring of joy and sorrow. The giant's emotional capacity—expressed outwardly in the tears that do not trickle down for nothing, and inwardly in the prayer that will not go unanswered—is what brings the sunlight to shine upon the earth and effects the revival of the East, which becomes synonymous, in turn, with boundless sentiment. The poetic giant prays in such sentimental fervor that he unleashes a cascade of colors and lights upon the world—but he is not praying to God. His face is turned upward and eastward; it is the "East" that he is praying both to and for. This is a song of prayer completely devoid of divine presence. In God's stead, the ideal of a spiritual prayer grounded in emotional intensity enlarges and links together the two poets—metonymic of two Eastern cultures—ad infinitum.

The poem's recurring trope of light was ubiquitous in 1920s and 1930s China, assuming different meanings—from Kantian enlightenment (qimeng 啟蒙) with its imperative of shedding of the veil of Confucian tradition, to the promise of a hopeful dawn after decades of foreign oppression in Chinese

FIGURE 2.1 Cover of *Xiaoshuo yuebao* [Fiction monthly] 14, no. 9 (1923), special issue on Tagore.

cinema and drama. In reference to Tagore's writing, Chinese critics often employed light imagery to discuss the poet's impact on his readership. Zheng Zhenduo, for example, whose translations, from English, of Tagore's poetry, remain canonical in China to this day, defined Tagore's poetry as "a light shining forth the truth of human life."[46] Light is a prevalent trope in Tagore's poetry as well, especially in the collections translated into English around 1913. The first page of *Gitanjali* reads: "The light of thy music illuminates the world," and the word "light" in its various uses—from sunlight and candlelight to the light of reason or the light of a smile—appears sixty-one times in this slim volume of 103 short poems.[47] In "Sunrise Over Mount Tai," light symbolizes a very specific function: hope for a mutual East, in which the two poets stand unlimited, enlarged by their sentiments to shine the light of the East—the one and true sunlight—upon the world. Sentiment thus serves here not simply to enlarge and connect the two poets, but to actively predict the dawn of an Asian revival.

The understanding that Xu Zhimo invokes here, of China-India connections as emotionally stimulated, draws heavily upon Tagore's oeuvre, with one important difference: Xu's was not a view of the East that resisted nationalism. Nothing in this poem or in Xu's other writings suggests an understanding of a mutual Eastern sensibility as an active resistance to colonial thought. Xu was more interested in a notion of the East as an emotional force that enables, through poetry, a human connection. In this way, Xu selectively related to Tagore's view of "science" as hindering the spontaneous flow of human interaction. But he did not mention something Tagore himself relentlessly emphasized—that is, science's role as an epistemology in service of the nation.[48]

As a counter to "science," Tagore posited a paradigm he often referred to as "religion" to capture those dynamics that do facilitate spontaneous growth via unhindered sentiments.[49] For Tagore, religion meant not a system (of doctrine, faith, or worship), but a human understanding of the universe that occurs through an emotional experience (rather than rational thought). Much like we see in the song of prayer that links the two giants in "Sunrise Over Mount Tai," Tagore believed that art carries the crucial responsibility of mediating and disseminating spontaneous growth. *Personality* (1917), which was translated into Chinese in 1921 and had appeared in five different editions by four different publishing houses by 1924,[50] offers a good example of this thinking:

The darkness of the cave has yielded its stillness to man's soul, and in exchange, has secretly been crowned with the wreath of art. Bells are ringing in temples, in villages, and populous towns, to proclaim that the infinite is not a mere emptiness to man. This encroachment of man's personality has no limit, and even the markets and factories of the present age, even the schools where children of man are imprisoned and jails where the criminals are, will be mellowed with the touch of art, and lose their distinction of rigid discordance with life.[51]

Like the bells ringing in temples, Tagore believed that poetry reverberates and is capable of transforming the world through Eastern spirituality: "Let the awakening of the East impel us consciously to discover the essential and the universal meaning of our own civilization," he urged his listeners in China.[52] The perception of art as reverberating inspired Xu Zhimo, as well as other poets of the May Fourth generation, to imagine poetry as an agent of social cohesion. Like the prayer of the emotional giant, the link these poets fashioned between emotional stimulation, song, and real-world resonance hinged upon a new concept of religion that emerged from reading a sentimental East in the writings of Tagore.

Religion Reconceived

We have seen that Tagore was first introduced in *New Youth* in 1915 via his Western persona: a prophet of spiritual resurrection. Yet by 1923, in the Tagore issue of *Fiction Monthly*, a much more nuanced perception of religion's role in Tagore's spirituality had begun to take shape. In perhaps the most in-depth analysis of Tagore to be executed by a May Fourth writer, Wang Tongzhao argued: "We know that Tagore modified Indian philosophical thought in accordance with the present era. And yet, the core of Tagore's thought remains distinctly Indian, and has not been adjusted by outside influence."[53] What we might read at first as Wang Tongzhao essentializing Tagore's Indianness, was in fact Wang's way of responding to Western, particularly Christian, attempts to appropriate Tagore's thought (such as those I mentioned earlier in the chapter)—to make Tagore figure as a new (Indian) Jesus. In contrast to such generalizations, Wang offered a careful analysis of Tagore's thinking about religion in relation to the dissemination of the concept of religion in Asia:

Religion in India is different by nature from other religions. The definitions we always had for religion, though provided by different thinkers, all submit religion to the divine and agree that religion means having only one faith. If we go back to the roots of this idea, it is an oppression of individual emotions and character and a subordination to a ruler (god). Like Muhammad and Jesus, other religions all manifest this important component. Only Indian religions are different. Already in antiquity, Indian religions did not believe in an omnipotent one God. While Indian religions advocated faith in many gods, the other [monotheistic] religions failed to recognize the divine in human personality [*you shen de renge* 有神的人格], and instead of nurturing human emotions and imagination, stifled them by subjecting them to the worship of the one.[54]

In this passage Wang echoed Tagore's critique of Christian imperialism, voiced for example in *Nationalism in the West*, where he admonished imperialist forces for "making peace-offerings to each other's barking dogs with the meat which does not belong to them; holding down fallen races which struggle to stand upon their feet; with their right hands dispensing religion to weaker peoples, while robbing them with their left."[55] By illuminating the imperialist-introduced slippage between "religion" and "Christianity," Wang suggested the need to move beyond an understanding of religion as monotheism, by and through reading Tagore. This invitation to turn to India in order to undo previous definitions of religions introduced by Western Christianity was a call to develop a new terminology to engage with religion and human life through transregional cultural affinities.[56]

During his visit, Tagore was asked to speak about his own religion. Wary that he might be perceived as a missionary, Tagore was reluctant. Finally, he explained that arguments to support a belief in God were wholly different from an experience of realization, in the same way that a theory explaining light lies in a different realm than the actual human perception of light. Tagore's focus on the realm of perception, on sensorial and emotional response, located "religion" as that which cannot be explained by a doctrine but only sensed and experienced. "My religion essentially is a poet's religion," Tagore offered in response to audience questions in China. "Its touch comes to me through the same unseen and trackless channels as does the inspiration of my music."[57]

Tagore's notion of the "poet's religion," cemented in a 1922 essay that bears this title, appealed to Wang Tongzhao and other leading voices of May

Fourth poetry and criticism. There is more to poetry than aesthetics, Wang argued. Poetry connects the reader to the boundless universe and binds readers to one another. If philosophy teaches us how to think, literature teaches us how to feel. Indeed, Wang suggested: "Once we thoroughly grasp this truth, as if it is burning in our mouths, we could then use the intensity of our emotional fervor, the light emanating from the flame in our hearts, to gasp in admiration, to volatize, to disseminate the pleasure I feel, so that others could, through writings and speech, unite their gratified soul [*linghun* 靈魂] with my own self [*ziwo* 自我]."[58] Broadening the concept of religion through Tagore, Wang urged, promises to open up a whole register of pleasure. More than that, words, whether written or spoken, bring us closer to one another. Who is this *we* that Wang Tongzhao mentions? Is it *we Chinese*, or *we, China and India*? Or *we, the people of the universe*? While Tagore was very direct about his resistance to nationalism and his promotion of internationalism and interregionalism, the Chinese poets who read him were not necessarily so. For Xu Zhimo, as well as for Wang Tongzhao, the universal, the regional, and the national were often conflated. Even "Sunrise Over Mount Tai" itself, which celebrates the revival of "the East," offers no specification for which version of the East is rising, or what the ramifications are, given its ascendance in the world. May Fourth authors and critics crisscrossed between the "national" and the "universal" quite often.[59] Wang Tongzhao redeployed Tagore's ideas to discuss China's own need to open up to new perceptions of religion and new understandings of poetry's function. This tension between the national and the regional tells us much about the context in which Chinese writers committed literature to the task of facilitating communication. While deliberations of Tagore's notion of sympathy were couched in terms such as "humanity" and "universe," the ideal of an Eastern spirituality literary expression was often used as a mean to discuss the needs of China. The Chinese version of "The Poet's Religion," translated in 1923 by Hu Yuzhi 胡愈之 (1896–1986), then editor of the influential *Eastern Miscellany* (*Dongfang zazhi* 東方雜誌) demonstrates these complexities.

In this essay, Tagore focused on the idea that poetry is a connecting medium. The notion of connectivity, embedded in all types of relations, was at the heart of all worldly affairs for Tagore. The original reads:

> What is the truth of this world? It is not in the masses of substance, not in the number of things, but in their relatedness, which neither can be counted, nor

measured, nor abstracted. It is not in the materials which are many but in the expression which is one. All our knowledge of things is knowing them in relation to the universe, in that relation which is truth. . . . There is the dancing ring of seasons, the elusive play of lights and shadows, of wind and water; the many colored wings of erratic life, flitting between births and deaths. The importance of these does not lie in their existence as mere facts, but in their language of harmony, the mother tongue of our soul through which they are communicated to us.[60]

Hu Yuzhi translated the last sentence to read: "The importance of these facts [*shishi* 事實] does not lie in their existence [*cunzai* 存在] but in the words that mediate them [*tamen de tiaohe de yanci* 他們的調和的言詞]. These words are the *national language* [*guoyu* 國語] of our soul. With words, facts resonate with us [*gantong* 感同]."[61] Hu's translation was more of an interpretation, and a very particular one. Replacing "the importance of these does not lie in their existence as mere facts" with "the importance of these facts does not lie in their existence" privileges communication over substance even more than in the original. Whereas Tagore's "language of harmony" opens itself to different readings—from language as harmonizing to the harmonization of language—Hu Yuzhi concretely discusses words as mediators. The term that he uses here, *yanci*, may also be understood as "expression," thus narrowing even further the range of language to the concrete expression of it via poetry. In transforming "the mother tongue of our soul" into "the national language of our soul," the translation reads as committed to the soul of a national community. "National language"—*guoyu* in Chinese—was italicized in the original. While the term *guoyu* was used during the Republican era to designate modern standardized Chinese, Hu plays on the slippage here between "Chinese" and "national language" to render Tagore's ideas as more localized and concrete.

The Tagorean notion of "the poet's religion" located poetry as a medium linking man and the forces of the universe. In "Sunrise Over Mount Tai," as well as in the critical writings and translations of Wang Tongzhao, Zheng Zhenduo and Hu Yuzhi, the emotional effect of reading or singing poetry is understood as so volatile that it links the individual to others, creating a social harmony. New poetics thus emerged and self-identified as an Eastern vision of emotion, religion, and poetry—a Pan-Asian poetics so to speak. The focus of these poetics on prioritizing relations over substance honed the

Chinese conception of literature as creating a social impact. Alongside Xu Zhimo, another influential poet who dedicated the early stage of her career to exploring the possibilities of poetry to forge relations, was Bing Xin, who developed the Pan-Asian poetics ideal by invoking the interpersonal through emotional stimulation.

Bing Xin's Poetry of the Interpersonal

In a lengthy essay about the work of Bing Xin, one of the most prolific writers of fiction and poetry in twentieth-century China, the celebrated author and critic Mao Dun 茅盾 (1896–1981) challenged an assumption that contemporaneous readers made concerning factors that shaped the poet's work:

> Everyone who has read Bing Xin points out that she was influenced by Christianity and Tagore's philosophy. We can only take this idea as a half-truth. Generally speaking, a foreign ideology [*sixiang* 思想] cannot simply impact a person's mind with no background. Foreign ideology is like a seed. It must be dropped on amiable soil to sprout. This amiable soil is one's living environment.[62]

Bing Xin was indeed deeply inspired by Tagore's poetry, and she herself noted as much on multiple occasions.[63] A sizable body of scholarship in China and the West has pointed out allusions to Tagore's work and life in Bing Xin's writings, from the late 1920s to the present.[64] Nonetheless, Mao Dun's caution regarding the notion of Tagore's "influence" on Bing Xin is worth recalling here: analyzing a literary work as "influenced by Christianity or Tagore's philosophy" blinds us to the tensions from which literature often emerges, such as the tension between foreign thought and our own cultural context and upbringing. This very tension, Wang Tongzhao has suggested, kindled the transformation of the meaning of religion in China from a closed system of beliefs to an open channel of exchange with the universe. Reading Bing Xin with these paradigmatic shifts in mind reveals not so much Tagore's influence, but rather how what I call Pan-Asian poetics can explain intertextuality in Bing Xin's work, and the work of other May Fourth writers as well.

Though she shared, as Mao Chen eloquently put it, the May Fourth writers' "interest in influencing—and in some cases articulating—the attitudes of a socially engaged reader,"[65] Bing Xin, like Xu Zhimo, did not openly support Tagore's resistance to nationalism. Instead, she engaged with Tagore's ideas on religion and art through her analysis of the act of reading in her essays and poems. In an essay titled "Letter to Tagore" dating to 1920, Bing Xin wrote: "Your absolute faith in 'the harmony between the universe and the individual soul,' how you gather a 'natural sense of beauty' and give it free rein in your poetry—these have seeped through the sea of my mind. And my thoughts, which I had no words to express, trembled like strings, sounding divine, faint music, with no notes or sound."[66] Here, with Tagore's poetry resounding in her mind, Bing Xin imagined a dialogue, an act of reciprocal communication, taking place via the poetic medium.

The belief in the power of poetic communication undergirds Bing Xin's own poetry and demarcates a territory expressed by the May Fourth commitment to unite and strengthen Chinese society through poetry. This was a political commitment, yet ever since the renowned critic A. Ying coined the term "philosophy of love" (*ai de zhexue* 愛的哲學) in reference to Bing Xin's poetics in 1930, her poetry has been viewed as subjective, apolitical, and self-indulgent—engrossed in abstract private emotions such as motherly love, love of nature, and Christian love of God.[67] The resemblance of this reception to the criticism leveled at Tagore by other Marxist critics is, of course, not coincidental. Such casting of religious figuration as inherently apolitical—a view persistently voiced by Marxist thinkers during the May Fourth Movement—likely informed later conclusions that Tagore's visit was a colossal debacle. But if we are to understand the role that thinking about religion assumed in Pan-Asian aspirations, we need to locate Bing Xin's poetry within a view of religion that was not at all abstract, but rather a specific tool for exploring and constructing a literature of social cohesiveness.

Published in 1923, the anthologies *Myriad Stars* (*Fan xing* 繁星) and *Spring Water* (*Chun shui* 春水) became immediately popular and are considered defining works of new poetry. More specifically, these poetry collections are exemplars of the short poem form (*xiaoshi* 小詩)—a trend that was widespread for a brief period of time in China, from 1921 to 1924.

Short poems are composed of one to eight verse lines, which may or may not rhyme.[68] They are written, with no specific meter, in free verse. Thematically, the short poem portrays a specific moment within a sentimental experience: the fleeting instant of emotional eruption. The origin of the short poem form in China is a contested topic. Scholars dispute whether it was introduced through "foreign influence"—namely, the Japanese haiku and Tagore's early English translations of Gitanjali and Stray Birds—or whether it is an originally Chinese form dating as early as the Shijing 詩經 (Book of Odes) and culminating during the Tang dynasty era.[69] Although how and when the short poem form came to be may not offer much help for examining the modern problem of emotional stimulation through poetry, it is certainly worth mentioning that English translators and promoters of Tagore's work in Europe and America, such as Ezra Pound and Yeats, were deeply engrossed in Japanese haiku in the 1910s. Investigating the form of the short poem thus sheds light on China's participation in a transnational network circulating ideas on poetic stimulation—not unlike the back-and-forth route of modern-day "spirituality" between the East and West.[70]

The short poems in Bing Xin's collections read like snippets from a personal diary. Many of them locate the speaker in a natural setting, the sensations of which stimulate a sense of profound understanding of the universe. The sound of the sea, the scent of a flower, the reflection of the moonlight, the touch of rain—all evoke in the speaker a knowledge of the forces that govern life, and of the poetic act as a never-ending attempt to capture the fleeting nature of life in its constant movement. The poems focus on interactions: desired and missed encounters, pining for a connection with people, nature, and God. The moment of emotional eruption, the defining emblem of the short poem form, often arrives through the possibility of encounter and communication:

> Flower and stone by the side of the road!
> In this split second,
> You and I
> Meet within limitless life,
> Part forever within limitless life;
> When I return,
> Among countless of your kind,
> Where would I find you?[71]

In this poem, an encounter with nature invokes a religious understanding of life as limitless. And yet, paradoxically, this understanding occurs as an intense feeling, erupting within a split second, of ephemerality. Momentary yet intensely experienced, the encounter with nature crystallizes a process of perception (I notice this flower and this stone—Bing Xin uses *huaer* 花兒 and *shizi* 石子 to distinguish their singleness) and realization (I will never see them again). She emphasizes the fleeting nature of this process on a structural level with her use of enjambment, especially when she describes the encounter itself: "You and I/Meet within limitless life." Thematically speaking, the poem depicts an encounter between the speaker and nature, conveying a strong sense of human mutuality. Without turning the stone and the flower into metonymies or metaphors for people, Bing Xin manages to communicate a sense of human-to-human encounter. She does this by personifying the stone and the flower in a single line, immediately engaging the reader's attention not only with its relative brevity ("You and I") but also by the need to move quickly to the next line and complete the thought. This line, the only line in the poem that exhibits enjambment, is thus highlighted as the center of the emotional action.

The majority of Bing Xin's short poems present a conversation, either with a human being, higher powers, or natural phenomena. Many of the poems strike a conversation with a character named "my friend," in what seems like a direct address to the reader. Bing Xin borrowed this convention from Tagore, but her use of this address is distinct: she highlights not a one-way message, but an eagerness for connection and response, particularly present, for example, in the closing poem of *Myriad Stars*:

My friend!
I already departed,
This one last page,
I leave for you[72]

Extending an invitation to the reader to share the poetic space takes the effect of relations to an active sense of mutual creation. In Bing Xin's vision, the act of writing is always a relational endeavor—a desire to unite. The connection between the self and nature animates a constant inclination toward the interpersonal.[73] This idea was fundamentally religious in the sense that Wang Tongzhao referenced in his analysis of Tagore's religious poetics. God, in these poems, serves as the means for reaching human resonance:

God!
Even if the sky is overcast,

And men are lonely,
Only one soul is needed
To guard your solemn, still night,
And the desolation of loneliness
Is immediately dissolved from the universe[74]

This poem demonstrates the active function of religion—albeit one not grounded in Christianity—that Bing Xin was often said to employ in her work. Here the human soul overcomes loneliness through its connection to the quiet, still night. Yet the loneliness of the individual soul is not abated through a connection to God; rather, loneliness vanishes from the universe at large. In its stead, people are connected to one another. Only one soul is needed to achieve the right sentiment and then draw others. The short poem, with its depiction of the moment of emotional upsurge in a structural combination of free verse and limited scope, enabled Bing Xin to investigate a flash-like experience of connecting with higher powers. In this way, Bing Xin turned emotional abundance into a means of effecting social cohesiveness.

Bing Xin wrote one of her last poems, "Yearning" (Xiangsi 相思), in 1925—a year after Tagore departed and as the form of the short poem began to decline in China (she would devote the remainder of her prolific career to writing fiction and essays). At first glance, the poem reads as a celebration of the subjective individual escaping from the "human chambers" but not from her own emotions:

Escaping yearning,
Donning fur
I leave the quiet human chambers brightly lit

The small path and the moonlight peep at each other,
Withered branches—
On the snowy ground
Writing mutual longing all over, left and right[75]

But a closer look reveals something different. Even as the speaker attempts to leave the social realm and escape from thoughts of longing for another, she is struck by the mutuality that governs nature: the moonlight dialoging with the small path, the branches writing a lattice of intertwining lines. The world moves in connections. Not only does the universe abound in communication, but these communications become manifest through writing. The branches write a poem of longing on the ground in nonlanguage. The poet uses words to relay her experience of nature, which serves in turn to bring her back to the realm of humans. The connection with nature reveals itself to be a means to the end of a fundamentally social human connection.

Conclusion

Situating Chinese new poetry's response to Rabindranath Tagore within the context of shifting ideas on religion and literary effect sheds light on the larger task that Republican-era literature took upon itself: to transform Chinese society. Tagore's notion that poetry mediates a religious connection between man and universe via emotional stimulation inspired May Fourth poets such as Bing Xin and Xu Zhimo to cultivate an interpersonal poetic form. This encapsulates Tagore's radical potential as both a poet and an advisor: an invitation to create an interpersonal, transregional community of readers; an Eastern alliance of spirituality resisting colonialism and nationalism. But was this potential realized, politically or poetically?

Bing Xin's development of the short poem as manifesting an idea of resonating individual emotional terrains, Xu Zhimo's imagination of the East rising in song of prayer, and Wang Tongzhao's vision of religion as opening a Chinese-Indian literary front are just a few examples of how Chinese writers and poets engaged with Tagore's project of an Eastern spirituality. In this sense, 1920s Chinese literature shows a distinct move away from reading Tagore, and, for that matter, from reading "the East" through a generic prophetic image promoted by Anglo-Americans in the post-Nobel excitement, and through which Tagore was first introduced to Chinese readers in 1915.

It is, however, important to pay attention to the fact that while the legacy of Tagore's Pan-Asianism profoundly inspired Chinese writers, they did not voice its most critical concern: denouncement of the nation as a viable category for modern societies. The Marxists misread Tagore's view of the East as abstract and apolitical. The poets grappled with it in a much more nuanced way, submitting to the notion of the spirit presiding over the machine and thus honing a fundamentally political idea of literature as vehicle for social cohesion. Yet even the most concretely explosive legacy Tagore helped to initiate in Chinese literary culture—namely, the shifting meaning of "religion" from its monotheistic imperial roots as grounded in submission to The One to a transregional shared view of erupting sentiment—did not facilitate a truly radical vision of Chinese society disengaging from the political form of the nation-state. This should not come as a surprise. Such a vision did not materialize in India either, as demonstrated by recent tracing of the roots of contemporary Hindu nationalism to a cynical reading of Vivekananda's call to the West to turn to India, "mother of spiritual humanity."[76] The historical pliability of such categories as "spirituality," "humanity," and, of course, the "East" still informs an interplay between national urgency and transregional aspirations in both China and India. Thus, while the May Fourth envisioning of Pan-Asian poetics of social transformation remained indebted to their exchange with Tagore in writing and in person, the interplay between the national and the transregional—which Tagore dreamed of making irrelevant—remained steadfast. And it continues to this day to arouse battles over the "true" meaning of Tagore's words and the relation between an "Eastern sensibility" and the "Chinese people."

Despite the bitterness with which Tagore initially left China, his relationship with China and Chinese authors did not end there. Tagore dedicated his *Talks in China* to Xu Zhimo, with whom he remained in close contact, and Bing Xin continued to translate Tagore's works until the 1960s. But the presence of Tagore and his ideas should be understood as extending beyond any single individual's encounter with the poet. Tagore's work, as Wang Tongzhao explained, had a major contribution in making Indian thought a meaningful horizon for the May Fourth literary imagination. Once this happened in the early 1920s, Chinese authors continued to draw upon Indian philosophy and literature. The writer and scholar of comparative religion and folklore, Xu Dishan 許地山 (1893–1941), whose literary project is the subject of the next chapter, was a key figure in this respect.

Between 1924 and 1925, Xu spent a year in Oxford and from there traveled back to China through India, where he spent several months at Calcutta University improving his Sanskrit and meeting with local cultural leaders. A critical destination on the itinerary of Chinese writers who traveled to India from the 1920s and onward was Visva Bharati—the university Tagore founded in Santiniketan, Bengal.[77] Xu Dishan met Tagore there, and the encounter left a strong impression on him, as he wrote to his wife in 1933:

You remember how in 1926 as I was heading back to China from England, I deliberately passed through India to pay a visit to sage poet Tagore. I was staying in Varanassi and hitchhiked to Santiniketan, close to Calcutta, to visit the international university that Tagore has founded. I also visited him in his home. He has been my admired senior mentor and bosom friend all along. I remember the beautiful silver ripples of his long hair floating freely, draping his shoulders, and his cheerful, yet exquisitely elegant manner of speech. The deep impression he left has remained with me to this today. He proposed that I compose a Chinese-Sanskrit dictionary to strengthen the connections and exchange between Indian and Chinese scholarship, as well as the friendship between the two countries.[78]

Xu Dishan began working on a Chinese-Sanskrit dictionary, though he was never able to complete it. But the Sino-Indian literary network that Tagore helped to create branched out to realist fiction and scholarly research largely thanks to Xu's contribution. In the next chapter I elaborate on the circumstances and implications of these endeavors.

THREE

Folklore, (Il)literacy, and Cyclical Realism

FOLK-TALES OF BENGAL, a highly acclaimed collection of twenty-two tales, was originally composed in English in 1883 by Reverend Lal Behari Day (1824–1894), an active member of the Bengali Renaissance Movement, which prevailed from the late eighteenth to the mid-twentieth century. The book circulated widely and was reprinted numerous times. A 1912 decorated edition with colored illustrations by the renowned illustrator Warwick Gobble (see figure 3.1) traveled back to Asia across the Indian Ocean, and into the hands of Xu Dishan, by then a leading figure in China's literary circles. In 1929, just a year before he would publish a survey of Indian literature in Chinese—and thus launch the study of Indian literature in China—Xu Dishan translated Folk-Tales of Bengal into Chinese.[1]

Xu was intrigued by the motivation for writing the book, which Reverend Day had specified in his preface:

Captain R. C. Temple of the Bengal Staff Corps, son of the distinguished Indian administrator Sir Richard Temple, wrote to me to say how interesting it would be to get a collection of those unwritten stories which old women in India recite to little children in the evenings, and to ask whether I could not make such a collection. As I was no stranger to the Mährchen of the Brothers Grimm, to the Norse Tales so admirably told by Dasent, to Arnason's Icelandic Stories translated by Powell, to the Highland Stories done into English by Campbell, and to the fairy stories collected by other writers, and as I believed that the collection suggested would be a contribution, however slight, to that daily increasing literature of folk-lore and comparative mythology which, like comparative philosophy, proves that the swarthy and half-naked peasant on the bank of the Ganges is a cousin, albeit of the hundredth remove, to the fair-skinned and well- dressed English-man on the banks of the Thames, I readily caught up the idea and cast about for materials. . . . I have reason to believe that the stories given in this book are a genuine sample of the old old stories told by old Bengali women from age to age through a hundred generations.[2]

Two things stand out in Day's preface: first, the lure of folklore as a cultural equalizer, capable of making the differences between a well-dressed English-man and an Indian peasant disappear in a flash; and second, the role of female storytellers in bridging the gaps through the daily ritual of reciting stories.

In the introduction to his translation of Day's work, Xu shared the author's excitement about folklore and cultural exchange. But whereas Day had rel-ished the thought of cultural affinities with Europe, Xu was more interested in Chinese-Indian connections: "I have always felt that many Indian folktales made their way to China,"[3] he wrote. Like Day, Xu was fascinated by the trope of the old female storyteller that China also exhibits. These storytellers, in Xu Dishan's understanding, conjured transregional folktale imaginaries, sus-tained through oral myths that crossed the borders of the two cultures for hundreds of years. His lengthy introduction details a typology of tropes and plot devices that appear in both Bengali and Chinese folktales. Unlike Day, Xu did not see the folktales themselves as "old." Rather, he understood folk-lore as something that was continually produced, and argued that even the modern era had its own rituals of storytelling. As he put it, "Folktales emerge in every culture, in every time period."[4] Detecting continuity between the ancient and the modern, Xu Dishan approached folklore as a locus of both transhistorical and transcultural connections.[5]

In this chapter, I examine the fiction and scholarship of Xu Dishan, focus-ing on the prominent role of female characters and Xu's use of such charac-ters to invent a literary form I call "cyclical realism," a portrayal of social life that is lived in a nonlinear temporality, and expressed in narrative via rituals of the everyday. The continuity that Xu identified between old folk-tales and modern living—grounded in a history of contact between China and India—underscored an aesthetic of circularity that challenges the truth

FIGURE 3.1 Right: Cover of the 1912 edition of *Folktales of Bengal* (London: Macmillan). Xu Dishan translated from the same edition. Left: Illustration from the story "Phakir Chand," 22.

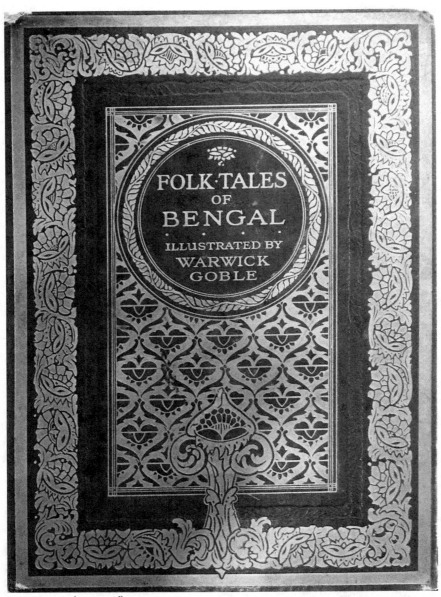

FIGURE 3.1 *(continued)*

claims of colonial bodies of knowledge, namely, folklore studies and comparative religion. Xu Dishan's thinking about Indian religions and folktales—influenced by his training as a scholar of Sanskrit, Buddhism, Daoism, and folklore studies at Yenching, Columbia, and Oxford Universities—helped shape a literature that offered a radical epistemic intervention in the widespread modern Chinese literary practice of realism by extending an invitation to the reader to think about modern living in new ways.

The Transregional Making of a Merchant's Wife

In 1921, eight years prior to the publication of his Chinese translation of Day's *Folktales of Bengal*, Xu Dishan published a story featuring a Chinese-Indian storyteller who uses folktales as a survival mechanism in an age of modern uncertainties. "The Merchant's Wife" (Shangren fu 商人婦) opens when the Chinese narrator withdraws to his cabin aboard a Singapore-bound ship to read a book titled *West Green Random Notes* (*Xi qing san ji* 西青散記). He sees a woman he noticed the day before as the ship docked in Penang and stops to inquire who she is. The mention of his reading material in conjunction with meeting the woman is brief yet telling. *West Green Random Notes* is a collection of writings by the eighteenth-century female poet and painter, He Shuangqing (賀雙卿 1715–1737). Born in the Jiangsu area to a farmer family, He taught herself to read and write by eavesdropping on classes taught by her uncle, the village teacher. In a letter included in *West Green Random Notes*, she writes:

> My uncle said that [in the records,] the story of the man who begged [and got drunk at funeral sacrifices and then boasted of having been wined and dined by friends when he got home] is acrimonious, and the story of [the father who was hauled to court by his son for] stealing a chicken is a fabrication. If he were a disciple of Confucius, he would have had the Master censor these two stories. I said: Uncle has a narrow view which I'm afraid prevents him from truly following [the Dao]. The Dao has no formula, the great teaching is not restricted.[6]

In this letter, He Shuangqing uses the question of what constitutes a proper story to reflect on the broader problem of understanding the Dao. She insists on her own right to define what constitutes a valuable story, beyond formulas that are passed on by male authorities for generations.

He Shuangqing's implicit cameo is also significant for she mirrors in many ways the protagonist of "The Merchant's Wife"—a mystery woman in Indian clothing who, the story reveals, learns to read in unconventional ways, questions what constitutes a proper story, and devises her own interpretation of the proper way to live her life in order to survive. The narrator recognizes there is something different about this woman, and his curiosity is piqued. "Her attire is Indian," he notes, "but her gestures and comportment do not resemble those of an Indian woman." When the woman addresses him in Chinese, he is baffled and asks, "How is it that you speak our language?"[7] She responds by sharing her life story.

Her name is Xiguan, she tells him, and she was born and raised in southern China, in a village near Fujian. While Xiguan was still a young married woman, her husband gambled away the family funds and decided to try his luck earning money in Singapore. He promised to send for her, but after ten years with no word, Xiguan decided to travel to Singapore and seek him out herself. Upon arriving, she finds her husband remarried and running a successful business. When the husband asks why did she not write before showing up, she replies, "Don't you know that I can't write? And that letter writer in our village, Mr. Wang, often writes the wrong words for people even to the point of getting the meaning wrong. That is why I didn't want to ask him to write for me."[8] Xiguan's decision to deliver her own message, rather than rely on the (mis)translations of a male letter-writer, is severely punished: her husband sells her to a Muslim merchant of woolen textiles who proceeds to take her with him from Singapore to Madras, India.

There are many questions to ask about "The Merchant's Wife," but I begin with Xiguan's unexpected yet transformative time in India. Xu Dishan's selection of this setting is significant not only because the majority of Chinese authors at the time were writing about Chinese characters located in mainland China,[9] but also because Xu Dishan explored his particular interest in folktales, which is manifested later in the story, through India. Stranded in a strange land, Xiguan is forced to assume a new identity as an Indian Muslim: "Ah Huye [the new husband] gave me a new name, Li Ya. He ordered me to unbind my feet, pierce a hole in my nose and wear a diamond nose ring. He said that their custom dictates that every married woman must wear a nose ring to signify her marital status. He also gave me fine quality

Kurta, ma-la-mu and a pair of *ai-san.* I was thus transformed into a Muslim wife."[10]

Closely watched so that she doesn't escape or kill herself, Xiguan has no choice but to accept her new identity. Her single source of support is the new-found friendship she makes with her husband's third wife, Akolima, who teaches Xiguan to read Arabic and Bengali. The description of how Xiguan learns to read is interwoven with descriptions of her husband abusing her sexually. Attributing her current circumstances to her previous lack of lit-eracy, Xiguan is eager to learn and does so rapidly, despite the two difficult and utterly different languages. Her experience of learning how to read for the first time is conveyed in a single sentence: "She [Akolima] also taught me how to read Bengali and Arabic [scripts]."[11] The brevity of the descrip-tion contrasts sharply with other passages in the text that provide, for exam-ple, elaborate details of clothing, jewelry, and local customs.

For today's readers of Xu Dishan's works, this depiction connotes another similar instance, in which he portrays an illiterate female protagonist who learns how to read Chinese in romanized script within a single week. This is Yuguan, the eponymous protagonist of Xu Dishan's well-known novella (*Yuguan* 玉官, 1939), who finds shelter from the persecutions of a family mem-ber in the home of a fellow female villager, an avid Christian, where she finds a Bible written in Romanized Minnan dialect. Her Christian friend teaches her how to read the Romanized script, and "in seven days Yuguan could read the thick book as fluently as running water."[12] How should we understand such tales of miraculously rapid literacy acquisition?[13] Whereas May Fourth writers often pitted the figure of the subaltern illiterate woman against that of a young male scholar who represented China's bright future,[14] Xu Dishan shunned this binary opposition by providing a nuanced explora-tion of literacy as thoroughly connected to orality. We can see this in the passages that immediately follow the description of Xiguan learning Ben-gali and Arabic.

Along with her newly acquired literacy, Xiguan enjoys listening to the folktales that Akolima routinely shares. The tales become the foundation of their friendship and the sustenance of Xiguan's daily hardships in a foreign country with a new culture and religion. One day, Akolima presents Xiguan with a copy of the Quran. She tells Xiguan that women are traditionally not encouraged to read this book, but it can be a source of comfort in times of physical and emotional turmoil. Thus, literacy constitutes both a resource and a form of rescue: the two women, one Chinese and one Bengali, find solace through a scripture women are forbidden to access. But instead of teaching the new Muslim convert to read the holy book and deepen her faith, Akolima reveals to Xiguan how folktales can rewrite, or retell the sacred word. This is Xiguan's account of the experience:

> Though no matrimonial love existed between my new husband and myself, I couldn't avoid having sex with him. Alas! This boy (she stroked his head) was born in my second year in Madras. I was over thirty when I got pregnant for the first time. The pain was harsher than anything I have ever endured. Luckily Akolima was there to care for me, comfort me, and teach me how to forget the pain at hand. Once, when the discomfort was unbearable, she told me: "Liya, you must endure. We are not as lucky as the fig tree. It is recorded in the Quran that Adam and Eve were seduced by the demon Aja to steal and eat the forbidden fruit. Once they did, they lost the divine garments that they were wearing. They felt ashamed of their nakedness and implored all the trees in paradise to lend them leaves to cover themselves. Because they disobeyed Allah, no tree dared helping them. Only the fig tree took pity on them and generously gave them its leaves. Allah praised the fig tree for this gesture and blessed it to bear fruit without blossoming first, thus saving the fig tree from butterflies harassing it. That is why we may not avoid the pains of bearing children. Whenever you are in pain, think of Allah's grace. He will take pity on you and give you peace." She helped me so much before and after my delivery. I could never forget her kindness.[15]

In the Quran, although Adam and Eve repent and are forgiven by Allah,[16] Akolima omits this detail in her telling. Instead, she uses the formal verb "recorded" (from *zai* 載—a term used in premodern Chinese historiography to denote recording in official documents) to describe what is written in the Quran. Not actually citing the Quran allows her to retell the story of the original Sura in a way that highlights the fig tree. But the Quran does not specify which tree Adam and Eve used to make their clothing or even mention that Allah praised the fig tree for offering its help. Here it is important to know that unlike other fruit-bearing trees, fig florets are hidden inside the fruit of the fig and are only pollinated by a particular type of hornet that is able to penetrate the fig. Thus fig trees are protected from common insects. Moreover, in Bengali, the common fig is called *dumur*, and a well-known saying goes: "You have become [invisible like] the *dumur* flower" (*tumi jeno dumurer phool hoe gele*). In Chinese, the common fig is called *wuhuaguo* (無花果), which literally means the flowerless fruit.

Was Xu Dishan familiar with this Bengali proverb relating to the fig tree? Did this emphasis on the fig as flowerless—shared by both Chinese and Indian traditions—facilitate the meeting ground for Akolima and Xiguan? Whether drawing on a textual exegetical tradition or an oral one, Akolima changes the original scripture in response to Xiguan's physical pain. The story of a tree that is spared the pain of insects probing into its flowers—allegorical of Xiguan's abuse by her husband—is offered to bring comfort. It is not faith, the act of conversion, or reading the true word of the scripture that comforts, but the story and its specific telling by a compassionate friend. In this way, a folktale intervenes in the act of reading, rupturing the sacred text with orality. How, then, should the reader understand Xiguan's literacy? Without it, she was kidnapped and enslaved, but no sooner does she acquire literacy than its significance is overshadowed by the power of oral storytelling. Retelling the texts in the scriptures in ways relevant to their lives, Xiguan and Akolima soothe the physical pain inflicted upon their bodies, and, in so doing, render their lives livable.

Soon after Xiguan's delivery Akolima is banished from the household, and Xiguan finds herself lonely once again. She manages to escape in the dead of night. During her flight, she stops to look up in the sky and notices Venus. Another folktale that Akolima shared with her comes to her mind. Venus, Akolima told her, was once upon a time a seductive woman who metamorphosed into a star after seducing too many men. Remembering this folktale, Xiguan experiences a profound spiritual awakening:

> As I was gazing at the morning star, a voice seemed to be coming out of its starry glow, and said: "Xiguan, do not take me for a man-luring woman. You should know that shiny things couldn't delude anyone. I am the first to appear among all the stars, to tell you that darkness is approaching, and the last to disappear, drawing you close to the rays of the sun. I am the brightest star in the night, and I can be your own guiding star." Facing Venus, my anger was relieved, and I felt gratitude. Since then, whenever I would see Venus, I felt a unique connection with it.[17]

Xiguan finds confidence in her choice to escape from physical and emotional oppression and, from that point on, takes control over her body and herself.

Making the story that she heard from Akolima her own, she creates a ritual of gazing at Venus, her own personal way of connecting with the universe. But then, Xiguan's travel plan changes once again: she misses the boat that is supposed to take her to a different part of India and ends up in a small town near Madras. There, she makes a new friend—this time, a Christian missionary named Elizabeth. The pattern of woman-to-woman compassion is repeated: Elizabeth, like Akolima, teaches Xiguan to read in a new language—in this case, English. Xiguan attends an adult missionary education program and eventually becomes a Christian.

The extent of Xiguan's journey is striking: in less than three years, she moves between three locations (China, Singapore, and India); converts to two different religions (Islam, then Christianity); and learns to read three different languages (Arabic, Bengali, and English), none of which are her native tongue. When the narrator meets Xiguan, she is on her way back to Singapore in an attempt to locate her husband. She wants to find out from him who sold her, as she believes her husband incapable of coming up with such a plan. After listening to her story, the narrator responds: "It is admirable how you found your own way in this life of constant drifting." To this, Xiguan replies: "I am not that smart. It is the guide up above who directs me."

But which guide is she talking about? Allah? Jesus? Scholars who study Xu Dishan's work often mine his fiction for clues that might indicate whether he identified more as a Christian or a Buddhist.[18] It is tempting to read "The Merchant's Wife" as a triumph of Christianity offering liberation to the disenfranchised Fujianese woman, if only because the conversion to Christianity takes place late in the narrative. Yet despite converting to two different religions, Xiguan remains vague about the identity of the "guide up above," which makes her piousness somewhat hollow.[19] After this ambiguous statement, however, Xiguan adds a comment that suggests a different interpretation: "The two most moving books that I read in school were *The Pilgrim's Progress* and *Robinson Crusoe*. These books consoled me and gave me an example to follow. By now I am truly a female Crusoe."[20]

Missionary literacy pedagogy often targeted illiterate women, who, during the nineteenth century became the focal point of the civilizing mission. Pivotal to the discursive distinction between "civilization" and "savagery" that geography and social sciences textbooks exported across the colonial world in the latter part of the nineteenth century was "The Woman Question"—a notion that linked women directly to the evolutionary structure of civilizational progress.[21] Emerging in Victorian England and quickly spanning Asia, the Middle East, and the Americas, the idea behind the woman question located the condition of women in a certain country—particularly the numbers of literate women, the customary marital age, and body-related practices (tattoos, ear and nose piercing, foot-binding, self-immolation, wearing a headscarf)—as the yardstick for measuring that country's level of civilization.[22] Chinese and Indian male intellectuals read about the woman question in global bestsellers such as John Stuart Mill's *The Subjection of Women* (1869) and Herbert Spencer's *Social Statics or the Conditions Essential for Human Happiness*, which included a chapter titled "The Rights of Women" (1851). As a result, such male liberals, often with the support of missionaries, launched the first campaigns in China and India to end foot-binding and widow self-immolation (*sati*), raise the marriage age, and provide women with vocational education.[23]

Shaopeng Song has mapped one of the routes through which Protestant missionaries introduced this correlation between female subjugation and savagery in China, by way of India. In 1900 Young J. Allen, whose editorial work I mention in chapter 1, and who wrote extensively about the condition of women in China, translated into Chinese and published William Ewart Gladstone's (1809–1898) essay "On The Position of Indian Women Then and Now," which urged missionaries to focus their efforts on women. Their innate pristine emotionality, Gladstone argued, rendered women more susceptible to religious conversion. Song charts how this linkage between civilizational level and women's condition thus traveled from Europe to India and then to China through British and then American agents of the Bible, respectively.[24]

Robinson Crusoe and *The Pilgrim's Progress* were both foundational texts for the Protestant Missionary Movement in the nineteenth century. Protestant missionary emphasis on literacy as a miraculous event forged a close connection between translation and evangelization. Literature, particularly *The Pilgrim's Progress*, was so successful in raising conversion rates that it was often preferred over scriptures as teaching material.[25] The fictional character of Xiguan—a Chinese woman who learns how to read in English in a British missionary school in India—links the China-India history of missionary pedagogical exchange to the specifics of how women became entangled in the discourse of literacy and civilization. This history contextualizes Xiguan's comment but not as a victim in any way: by naming herself a "female Crusoe," Xiguan personalizes the original Defoe and undoes, in that, the missionary pedagogy that taught her how to read it. Far from being a passive form of reading, the literacy Xiguan has gained in English is an active, agentic form that weaves the stories she reads into her own life.

But what exactly does she mean when she describes herself as a female Crusoe? In both *The Pilgrim's Progress* and *Robinson Crusoe*, the male protagonists set out on long journeys with a distinct purpose. Both journeys also have closure: in *Crusoe*, Robinson goes back home, and in *The Pilgrim's Progress*, Christian finds the celestial city. Xiguan's story, in contrast, follows a pattern of wandering that is not linear. Salvation in her story comes in a different form—specifically, through textual sources that she makes her own. Despite learning how to read in three languages, Xiguan returns again and again to an oral form of storytelling. When the boat reaches Singapore, she informs the narrator that she has decided to stay there for a few days to try to find her husband on her own; to see if he is willing to take her back. "If I'm unsuccessful, I will return to India," she says. Then she adds, "Ah, I have become an Indian now!"[26] When we leave Xiguan, she is just as she was when we first met her: en route.

Missionary Education and Colonial Folklore

The author of *Folktales of Bengal*, Lal Behari Day, had something in common with Xu Dishan: both belonged to the first generation of scholars who trained in English in the first modern schools in their countries. Day was a student at the General Assembly Institution in Calcutta, founded and run by the Scottish missionary Alexander Duff (1806–1878). A model student and convert, Day had won three essay competitions held at the General Assembly, with such topics as "Most Accurate Knowledge of Scripture Proofs for Doctrines," "Conversion of St Paul: Viewed as an Argument for the Truth of the Gospel," and "The Falsity of Hindu Religion."[27] Xu attended missionary schools in Fujian in his youth and became a student and a teacher at the missionary Yenching University in Beijing from 1918 to 1935. Scholarship on the development of modern universities in China has traditionally located Japan and Germany as the two sources from which Chinese educators drew their vision for educational reform. These studies mainly focus on Peking University, the hub of radical student movements throughout the twentieth century.[28] Just as influential in defining new goals for higher education as Peking University, however, were a small number of missionary colleges, namely, Yenching in Beijing and St. John's University in Shanghai.[29] The colonial legacy upon which these institutions were founded compels us to look toward India—arguably the first testing ground for projects of missionary education in Asia—in order to get a better grasp of the complex relationship between Anglo-American-imported knowledge and local negotiations of this knowledge.

I mentioned in the introduction that the first institution of Orientalist scholarship, the Asiatic Society, was established in Bengal in 1784, and legitimized Indology as a new field of European scholarship. By the mid-nineteenth century, Indology branched out to new disciplines such as comparative religion and modern linguistics, and Indian pundits and students became more and more involved in the intellectual activities of the society.[30] The Bengali Renaissance—a Bengal-based movement that called for national revival through modernization of India's past religious traditions, was the offspring of the collaboration between British colonial scholarship and missionaries' importation of Western science and technology. Modern universities, especially the University of Calcutta, where Lal Behari Day taught English, were the seedbed for the development of the Bengali Renaissance. By 1916, the founding year of Yenching, the University of Calcutta was the largest in the world with 27,000 students and extensive connections with universities around the globe.[31] Xu Dishan, who taught Sanskrit and Buddhist literature in Yenching, spent time at the University of Calcutta in 1926 and 1933, on both occasions studying Sanskrit and conducting research.

Decades earlier, missionaries in China would turn to their more seasoned peers in India to learn "what works" in programs of evangelization and literacy. As we saw in chapter 1, missionary journals contain many advertisements for reading primers or Christian education materials that specifically highlight the previous success of these materials in India. It is very likely that Xu Dishan first learned English and read about India in missionary school in southern China through such primers, or "India Readers," used by missionaries in British-run schools in India. We have evidence showing that missionaries who worked in China in these years avidly encouraged the "India model" of English-language training there. India Readers were used in China's southern provinces, where missionary presence in elementary school education was particularly strong.[32]

Moreover, Day and Xu were both informed by their specifically colonial introduction to folklore and its study—a project that was, from its inception, imbricated with the larger imperial civilizing mission. Sadhana Naithani has shown that the study of folklore in the colonial world differed from the same scholarship in Europe in terms of both theory and practice. Nineteenth-century European folktale collectors (the Brothers Grimm are a familiar example) were trained philologists who set out to excavate ancient proverbs, myths, tales, and songs so as to ascertain the roots of what was believed to be their nation's identity. The first folklore researchers in Asia, by contrast, were nonspecialists. British officers studied folktales and folksongs in India as a side project and depended upon the help of local informants for communication and translation.[33] Richard Carnac Temple (1850–1931), who inspired Day's project, is an important case in point. Serving as Chief Commissioner of the Andaman and Nicobar Islands, Temple also spent time collecting folktales, legends, and versified tales in Punjab. Coining the term "colonizer-folklorist," Temple argued that folklore collection would aid in governance by smoothing communication between colonizers and natives.[34] Temple and other aspiring folklorists believed that folklore collection not only provided essential knowledge of the empire, but was an act of benevolence the British Crown extended toward the local population—designating its representatives custodians of the ancient traditions of the people they conquered. Lal Behari Day's introduction to *Folktales of Bengal* demonstrates how well this message was received. Indian collectors gradually became convinced of the importance of preserving their cultural roots—enamored, as we saw in Day's intro, by that elusive promise of comparative folklore: that the Englishman and the Indian peasant might prove to be distant cousins.[35] These collectors paved the way for the professionalization of folklore studies in India, which, during the 1920s, and as British officers began to lose interest in collection activities, were shaped anew by Indian folklorists dedicated to understanding their own "primitive cultures" and developing a distinct national identity.[36]

Professionalized folklore research executed by local specialists boomed across Asia in 1920s. Lydia Liu has shown how in China, the new discipline of folklore studies—*Minsuxue* 民俗學 in Chinese—dovetailed with an effort to define a uniquely Han Chinese ethnic identity through field research on rural minorities.[37] Folklore studies flourished in Chinese academia, inspiring the establishment of study groups, journals, extensive fieldwork, and data collection surveys of folksongs, proverbs, and riddles in local dialects.[38] Spearheading the research was the Folklore Movement at Peking University, with its pioneering publication *Folksong Weekly* (*Geyao zhou-kan* 歌謠周刊, 1922–1925), which boasted the era's most well-known literature scholar, Zhou Zuoren, as its editor. Dedicated to the execution and documentation of a large-scale survey, the journal reported on the collection and recording of folksongs all over China. A preliminary typology of ballads (*minge* 民歌) and children's songs (*erge* 兒歌) guided the contributors in their efforts to preserve and analyze a repository of common people's literature (*pingmin wenxue* 平民文學) as testament to national sentiments in their most primordial state.[39] Xu Dishan worked closely as Zhou Zuoren's assistant (Zhou was appointed the first chair of the Chinese Literature Department in Yenching in 1922), while studying and teaching courses in folklore and social anthropology.[40]

Lal Behari Day and Xu Dishan both studied folklore through the mediation of colonial education, which trained Asian folklorists to tie field research of the so-called original peoples to national strengthening in a competitive modern world order. And yet, while Day ultimately saw the global reach of folktales as a means to prove kinship between the Bengali and the Brit, and to validate his own culture, Xu had a more radical vision in mind. Drawing from Bengali folktales to ascertain the exchange between Chinese and Indian folk traditions, Xu Dishan reframed the purpose of folklore studies. In his view, folktales were not a source from which to glean the savage origin of mankind, but rather a means of coping with everyday life in times of flux through regional rituals and relations of storytelling. For Xu, these rituals and relations were powerful because they fostered regional forms of solidarity—such as the solidarity shared between Akolima and Xiguan.

The notion of regional solidarity through storytelling helps us to better situate the inversion of the hierarchy between literacy and orality that takes place in "The Merchant's Wife." By rewriting the Quran and two evangelical blockbusters as means for his protagonist to cope with challenges of modern life—such as financial duress, patriarchal oppression, migration, and colonial education—Xu Dishan offers an intervention in the way modernity is understood. Instead of affirming a narrative of cultural evolution from storytelling to literacy, and from Asian barbarianism to European enlightenment, in Xu's work orality continually returns, not as a savage past that haunts a progressive present, but to offer a source of consolation.

A History of Savage Life

Much like his literary characters, Xu Dishan spent his life crisscrossing various geographical borders. Born in Taiwan a year before its colonization by Japan as a result of the First Sino-Japanese War, Xu's father, a Qing official, refused to serve under the Japanese colonial regime. As a result, the family spent Xu's childhood as refugees, moving between Taiwan, Thailand, Singapore, Guangdong, and Fujian. Between 1913 and 1918, Xu taught Mandarin in Rangoon, Myanmar. He then relocated to Fujian, where he converted to Christianity and joined the Minnan London Missionary Society before finally arriving in Beijing. Befriending key figures in the New Culture Movement, Xu Dishan was among the founding members of the influential Chinese Literary Association (Wenxue yanjiuhui 文學研究會 1920–1947), as well as a cofounder of *Fiction Monthly*. In 1920, Xu graduated from the department of Chinese in Yenching University and continued to study toward his bachelor of divinity degree.

In 1923, Xu set sail for New York, where he pursued a master's degree in comparative religion at Columbia University under the guidance of the first chair of Indo-Iranian languages there, A. V. Williams Jackson (1862–1937). A pioneering expert on Iranian languages and literatures, whose 1892 study on Avestan grammar (the language used in Zoroastrian scriptures) is considered seminal to this day, Jackson studied Manichaeism for several years in the 1920s and encouraged his Chinese student to write on the history of Manichaeism in China. Xu's thesis investigated Chinese sources on the introduction and ensuing religious persecution of Manichaeism from the ninth to the sixteenth century. Focusing on the failure of Manichaeism to endure in China, Xu argued that to understand the religious persecution of Manichaean clergy and believers, one had to look beyond doctrine-based objections to the new religion as heretical. Xu thus traced Manichaeism's persecution to the government's loss of tax revenues due to the growth in Mani believers and clergy, who were exempted from paying taxes—a privilege reserved for religious institutions and famously abused throughout Chinese history.[41]

This emphasis on material concerns in understanding the history of religions remained central in Xu's scholarly and creative writings throughout his career. His intellectual passion for the nonscriptural aspects of religions, particularly rituals and myths, led him to depart from the theologically inflected work of many of his colleagues at Yenching.[42] As a result, Xu devoted his attention and his training abroad to emerging disciplines in Chinese academia such as comparative religion and folklore. He was deeply invested in folklore studies during these two decades and published, as early as 1920, several studies of folksongs and folk customs in journals such as *New Society* (*Xin shehui* 新社會), which Xu Dishan established with Qu Qiubai.[43] But significantly, Xu was not involved in the Peking University Movement and did not publish anything in *Folksong Weekly*. The reason, in my view, is most likely the strong progressive stance that *Folksong Weekly* writers assumed in relation to issues such as rituals and superstitions. For Xu, these were an integral part of any folklore research that aims to understand culture in a fundamental way, but the *Folksong Weekly* writers did not include rituals or religious practice in their typologies. Instead, they regarded supernatural elements in songs as superstitions (*mixin* 迷信)—a primitive predecessor of modern religion.[44] The Peking Movement's approach argued that superstitious elements should only be studied as a way to avoid regressing to backward beliefs in demons and ghosts.[45] Xu's understanding of the superstitious elements in folklore was different. Emphasizing that folktales "emerge in every culture, in every time period," he developed a radically different conception of both folklore studies and the relationship between the so-called savage and civilized.[46]

In 1932, Xu formed a research group along with Jiang Shaoyuan 江紹原 (1898–1993), a scholar of comparative religion at Peking University, and three colleagues, social scientists from Yenching who were working in folklore studies and anthropology: Wu Wenzao 吳文藻 (1901–1985), Huang Huajie 黃華節 (b. 1901–?), and Li Anzhai 李安宅 (1900–1985). This group of scholars operated separately from the Peking Movement and offered a different approach to folklore research. Their leading project was a study titled *A History of Savage Life* (*Yeman shenghuo shi* 野蠻生活史). In a call for papers published in *Tianjin da gongbao* (天津大公報) to solicit contributions to their compendium, Xu wrote a short satiric history of mankind, describing its rise from among the animals to dominate nature, leading over the centuries to ever more bitter and destructive wars. The grace of science, Xu narrated, has turned into tanks and bombs. Life in savage societies was in many ways much safer: "We should never forget that 'Man' originated among the rest of the animals. If scientists love the term 'evolved' so much, then let them have it, it doesn't change this mere fact."[47] Thus undermining the validity of evolution as a frame for understanding human history, *A History of Savage Life* aimed to highlight the connections that we have with our past: Is modern medicine that different from primitive potions made from animals feces? Is modern jewelry truly so different from tribal attire? Are habits we perceive as sexually deviant so divorced from our modern-day infidelities within the institution of marriage? These were the type of questions the research group raised.

Twelve volumes of 100,000 characters each were planned, covering the following topics: consumption of food and narcotics, sexual habits, prostitution, theft, slavery, corporeal punishment, murder, medicine, sorcery, superstition, attire, and warfare. By revealing the strong connections we still have with our savage past, Xu concluded, "we hope that our work will introduce the true face of what we now term 'culture,' so that our readers will know that humanity, till this day, continues to be 'savage' or 'half-civilized.'"[48] This last sentence tied together the whole meaning of the project, both politically and theoretically. By bringing forth a new definition of culture, *A History of Savage Life* aspired to challenge the hierarchical understandings of savage/civilized. In this respect, Xu Dishan and his colleagues offered a radical alternative to the mainstream national and ethnically driven folklore studies of the Peking Movement. Whereas the latter focused their efforts on essentializing a Han origin and its modern turn away from its superstition-ridden past, Xu Dishan and his collaborators located the primitive and the superstitious not as objects of fantasy or imagined origin, but as part and parcel of the modern era.

Cycles of Creation and Destruction

The argument that the savage is very much part of modern civilization was foreshadowed in Xu's definition of religion, which he solidified about a decade earlier. In a 1922 essay titled "The Rise and Fall of Religions" (Zongjiao de shengzhang yu miewang 宗教的生長與滅亡), Xu developed an approach to religion as an object of study that is separate from theology.[49] He defined it thus: "Religion has always been a living thing and cannot be contained within a simple fixed definition. All religions operate throughout history in dynamic cycles of creation and destruction. They are not a set of doctrinal truths but a dynamic process of dealing with nature."[50]

Earlier in the essay, Xu invoked the works of Max Müller (1823–1900), the renowned Sanskrit philologist whose work cemented the hegemony of comparative grammar and founded the discipline of historical linguistics (see my discussion of Müller in the introduction and chapter 1). Müller's initial career as a prominent Indologist led him, in tandem with the growing momentum of Orientalist scholarship on the Near and Far East, to develop a disciplinary framework for comparative research of religious traditions worldwide. Defining religion as a human "faculty of the infinite,"[51] Müller and his colleagues established a typology of recognized "world religions." Hinduism was one of the first world religions to be consolidated as such. As Richard King illuminates, the tenets of monotheistic traditions—particularly the privileging of scriptures over rituals—were used to recognize and assess Hinduism as religion. King's analysis reveals much about the critical role that Christianity assumed in informing European scholarship of Vedic texts:

> The philosophical orientation of the *Upaniṣads* and the *Gītā* seems to have appealed to Westerners with a variety of interests and agendas. The texts appealed to the anti-clerical and anti-ritualistic sentiments of many Western intellectuals and proved amenable to abstraction from their own context via an emphasis upon interiority. The allegorization of Vedic ritual found in the *Upaniṣads* could be applied to all religious practices and institutions, proving amenable to the growing interest in non-institutionalized forms of spirituality. On the other hand, for Christian missionaries the *Upaniṣads* could also be used as evidence of an incipient monotheism within the Hindu tradition. For the liberal Christian this provided a platform for inter-faith dialogue between Christianity and Hinduism and a recognition of some commonality between faiths. Max Müller, for instance, was interested in the comparability of Indian religion and his own liberal version of Christianity and became increasingly preoccupied by the possibilities of a Christian Vedānta in his later years.[52]

King highlights how Vedic textuality mediated the spread of Christian imperialism to Asia at large, particularly through the tension between literacy and oral traditions. The appropriation King describes of the Upanishads and the

Bhagavad Gita—the manifestation of which missionaries sought hard to find in these texts—is key, epitomized in the obliteration of their ritualistic elements in favor of an "emphasis upon interiority." Studies demonstrate that in America and Britain, the modern separation between church and state, which begot freedom of religious worship as a major part of the discourse of natural rights, relegated faith to the human interior, all while maintaining the modern paradox that interior faith leads the believer to connect with the exterior divinity.[53] New bodies of knowledge such as comparative religion quickly adopted this privileging of the written word, thus removing elements of oral traditions from the (re)construction of Indian religious texts. The privileging of the written word stipulated the terms and conditions for what could and could not be considered "religion." In so doing, it also supported and sustained an imperialist world order grounded in evolutionary logic, according to which certain civilizations evolved to be recognized as belonging to a known religion while others did not fulfill the universal standards of such a belonging. Examples abound. One need only glance at the preface to Müller's monumental fifty-volume translation project, *Sacred Books of the East* (1879–1910), referenced by Xu Dishan in "The Rise and Fall of Religions:"

We must try to imagine what the Old Testament would have been, if it had not been kept distinct from the Talmud; or the New Testament, if it had been mixed up not only with the spurious gospels, but with the records of the wrangling of the early Councils, if we wish to understand, to some extent at least, the wild confusion of sublime truth with vulgar stupidity that meets us in the pages of the Veda, the Avesta, and the Tripitaka. The idea of keeping the original and genuine tradition separate from apocryphal accretions was an idea of later growth, that could spring up only after the earlier tendency of preserving whatever could be preserved of sacred or half-sacred lore, had done its work, and wrought its own destruction. . . . If we are once satisfied that the text of the Avesta, or the Veda, or the Tripitaka is old and genuine, and that this text formed the foundation on which, during many centuries, the religious belief of millions of human beings was based, it becomes our duty, both as historians and philosophers, to study these books, to try to understand how they could have arisen, and how they could have exercised for ages an influence over human beings who in all other respects were not inferior to ourselves, nay, whom we are accustomed to look up to on many points as patterns of wisdom, of virtue, and of taste. . . . Shall we say then that they were forsaken of God, while we are His chosen people? God forbid! There is much, no doubt, in their sacred books which we should tolerate no longer, though we must not forget that there are portions in our own sacred books, too, which many of us would wish to be absent, which, from the earliest ages of Christianity, have been regretted by theologians of undoubted piety, and which often prove a stumbling block to those who have been won over by our missionaries to the simple faith of Christ.[54]

The underlying narrative, evident here, of a mutual evolutionary process that impacted religions worldwide was one of the core methodological assumptions of comparative religion scholars, in the same way that it undergirded the metanarrative of a transfer from savage to civilized in folklore studies. Müller urged his readers to take any religious tradition as valid research material and not shy away from an amalgam of the spiritual and the mundane—or, as he calls it, confusion of the vulgar and the sublime. But the presumption of a historical shift away from confusion, towards an enlightened, textually-based religion—that is, the Christian faith—was the premise driving his project forward.

Xu Dishan, however, proposed a different understanding of religion, and we can now investigate further the meaning of the definition I cited above: "Religion has always been a living thing and cannot be contained within a simple fixed definition. All Religions operate throughout history in dynamic cycles of creation and destruction. They are not a set of doctrinal truths but a dynamic process of dealing with nature."

This definition certainly aims to encapsulate religions as historical instances with universal commonalities. In this sense, it fits the premises of comparative religion. But the resemblance ends there. For in Xu's view, religions do not evolve from oral chant to silent reading of scriptures so much as they operate in cycles of creation and destruction, with religious practices—the dynamic process of dealing with nature—constantly appearing when a new religion is born, and then disappearing when a religion is no longer practiced. In underscoring a cyclical structure for religiosity, Xu built upon his study and personal experience of Hinduism and Buddhism in Myanmar, India, and China. Cycles of rebirth and the creation and destruction of worlds are integral to both religions' perceptions of historical time.[55] In turning to Indian and Chinese religious traditions to come up with his own definition of religion, Xu nevertheless could not simply do away with the European frameworks that structured his own training. On the contrary: in "The Rise and Fall of

Religions" he dialogs directly with seminal works in comparative religion and folklore studies such as Müller's *Sacred Books of the East* and *The Golden Bough: A Study in Magic and Religion* by James Frazer (1854–1941).[56] Yet in his conversation with these works, rather than embracing their narration of a developmental human history, in which religions evolve from the savage, the ritualistic, and the superstitious into scripture-based faiths, the history of religions Xu Dishan defined is a cyclical history, revealing the repetition of certain elements in ancient as well as modern times, with one constant commonality: religions exist to mediate between people—and that which is beyond their control—to facilitate ways to "deal with nature." Departing from prevailing cultural and scholarly trends, Xu Dishan rejected an Orientalist-evolutionary narrative and, likewise, did not participate in the fervent search for an authentic Han nationality—a search that similarly located folk religious practices as a primitive stage from which China had to emerge.

If, as Wang Tongzhao suggested (see chapter 2), the opening of the May Fourth literary imagination to Indian thought expanded previous definitions of religion that were based on imperialist monotheistic grounds, Xu Dishan pushed these boundaries both politically and aesthetically. Trained as a scholar of comparative religion and as a folklorist, Xu critiqued the colonial legacy of his education by envisioning a different fate for religion in the modern era. The episteme of rebirth cycles enabled Xu to imagine a religion capable of constant renewal precisely because it was not bound to a particular doctrine. He thus located the function of religion in human history by moving away from enshrining religions of the book as the apex of human development, as well as from positing Buddhism or Hinduism as "distant cousins" or worthy opponents to monoletheism. Xu Dishan radicalized a notion of religion that does not evolve but rises and falls, and which recognized the place of the material, the ritualistic, the oral, and the mundane in the religious life of modern Chinese society. Upholding practice rather than scripture and doctrine and emphasizing cross-cultural storytelling and rituals, Xu conceptualized religion as a survival mechanism in both his scholarship and his fiction.

Cyclical Realism: Life as Web

In 1922, the same year that "The Rise and Fall of Religions" was published, Xu Dishan's short story titled "The Web-Mending Spider" (Zhui wang lao zhu

綴網撈蛛) appeared in *Fiction Monthly*. The story, which focuses on a Chinese Christian convert who is persecuted by her local church, disengages from it, and sets out to Malaya on a quest to find her true faith, opens with a short passage that the protagonist, named Shangjie, later cites to describe her life: "I am like a spider. Fate is my web. The spider gobbles down every insect, whether poisonous or not, and then goes back to weave. The first gossamer that they weave will be blown away by the wind, no one knows how far. But they will wait to patch it up with something, anything, and then their web will be complete once more."[57] Xu Dishan's female protagonists—while often illiterate—are savvy users of figurative language. Much like Xiguan, the "female Crusoe" and the old clothes mender whose story I discuss at the end of this chapter, Shangjie calls herself a web-mending spider to describe a life of subsistence. As a poignant metaphor for this protagonist's travails, the idea of repeated web mending expressed here nevertheless extends beyond the story itself to suggest a new narrative structure that characterizes Xu Dishan's fiction more broadly and offers a critical intervention in modern Chinese literature's engagement with realism as form. This narrative structure, which grounds the representation of human life and social reality in recurring patterns of creation, repetition, and destruction, grew directly from Xu Dishan's Hinduism- and Buddhism-inspired idea of how religions work.

In the *Fiction Monthly* issue that published "The Web-Mending Spider," Mao Dun—then editor of the journal—made the following prefatory comment:

> "The Web-Mending Spider" by Xu Dishan at first glance reads like a story about a religious believer, but I say that this story actually embodies the tragedy of human life trapped in the web of fate, whereas one will not necessarily fulfill their expectations even if they work hard. But this view of fate is different from the determinism advocated by naturalism, for it harbors a spirit of relentless struggle.[58]

Mao Dun's words here shed important light on Xu Dishan's intervention in May Fourth literary realism. Being a vociferous proponent of realism and naturalism in Republican China, Mao Dun notes how "The Web-Mending Spider" is situated both within and without a realist framework as it was practiced at the time: the story portrays the tragic aspects of human life with precision yet offers a view of fate that is "different from the determinism advocated by naturalism." Indeed, the spider web as a metaphor for the course of life exemplifies a fundamentally different rationale than the linear determinist narrative that characterized the European realist and naturalist fiction—especially the works of Leo Tolstoy, Victor Hugo, and Emile Zola—which inspired many Chinese authors in the 1920s and 1930s.

Whereas late Qing intellectuals began to conceive of socially engaged literature as critical for national transformation, by the early Republican period, Chinese writers produced what they viewed as socially effective fiction mainly by employing the generic frame of realism (*xieshi* 寫實), understood as a literary representation of social life with scientific accuracy. In 1915, Chen Duxiu proclaimed in *New Youth*'s inaugural volume that science dominates all realms of life: in philosophy it is materialism and experimentalism, in politics it is eudemonism, and in literature and aesthetics it is realism and naturalism.[59] Chen and others—most notably Zhou Zuoren, whose 1918 milestone essay "Literature of Humans" (Ren de wenxue 人的文學) pioneered a critical engagement with literary realism in China[60]—reflected the permeation of a scientific understanding of human life that was deeply informed by evolutionary theory. The task of exposing social realities as underscored by a strong sense of biological determinism, under which contingency only the fittest survive, was perceived as the road to enlightenment and change. As Andrew Jones has succinctly put it, Chinese writers of new literature assumed the task of "pushing the developmental process forward, of enlightening the nation so as to enable its movement up the evolutionary ladder of a 'civilization' (*wenming*) exemplified by the imperial powers of the West."[61]

Despite being a leading member of Chinese intelligentsia, Xu Dishan steered his writing away from developmental conventions that depicted the weaker members of society as destined to their own extinction. Instead, he offered what can be called a cyclical realism: fiction that portrayed society's most oppressed members—disenfranchised, illiterate women—as sustaining a circular web-like structure through their everyday rituals, like the storyteller who every evening tells the same stories passed down from generation to generation but also modifies them as she goes along.

In his stories Xu Dishan depicts human life as a recurring act of mending one's fate. The image of the spider's web captures this perfectly, with its simultaneous reliance on a line (the single gossamer creating the web) that is also necessary for the patching, repetition, and circulation of the web's expansion and progress. In "The Merchant's Wife" we saw how

Xiguan negotiates her fate through the personalization of rituals and scriptures of the two monotheistic religions to which she converts. Her path is anything but linear and determinist: it is amenable, subject to change, and shaped not by an evolutionary rationale but by her particular way of engaging with texts and reading. Xiguan's retelling of stories from the scriptures and her invocation of folktales and proverbs locate literacy as a means to question the truth claims of doctrinal scriptures. A specialist in comparative religions, Xu's renegade definition of what religions are and how they work in people's lives shaped not just his scholarship, but his narrative craft as well. His study of Hindu and Buddhist conceptual frames informed more than thematic choices, which often situated religious worship, conversion, and faith-based notions of fate at the heart of his stories. Indian folklore and religious thought, particularly in its historical exchange with Chinese culture, shaped a new narrative form of realism that hinged upon repetitive cycles of ritualized existence: tearing, mending, and retelling. Xu Dishan continued to develop these ideas throughout his literary career. In 1934, his engagement with literacy and personalized rituals was brought to a crescendo in the short story "Chun Tao" (春桃, 1934)—regarded by many as his best work.

Text Is Paper

Titled after its female protagonist, "Chun Tao" tells the story of three refugees—Chun Tao, Liu Xianggao, and Li Mao—who escape their hometown in Liaoning Province after the 1931 Japanese invasion of Manchuria. Chun Tao and Li Mao married on the day of the invasion but were separated during the flight from Shenyang to Beijing. Li Mao joined the insurgent forces but became a beggar after losing his legs in a battlefield accident. A few years later, they chance upon each other again in Beijing, where Chun Tao, who is now living with Liu Xianggao, earns money by collecting and selling wastepaper. Chun Tao and Liu Xianggao's relationship is shaken by her lawful husband's return. Chun Tao decides to take Li Mao in, and all three of them live in the same household. The narrative revolves around this strange family structure—an ad-hoc set-up dictated by the conditions of war—and the ways the characters negotiate its terms.

The problem of marriage as a form of possession comes up in the story numerous times, beginning with the first dialog between Chun Tao and Liu Xianggao as the story opens: "Wife," says Liu Xianggao as he greets her, "you came home late today!" Chun Tao quickly responds: "I already told you, don't call me wife!"[62] This type of exchange occurs throughout the text, not just in arguments regarding the definition of the relationship, but also in debating the meaning and significance of documents and official labels. When Liu Xianggao presents Chun Tao with the household registration forms—the *hukou* (戶口) papers that require them to disclose their relationship status, she disregards the papers as nonapplicable to their situation, hence not worthy of submitting.

The narrative itself mirrors Chun Tao's refusal to be boxed into a category dictated by social norms. Though Chun Tao and Liu Xianggao sleep in the same *kang* (a heated sleeping platform), the text remains vague concerning the sexual relations actually taking place. Liu Xianggao and Chun Tao's intimacy is expressed in other ways: "From dusk to dawn, she would brave the scorching sun or freezing wind all covered in dust. Partial as she was to cleanliness ever since she was born, she would wash herself thoroughly every day when she came back home. Liu Xianggao was the one who fetched the water."[63] The allusion here to the New Testament passage in which Jesus washes the feet of his disciples, and then instructs them to do the same for each other, is meaningful.[64] But in the story, foot washing and water fetching do not symbolize acts of devotion or rites marking faith in the holy Christ. For Chun Tao, washing up after a laborious day is an everyday ritual. It demonstrates compassion and love not between God's son and his disciples but between two lower-class refugees.

Chun Tao, known to everyone on the street as "Aunty Liu the wastepaper collector," comes up with the idea to make a living by exchanging the mountains of wastepaper generated by the war for matches. Liu Xianggao, who is literate, sorts the piles of paper in the evenings. Often he chances upon rare Qing documents, which yield a handsome fee when sold to collectors, in comparison to the wastepaper sold by weight. The streets of Beijing in the 1930s were filled with migrants and refugees such as Chun Tao, all searching for means of livelihood. Paper collectors, usually women and young boys, were a common sight, selling the wastepaper for reuse in the manufacture of course paper, or exchanging it for matches.[65] This form of labor becomes an important meaning-making device in the story.

Whereas in "The Merchant's Wife," Xiguan's acquisition of literacy in three different languages leads her to infuse literacy with oral storytelling, wastepaper collecting in "Chun Tao" undermines the very notion of literacy as a salvation technique. For Liu Xianggao, the value of *hukou* papers and marriage certificate papers lies in the meaning of the text printed on them; but for Chun Tao, who refuses to learn how to read, paper is worth its value in weight. For both characters, wastepaper (*zizhi* 字紙 in Chinese)—literally, paper with characters or text written or printed on it—becomes a commodity, a means of livelihood. In both Chinese and Judeo-Christian traditions, literacy is valued as a vehicle for accessing meaningful messages that generate true faith or convey membership in the bureaucratic scholarly class, but in Xu Dishan's story literacy and its paper medium are framed instead by the material conditions of wartime imperatives. The *hukou* document and the marriage certificate, representing the word of law, are demoted in Chun Tao's reasoning to the same status as wastepaper sold by the pound. The narrative is hypersensitive to economic issues and emphasizes the material aspects of survival that structure the storytelling strategy as well. Prices, commodities, and value come up again and again throughout the text—a typical strategy in realist fiction's detailed thematic emphasis on poverty and subsistence. The prices of different products are constantly mentioned, as is the revenue potential of different locations: "Anything that is thrown out in the Forbidden City area is excellent. The wastepaper found by schools and foreign companies is not a sure bet: it's heavy, it smells and the profit it yields is unstable—one can never [really] make a profit."[66]

Depictions of Chun Tao's appearance are also commodified, mediated through the gaze of the male characters in the story:

She changed into blue pants and a white top. Wearing no makeup, her face still radiated with natural beauty. If she were to consent to a marriage, a matchmaker would quote her price in no less than a hundred and eighty.

On one of the walls [in Chun Tao and Liu Xianggao's room] was a tobacco company advertisement, reading: "It's just better" [see figure 3.2]. If Chun Tao were to take off her tattered hat, she wouldn't even need to wear something from Ruifuxiang[67] or one of those Shanghai tailor shops. She could just pick up a rundown qipao that went out of style, sit on a patch of grass somewhere and look exactly like that modern girl in the ad. Xianggao always joked that this is her picture they have up there.[68]

FIGURE 3.2 Hademen cigarettes advertisement. Caption to the left reads: "It's just better" (*haishi ta hao* 還是他好).

It thus becomes clear that when Chun Tao refuses to fill out her relationship status as "married" in the *hukou* registration papers, she is refusing to put a price tag on her person. Unlike Xiguan, Chun Tao is rarely quoted in direct speech. Yet, the tension created between the narrator's commodified depictions and the character's resistance to having price tags and official documents define her status, evoke a similar relation to literacy and textual meaning as in "The Merchant's Wife." Scriptures lose their sacred status in "The Merchant's Wife" when they are reshaped, and stories such as that of the fig tree or the star Venus are transformed into personalized rituals of everyday survival, whereas in "Chun Tao" textual meaning is radically undermined altogether. Chun Tao views paper as a source of income rather than a source of meaning and reframes her own illiteracy not as a hindrance on the way to liberation, but a profound critique of the way textual meaning is manipulated for establishing ownership.

This becomes more apparent when Chun Tao, on one of her daily work routes, chances upon her lawfully wedded husband, Li Mao, now a cast-off war veteran and an amputee, and decides to let him live with her and Xianggao. When Li Mao protests the proposed arrangement, claiming that he will be mocked as a cuckold, Chun Tao snaps:

"A Cuckold?! The rich and powerful may worry about becoming cuckolds. But you? What are you famous for? No one will even remember you after you are gone, what does being a cuckold or not being a cuckold matter? Now, I am who I am. What I do cannot disgrace you."

"But we are husband and wife!" Li Mao exclaims. "You know the saying, 'even a one-night marriage merits a hundred days of joy.'"

"I wouldn't know anything about a hundred days of joy," Chun Tao retorts. She elaborates:

> You do the math; many hundreds of days of joy are already long gone since we got married. In the past four, five years we both had no idea where the other was. I never imagined that I could meet you here. I was alone, had to eke out a living, and needed someone to help out. We [Xianggao and I] have been living together for several years. Calling it conjugal love would naturally be unfair and mean to you. I took you in today because my father and your father were close, and we come from the same village. But if you call me your wife I wouldn't have anything to do with you. You can try suing me but you might just lose.[69]

Reinforcing her independence from a conventional marital system, Chun Tao devises a financial plan to make the new family system work: "I have been thinking we need an extra hand around here for a while now. Luckily, Mao showed up. He cannot walk so he will stay and run things around the house like sorting out the wastepaper. You will handle the selling, and I will continue collecting. We will open a company, all three of us."[70] In her acknowledgment of each household member's capabilities for production, Chun Tao rationalizes the new arrangement she is proposing, calling it "a company" instead of "a family" to emphasize its potential economic advantages. By constructing a model of codependence—which is a business model, to be sure, but one that also provides a home and a shared bed for the three refugees—Chun Tao challenges traditional models of polygamy, as well as the monogamy model that was the backbone of May Fourth reforms to the Chinese family structure.[71]

When both Liu Xianggao and Li Mao experience difficulties accepting the new arrangement, the two men discuss selling Chun Tao to Liu Xianggao. Unlike Xiguan who is sold and has no choice but to accept her new life, new Muslim attire, and a new language, Chun Tao rejects this outside imposition: she tears the bill of sale to shreds. Frustrated, Liu Xianggao leaves without any explanation. Chun Tao, saddened and disturbed by his departure, responds the only way she knows how, by continuing her arduous daily routine. When she returns home one day, she finds Liu Xianggao welcoming her, regretful, and willing to accept the new living arrangement: "I cannot leave you, nothing is complete without you." As Chun Tao enters the room to join the two men and the new family that has finally been agreed upon, life returns to the routine: "She went inside without speaking, took off her hat and performed her daily baptism (*xing ta mei ri de xili* 行她每日的洗禮). After that, they all talked business under the gourd shed. The possibility that Liu Xianggao would rent a booth in the market to sell wastepaper from the Forbidden City area came up, and they also discussed moving to a larger house." As night draws near and the story ends, life resumes its course: "The courtyard was quiet. Only the scent of roses still lingered in the air. From the small room one could hear the same old 'wife' and 'I don't like this! I am not your wife!' dialog."[72]

This closing paragraph ties together the themes of the text at large. The repetitive nature of Chun Tao's life—labor by day, rest by night—is epitomized in her daily bathing, described as a personal ritual. "Daily baptism" is a contradiction in terms: baptism is meant to be taken only once, to mark the singular event of one's taking on the word of God. The term "baptism" (*xili* 洗禮) was a new term in Chinese, first appearing in the 1919 *Union Version* Bible translation.[73] A reader at the time would likely have noticed this term and found its appearance strange in a text that does not otherwise mention religion explicitly. Yet, Xu Dishan depicts the daily cleansing as a ceremonial act, a respite after a long day of toil tied to intimacy with a loved one fetching the water. The story closes the same way it opened— "I am not your wife." In the beginning of the story, this statement reads as an angry rebuke, but by the end, when Chun Tao manages to assert her own definition of family, the reproach reads as a soft jab, one that is part of the daily cycle of making a living.

Similar to "The Merchant's Wife" but even more forcefully, "Chun Tao" demonstrates a type of realism that differs from the developmental narratives common in May Fourth literature. A female refugee such as Chun Tao should have lost the battle for survival by the conventions of evolutionary realism. But the protagonist in this story, painstakingly detailed in its descriptions of the everyday life of the lower classes in a particular historical period, emerges not only as a survivor but as the creative designer of her own survival. Like Xiguan, Chun Tao's path is not a linear one: she repeats the same route, collects papers that get recycled again and again, and engages in the same conversations, the same daily bath that is granted a position of ritual. But whereas Xiguan appropriates sacred textual meaning to meet her own needs, Chun Tao rejects textual meaning all together. In both stories the function of religion as personalized ritual is exemplified in how each woman's rituals offer her a way of coping with life's hardships. This is not a proposition for religious conversion to achieve salvation through faith, nor is religion cast as a bearer of enlightenment and liberation through education. Rather, Xu Dishan's fiction demonstrates his definition of religion as a "dynamic process of dealing with nature." His protagonists negotiate their fate—whether it entails forced marriage, violence, poverty, or war. They devalue the sanctity of the written word, be it scriptures or official documents, and create their own life stories: a female Crusoe or a nonwife with two husbands. Though in "Chun Tao" religion is not addressed as explicitly or thematically as in "The Merchant's Wife," both texts revolve around a process of dealing with modern life's hardships and demonstrate Xu's privileging of everyday rituals: gazing at Venus or cleansing the body of street dust. These short stories evoke a cyclical pattern, a spider's web woven and patched as needed, again and again, as the repeating structure of human life.

Fine Silk and Coarse Threads

Published in 1921 and 1934 (respectively), "The Merchant Wife" and "Chun Tao" inhabit important temporal junctures of Republican-era literature. The first is the heyday of the May Fourth Movement. The second is the cusp of the second Sino-Japanese War, a period in which many Chinese writers focused on portraying local experience of oppression under global capitalism and imperialist pursuits.[74] Between these two works, in 1925, Xu published a collection of informal short essays titled *Timely Rain in the Empty Mountain* (*Kong shan ling yu* 空山靈雨). The essays, featuring a distinctively Buddhist tropology, vary from personal reflections upon minute details of everyday life and childhood memories, to more profound contemplations on the illusoriness of desires and attachments and the ephemerality of all forms of life. One of these impressions, "The Old Lady Mending Clothes" (Bu poyi de lao furen 補破衣的老婦人) crystallizes the range of female protagonists we meet in Xu's fiction—from storytellers to laborers—all while revealing the author's perception of what it means to compose literature.

"The Old Lady Mending Clothes" begins: "She sat by the eaves. Not noticing the fine drops of rain gathering in the wrinkles that stretched across her face, she rearranged her basket. In the basket, fine silk pieces were mixed together with coarse threads and cloth bits. Not for a second did she pay attention to the thin drops beating down her head, face and body as she guarded the more exquisite fabric pieces from the rain."[75] The majestic old lady, her face like arid land finally watered by the delicate rain, is engaged in the mundane task of rearranging her valuables. This charged picture, the epitome of a peaceful bodhisattva uninterrupted by the rain, is disrupted almost immediately when it is revealed that this divine-seeming serenity masks the earthly reality of prior concerns—in this case, protecting one's livelihood.

When two brothers, neighborhood kids who nickname the lady "the clothes surgeon," arrive back from school, one of them asks her: "Doctor, how come you only use the fabric in the basket to mend other people's clothes and not your own? Look, there is a big hole right there on your shoulder!" The old lady offers a smiling reply and demonstrates a shrewd understanding of figurative language: "Sharp eyes! I was in such a hurry this morning that I did not sew this patch; I only pasted it with some glue and planned to mend the hole properly in the evening. Little did I know that the rain would tear it off! Well, since I am, as you say, a surgeon of clothes, I don't worry when my own clothes get sick!"

From this point, the conversation further develops the trope of surgery and turns into a discussion of the meaning of textual work. The older brother says: "Our father collects fine documents for his manuscript. He is the same as you, always flipping and rearranging, he . . ." "He is a different kind of surgeon!" the little brother interrupts. "Children, you are both right," replies the old lady. "Your father cherishes the document fragments in his booklets as I treasure my own pieces of fine silk. He gathers interesting thoughts from various places to use in time of need, and then sews them together to make a new idea. The only thing that is different is that he uses his head and I use my fingers." At this point the children's father emerges and adds: "Lady, you are absolutely right. We are the same you and I, both of us seek and gather nothing but scraps, bits to use in mending a cotton padded jacket."[76]

At stake here is a notion of writing, grounded in the ancient etymology of the Chinese *wen* 文 (one of the meanings of *wen* is a grid). This otherwise rather broadly used analogy of weaving to literary composition is subtly, yet crucially, modified by Xu Dishan to highlight repetition instead of creation. Textual work, the threading together of ideas or pieces of silk, is emphasized here as a reparative process—sewing bits and pieces to one another, and most importantly, constantly mending the extant. The equation of illiterate patching to scholarly editing is much more than an empty metaphor or a gesture towards the lower classes. This notion of writing as a labor of patching and mending locates composition as a practice of repetition, rather than innovation. The trope of patching, epitomized in an old lady who mends clothes or the spider that mends its web, evokes the same cyclicality that characterizes religions and informs the portrayal of the lives of Xu's protagonists.

Who is this clothes surgeon, this old lady who sews pieces of fabric together and weaves stories about mending and healing to recite to young children? Is she an incarnation of the old Bengali women whose evening rituals of storytelling so captivated Xu and prompted him to translate *Folktales of Bengal*? Is she simply a drifter and an illiterate refugee preoccupied with material subsistence? Or a Bodhisattva, simultaneously residing in the mundane desert of human existence and blessed by heavenly rain?

In the preface to *Folktales of Bengal*, after delineating a typology of narrative patterns and recurrent themes, Xu comments on how folktales almost always result in punishment for the evil characters and reward, in the form of marriage and childbearing, for the good characters: "almost all of them end in a perfectly satisfactory reunion."[77] Yet, Xu's stories never end with a conventional happy reunion. This is so for the stories I have examined here, but also in many others, where the ending is left open: a journey the characters embark on continues beyond the boundaries of the narrative; questions involving relationships usually remain unresolved. Far from mere coincidence or evidence of poor narrative craftsmanship, as some critics have argued,[78] I suggest this aspect of Xu's writing reflects his broader understanding of life and the meaning of religion within it. Xu's analysis of Hinduism and Buddhism's cyclical ritualistic patterns led him to perceive folklore not as the remnant of a bygone era, but as a key to revealing the permanent logic of life, in both antiquity and modernity: the duality of repetition and change. Building on yet also moving away from colonially informed premises of comparative religion scholarship, Xu's understanding of religion shaped his literary work. His realism constructs life not through linear Darwinism but through cyclical journeys, many spouses, retold stories, piles of papers, pieces of fabric, and daily rituals. His is a cyclicality that is repetitive but never formulaic. Xu's protagonists embody the endurance of folklore, modified in ways that escape a traditional "perfectly satisfactory reunion."

The stories of Xiguan and Chun Tao challenge the view—shared by groups as diverse as missionaries and Marxist revolutionaries in modern China—that literacy is a liberation technology. This move to empty literacy of its promise of redemption from a life of toil and poverty departs from the Peking Folklore Movement's fetishizing of oral traditions as the locus of original national sentiment. With older, uneducated female protagonists whose ideologies remain subtly phrased in ritual terms, Xu thoroughly critiqued an imperialist epistemology that explored the "savage" only in order to celebrate the evolution of mankind to (Western, Christian) civilization. Reading and writing to explore China-India folklore, Xu Dishan was intrigued by Lal Behari Day's depiction of Bengali traditions as well as by Tagore's ideal of Asian solidarity (I think here of Xu's letter to his wife after a visit to

Tagore's school, discussed in chapter 2). But Xu's critique went one step further by rejecting completely not just the equation of "religion" with "monotheism," but also the very distinction between (Eastern) spirituality and (Western) materialism, which was conceived in India and in China as result of a long negotiation with modern, ostensibly Christian frames of thought.

Conclusion

Modern Chinese literature was deeply engaged with representing the dilemmas of women caught between traditional patriarchy and modern possibilities, though few male authors other than Xu Dishan (if any) featured female protagonists in a majority of their works. Much has been written on Chinese modern literature's portrayal of female oppression as a symbol of both China's backwardness and its hope for redemption through women's liberation.[79] More recently, Haiyan Lee tied the Peking Folklore Movement to the production of women as emotional agents via the May Fourth project of emancipation. Doubly oppressed as slaves to men who were themselves slaves of the Confucian social and familial structures, women's fundamental lack of access to political power throughout Chinese history has rendered them, in the eyes of Folklore Movement members, an embodiment of pristine sentimentality, untainted by ideology or politics—arenas from which women were historically excluded. Viewing written language as a façade obscuring real, embryonic emotions, which can only be excavated via oral traditions (a legacy of European folklore research), the Peking Folklore Movement downplayed and often times glossed over the origin of many legends and songs in ritual practices. Brushing aside ritualistic elements, Lee argues, enabled folklorists to analyze female figures in folktales and folksongs for the purpose of discovering a hidden sentimental fountain bubbling under the veneer of the feudal Confucian culture. The figure of the emotional woman could thus provide a role model for creating a "national community of sympathy."[80]

Committed to revealing the simultaneity of savagery and civilization in modernity, Xu Dishan and his colleagues posed an alternative to the Folklore Movement. The premises that guided such projects as *The History of Savage Life* defined ritual and emotions as interlinked and inseparable. In both "The Merchant's Wife" and "Chun Tao," rituals stimulate emotions: the daily baptism ignites Chun Tao's affection for Liu Xianggao, folk beliefs shared to abate physical pain deepen the love Xiguan feels for Akolima. Inventing rituals as techniques for surviving the challenges of the modern world, these illiterate, disobedient female worshippers shed new light on the larger question of women's liberation in Chinese literature of the 1920s and 1930s. Rather than serving to illustrate a colonial economy of sentiment couched in national terms, these female protagonists, in their very survival, extend an invitation to imagine modern life's "relentless struggle"—in the words of Mao Dun—through a transregional horizon of shared folktales and rituals that effect epistemic disobedience to a shared experience of imperialist oppression.

Making a substantial intervention in the period's practice of literary realism that was deeply informed by a lifetime of studying Sanskrit and Indian religions, Xu Dishan's fiction and scholarship pioneered a more rigorous and philologically informed engagement with transregional culture that commenced in China in the late 1930s and 1940s and climaxed in the 1950s. Shaped to a large extent by a budding field of China-India studies and the era's touting of Third Worldism as a viable and exciting new path, this new foray into Indian literature is the subject of my next chapter.

FOUR

Śakuntalā in China

ON THE EVENING of May 7, 1957, Beijing's ground-breaking China Youth Art Theater (*Zhongguo qingnian yishu juyuan* 中國青年藝術劇院) debuted a performance of the classical Sanskrit drama *Śakuntalā and the Ring of Recollection*, rendered in Chinese as *Shagongdaluo* (沙恭達羅), to celebrate the five-year anniversary of the founding of the Sino-Indian Friendship Association. Previously, only a modern Indian drama, *Chitra*, by Rabindranath Tagore had been staged in China, on the occasion of his 1924 visit. Actors in that small-scale production of *Chitra* were not professionals, or even actors per se, as the cast included the poet Xu Zhimo and playwright Ding Xilin 丁西林 (1893–1974) among others. By contrast, the 1957 staging of *Śakuntalā* (as *Shagongdaluo*) was no amateur endeavor. The China Youth Art Theater's performance was a grand theatrical event aimed at the public and discussed in all the major media outlets of the time. It marked a high point in a decade that had already seen China and India's diplomatic, economic, and cultural exchange reach a historical peak.

The stage production of *Shagongdaluo* and the first translation of *Śakuntalā* from the original Sanskrit—done by China's foremost Indologist Ji Xianlin, and on which the script was based—were interrelated events. When published in 1956, the translation garnered enthusiasm and praise. As literary masterpieces were eagerly introduced to China from Asia, Africa, and Latin America, Ji Xianlin's translation was celebrated as a milestone achievement in Chinese literary circles. It has stayed in circulation, with second and third editions coming out in 1959 and 1978. Today it forms part of the curriculum in China's Central Academy of Fine Arts.[1] Ji Xianlin's career as a renowned scholar and diplomat spanned more than sixty years in which he composed seminal studies in fields straddling China-India historical interactions through the ages, from Tocharian linguistics and Buddhist literature to histories of the manufacture and trade of paper, silk, and sugar. His translational output from Sanskrit alone was staggering and included, alongside Śakuntalā, two other works by Kālidāsa: the drama *Urvaśī Won By Valor* (*Vikramōrvaśīyam*) and the long poem "The Cloud Messenger" (Meghadūta), as well as the complete *Ramayana*, numbering seven volumes in Chinese.

Although the 1957 production of Śakuntalā played an important role in China-India relations, the history of the translation and the reception of this drama take place in a broader context. The global clout of Śakuntalā— touted as a masterpiece by eighteenth-century orientalists and nineteenth-century promoters of the nascent field of world literature intersected with the modern reception and study of Sanskrit theater in China in the 1920s and 1930s, the founding of Indology as an academic discipline in China in the 1940s, and the growing significance of cultural diplomacy in the 1950s. China's part in the global history of reading and performing Śakuntalā demonstrates a transition from orientalist-informed readings of the drama in the 1920s and 1930s, effected through translations to Chinese from French and English renditions, to the late 1950s translation from the original Sanskrit, which grounded a reading and performance of the text in transregional historical research.

Most importantly for our purposes, the translation and production of Śakuntalā in China in 1956 and 1957 sheds new light on a fundamental tenet of socialist literary theory in modern China: that in portraying human life, art can produce a higher plane of reality by elevating the real (*xianshi* 現實) to the true (*zhenshi* 真實). This new direction for literary realism, launched in 1942 at the Talks at Yan'an Forum of Art and Literature (*Yan'an yishu tanhui* 延安藝術談會), had been studied almost exclusively within the purview of Chinese original literature. Yet, as I show in this chapter, the paradigm of *zhenshi* was significant not only in Chinese literary production, but also for the robust translation project championed by Chinese literary figures in the 1950s. I begin with a discussion of the 1950s as a watershed historical context for the translation and production of *Shagongdaluo*. I then move to a brief history of the modern translation of Śakuntalā, including its massive circulation outside of India in the eighteenth and nineteenth centuries, which paved the way for its early translations to Chinese in the first decades of the twentieth century. I also discuss influential essays by figures such as Zheng Zhenduo and Xu Dishan, who argued that Chinese drama (*xiqu* 戲曲) was deeply shaped by Indian theater. In the third section of the chapter, I turn to Ji Xianlin's translation itself. Although he was celebrated as scholar-diplomat and known most prominently for his harrowing memoir of the Cultural Revolution,[2] Ji Xianlin was also a literary critic who developed through his study of Indian literature an ideal of *zhenshi* as art "bringing to life."

The 1950s Watershed

Ji Xianlin's translation was published by People's Literature Publishing House (*Renmin wenxue chubanshe* 人民文學出版社), which was responsible for the majority of book-length translations of foreign literature.[3] The 1956 publication of Śakuntalā was part of an explicit campaign by China's Culture Bureau to introduce Indian masterpieces to Chinese readers during the 1950s.[4] Publications of new translations were often accompanied by large-scale cultural events that received broad media coverage. In May 1956, for example, an assembly commemorating "Three Paragons of World Culture" was held at the Beijing Capital Theater and featured the widely known author and Minister of Culture at the time, Mao Dun, discussing Kālidāsa, Fyodor Dostoevsky, and Heinrich Heine.[5] The 1957 production of *Shagongdaluo* was directed by the China Youth Art Theater's esteemed house director Wu Xue 吳雪 (1914–2006), a Norway-trained Ibsen specialist. Wu Xue prepared to direct the production by traveling to India to participate in an international theater conference, where he met and consulted with a Sanskrit drama scholar, as well as theater luminaries such as the celebrated actor Prithviraj Kapoor.[6] Wu Xue hired the leading film and stage music composer Liu Chi 劉熾 (1921–1998), who studied Indian films available in Beijing to familiarize himself with their musical styles, which he then incorporated in the original music he composed for the play. The iconic Indian Bharatanatyam dancer, Kamala Laxman, then visiting China and performing to audiences of thousands in sold-out venues,[7] personally choreographed and trained the actors and dancers to perform Indian-inspired dance routines accurately.[8] The production's fidelity to the original was vetted a month prior to the debut in a private performance attended by the Indian ambassador Ratan Kumar Nehru.[9] On opening night, all major figures in China's cultural circles were present, including the notable Peking Opera performer Mei Lanfang 梅蘭芳 (1864–1941), writers Mao Dun and Guo Moruo 郭沫若 (1892–1978), and the philosopher Feng Youlan.[10] The production was a hit: in addition to sold-out performances at the China Youth Art Theater, *Shagongdaluo* was performed at the Asia Film Week Festival held in July 1957, as part of a formal celebration held for all delegations of foreign filmmakers.[11] It was staged again in 1959.

The meticulous research and training in Indian musical styles and choreography that preceded the production—and, of course, the very translation of the play into Chinese from the original Sanskrit—indicated the commitment to and enthusiasm for producing rigorously faithful renditions of Asian cultural forms on the Chinese stage. This research-based approach was a distinct characteristic of the art world in China, spanning literature, drama, and dance between 1950 and 1962, when the Sino-Indian War redrew the terms for cross-cultural interaction with South and Southeast Asia. The twelve years between 1950 and 1962 witnessed dramatic transformation in Afro-Latin American/Asian geopolitics at large, and in China-India relations in particular. The period was shaped by the historic rise of a Third World Front outside the Soviet and US blocs, epitomized in solidarity movements aiming to resist the threat of new imperialism in an age of decolonization. Unified by the shared experience of fighting colonialism, alliances between recently decolonized countries fueled this surge in early Cold War diplomacy between Asia, Latin America, and Africa. Alliances formed as early as 1951 in response to the havoc wreaked by the United States during the Korean War, the urgency of the pending nuclear threat, and the uneven integration of places like the Philippines, Pakistan, and Turkey into the neo-imperialism of First World capitalist expansion. These alliances sought to diversify economic bases by developing local manufacturing and ramping up support for disarmament.[12] Conversations about these issues often took place at large scale conventions such as the Asian Peace Conference—held in Beijing (1952), then Geneva (1954), Colombo (1955), and, most famously, Bandung (1955)—where China and India were leading voices. Another emergent channel for communication between decolonized nations was "people-to people" diplomacy, which often took the form of cultural delegations and official visits of cultural figures.

In her study of "Chinese dance diplomacy" Emily Wilcox situates Chinese performances of art forms hailing from recently decolonized nations during the 1950s as a rigorous attempt to learn from other countries. Challenging the entrenched Cold War rhetoric that framed decades of cultural exchange as a mere communist front for geopolitical muscling, Wilcox shows how Chinese performances of Indian, Indonesian, and Burmese dance styles required intensive training with local specialists. Sometimes the training took place during a delegation's visit to other countries, and at other times—as in the case of the Laxman sisters choreographing dances for *Shagongdaluo*—during artists' visits to China. These carefully researched performances were very different from the early twentieth-century depictions of so-called oriental dances, which muddled together styles described as "Indian," "Persian," and "Arabic." As taught in dance schools established by Russians and in missionary schools, such dance forms consisted of "stereotyped poses with erotic costumes reminiscent of Hollywood films and cabaret, not serious attempts to represent complex and living cultural traditions."[13] By the 1950s, however, cultural diplomacy efforts among decolonized countries called for freedom not only from First World economic imperialism, but also from reliance on Western mediation to translate each other's cultural texts, whether dance, drama, or literature. Under this banner, rigorous research and translation from original languages became the new rule, whenever possible.

While China during the 1950s and early 1960s invested in developing thriving cultural diplomacy with countries spanning Asia, Latin-America, and Africa, the volume of exchanges with India was particularly substantial, for two intertwined reasons. First, between 1950 and 1962, China and India's shared commitment to peaceful mutuality and coexistence extended to leadership roles in regional geopolitics. Second, the 1940s and 1950s had seen the establishment in China of active academic study of Indian culture and of China-India connections. These two factors, the geopolitical and academic, intersected through figures such as Ji Xianlin, who was often called to participate in formal functions with South Asian diplomats and traveled in official delegations to India and Myanmar. As I show in chapter 2, the wave of Tagore translations from English into Chinese during the 1920s hinged upon Anglo-American Christian mediation and deeply informed a partial understanding of Tagore's ideal of Pan-Asianism. The 1950s, by contrast, saw a shift away from an episteme of Eastern spirituality towards a philologically informed study of the historical connections between China and India, encouraged and funded by increasing diplomatic contact.

Diplomatic relations between the Republic of India and the People's Republic of China were officially launched in April 1950, with India becoming the first nonsocialist country to establish an embassy in Beijing. The following twelve years, up until the outbreak of the Sino-Indian War of 1962, saw a tremendous amount of exchange and cooperation between the two countries as economists, engineers, scientists, politicians, public health specialists, women's rights activists, dancers, musicians, and literary writers, in official delegations and as individuals visited, taught, and learned from each other. Friendly relations reached a zenith in 1954 with the signing of the Panch-sheel Treaty of Mutual Non-Aggression (also titled the Five Principles of Peaceful Coexistence) between China and India, but then rapidly declined with the Tibetan Uprising of 1959 and the Dalai Lama's asylum in Dharam-sala. Arunabh Ghosh estimates that by 1958, about seventy delegations had traveled between India and China.[14]

By the Chinese debut of *Shagongdaluo* in 1957, contemporary Indian culture was becoming more familiar in China as films and popular music often played in Chinese urban centers. Between 1950 and 1962, more than sixty books of Indian literature were translated into Chinese, and the prestigious journal *Translations* (*Yiwen* 譯文), renamed *World Literature* (*Shijie wenxue* 世界文學) in 1959, published about eighty Indian titles. Translations from original Indian languages in books and in journals increased dramatically, representing the growth of Indology in China, from translations of Sanskrit and Pāli classics such as the *Joy of the Serpent* attributed to King Harsha, to works of contemporary progressive Indian literature, with writers such as Premchand featured prominently.[15] In October 1955, China exhibited a nationwide Indian Film Week featuring three popular Indian films: *Awara* (1951), *Do Bigha Zamin* (1953), and *Aandhiyan* (1952). More than two million tickets were sold and the films were screened in twenty major Chinese cities, across 120 theaters.[16] The nationwide film festival was part of a broader film-related exchange between China and India, which included media-covered visits by actors and directors between China and India, as well as a China Film Week, which took place in New Delhi earlier in 1955.[17]

In Ji Xianlin's 1958 essay titled "Indian Literature in China," he cites the films *Awara* and *Do Bigha Zamin* (and the popular songs therein) as examples of the increasing presence of Indian modern literature, film, and music in China.[18] Ji Xianlin was at the center of much of China's cultural diplomacy efforts in the 1950s: as an executive board member of the China-India Friendship Association (*Zhongyin youhao xiehui* 中印友好協會) and a delegate in several official delegations to India (including the first one in 1951), Ji Xianlin was sent in his capacity of an Indology specialist to represent China in the Asian Writers Conference in Tashkent (1958), and as part of cultural delegations to Myanmar (1951, 1959), Iraq, and Egypt. He also served as delegate to several key organizations including The Chinese People's Political Consultative Conference (*Zhongguoren zhengzhi xieshang huiyi* 中國人政治協商會議) and the Language Reform Committee (Zhongguo wenzi gaige weiyuanhui 中國文字改革委員會).[19] Thus centrally positioned in the scholarly and the diplomatic worlds, Ji is credited for founding the academic study of Indology in China when, in 1946, he founded the Department of Eastern Languages and Literature at Peking University, which he chaired until 1983.[20]

Other Chinese scholars working on Indian languages, religions, and texts included figures such as Jin Kemu 金克木 (1912–2000), who, like Ji Xianlin, was versed in Sanskrit and Pāli; the eminent historian Chen Yinke 陳寅恪 (1890–1969), whose work on Buddhism—much like Ji Xianlin's—was grounded in philological training he received in Germany; and the philologist and scholar of Indian literature Wu Xiaoling 吳曉鈴 (1914–1995), who translated another canonical Sanskrit drama by Kālidāsa, *Little Clay Cart*, in 1956 and 1957. In Chinese academic circles, more and more programs opened for the study of different Indian languages and sought to strengthen China-India connections based in knowledge of original languages. In 1954, Peking University established, alongside the existing Hindi program, an Urdu track. In the early 1960s, Beijing's Communication University of China, then known as the Beijing Broadcasting Institute, introduced degree programs in Tamil, Urdu, Bengali, Hindi, and Assamese.[21]

The late 1950s convergence of the two strands I have described here contributed to the new direction of research-based translation: The first was China-India's tightening relationship, informed by ideals of Third Worldism and underscored in the phrase often raised on banners and in the media: "Indians and Chinese are brothers" (*Hindi Chini Bhai Bhai* or *Yindu Zhongguo shi xiongdi* 印度中國是兄弟). The second was the development of Indology in

China. Ji Xianlin's translation of *Śakuntalā* not only represented the culmination of a diplomatic relationship, but also underscored a new phase in Chinese writers' modern engagement with Indian culture in the twentieth century.

Śakuntalā in the World

Very little is known about Kālidāsa (c. fifth century CE), the master poet of Sanskrit who composed arguably the most celebrated *nāṭakas* (often simply translated as "dramas") in Sanskrit literature—including, most famously, *Śakuntalā and the Ring of Recollection*. Kālidāsa's surviving oeuvre consists of six works: three long poems and three nāṭakas, the latter more fully described as heroic romances with themes and characters drawn from traditional sources. *Śakuntalā* is considered the nāṭaka par excellence.[22]

Kālidāsa based *Śakuntalā and the Ring of Recollection* on an episode in the *Mahabharata*, but his nāṭaka introduced significant modifications to the original epic. The play consists of seven acts, reflecting a classical nāṭaka plot structure with a successful union at the dénouement.[23] As *Śakuntalā* begins, King Duṣyanta of the lunar dynasty Purū is hunting an antelope in an area close to a forest hermitage inhabited by male and female disciples of the sage Kaṇva. As the king is about to close in on the antelope, Śakuntalā, the adopted daughter of Kaṇva, rescues the animal. She views the animals in the hermitage as her own flesh and blood and calls the antelope, in particular, her son. Śakuntalā and King Duṣyanta quickly fall for one another and their romance unfolds within the natural splendor of the hermitage, culminating in a Gandharva marriage—a marriage based on consensual consummation with no rituals or family involvement. But the period of bliss does not last long: when Duṣyanta is called back to attend to affairs of the royal court, he promises to send for Śakuntalā and leaves her with his royal signet ring.

As Śakuntalā passes the days daydreaming about her beloved, she ignores the request from the sage Durvāsas to be welcomed as a guest at the hermitage. In anger, Durvāsas first casts a curse on Śakuntalā that will make her unrecognizable to her husband, but later, mollified by Śakuntalā's friends, he modifies its terms: the king will recognize Śakuntalā only when he sees the ring that he gave her. Act 4 depicts a pregnant Śakuntalā finally saying teary goodbyes to the forest hermitage and heading to the city to search for the king. The depiction of nature—which has garnered for act 4 the title "The Core" in traditional criticism—manifests a religious dimension emerging from Kālidāsa's devotion to the gods Śiva and Kali. In the process of bidding Śakuntalā farewell, the hermitage and its inhabitants—humans, flora, and fauna—resonate in sympathy with her emotions. The realm of nature is thus presented as reverberating with the presence of the creative nature of Śiva through which humans and nature are interconnected.[24]

En route to the palace, however, Śakuntalā loses the ring. When she arrives, Duṣyanta does not recognize her and refuses to let her inside. Enraged, Śakuntalā calls to her earth mother to open up and receive her and is carried away by a female-shaped ray of light. Soon afterward, a poor fisherman finds the ring, and the king's memory returns. In deep despair, he begins to look for Śakuntalā, who has found refuge in the divine sage Mārīca's hermitage, where she gives birth to the baby boy Sarvadamana, later known as Bharata—the singular male heir to the Purū dynasty. After experiencing heroic adventures assisting in the war of Indra, King of the Gods, Duṣyanta is taken to Mārīca's hermitage. Once there, Duṣyanta recognizes his son as his own and is reunited with Śakuntalā.

In Kālidāsa's *Śakuntalā*, as in other Sanskrit dramas, the text incorporates elaborate staging directions that instruct the actors to express emotional states through miming, with particular emphasis on the use of hands and eyes for "translating ideas, objects and emotions into aesthetic statements."[25] Characters speak different languages based on their social status: Sanskrit is spoken by males of higher classes and Prakrit by women and lower classes. Great attention is paid to the actors' costumes and makeup and the acting is highly stylized. Two themes in tension push the plot of *Śakuntalā* forward and are grounded in the characterization of the two protagonists: the dialectic between sensual desire and sacred duty, epitomized in Duṣyanta's inner struggle between staying happily at the hermitage or returning to the city to fulfill his royal duty; and the tension between the forest, where the hermitage is located, and the settlement, where the royal palace is located. These themes structure the character of the female protagonist Śakuntalā, whose hermitage is a liminal space bridging the forest and the settlement.[26] The nāṭaka revolves around the drama of the innocent Śakuntalā, dwelling in a pristine forest setting, as she discovers and is yet bewildered by her own sexual desires. Her main characteristic is a staggering emotional sensibility: she is overflowing with love for the king and is viscerally connected to the flora and fauna of the forest. As the plot takes Śakuntalā from the haven of the forest to the settlement, she suffers as an abandoned lover, calls on Mother Earth to receive her, and finally experiences the bliss of her reunion with Duṣyanta. Kālidāsa's depiction of Śakuntalā as the ultimate lover ultimately came to inform the ideal "Śakuntalā" figure in India and beyond, while the less sensual *Mahabharata* version of her story became quite sidelined.[27]

The history of *Śakuntalā*'s translation and circulation—as arguably the first Asian classical text read, adapted, and performed across Europe and the United States—is well documented, but it bears summarizing here because it is part of the trajectory of the Western mediation of exchanges between China and India that I have been tracing from chapter 1. Kālidāsa's play was read and performed frequently during the period of the Mughal Empire (1526–1857), and *Śakuntalā*, specifically, was translated into several regional languages and extended into genres such as Braj-bhāṣā prose poetry. In the late eighteenth century, William Jones's pioneering English translation became a historic landmark in orientalist scholarship. Completed in 1789 in Calcutta, Jones's *Sacontala: or, the Fatal Ring*, along with his founding of the Asiatic Society in 1784, launched a new discipline of Indology. The nineteenth century saw numerous European universities install teaching positions and endowed chairs in the philological research of Sanskrit manuscripts.[28] Jones himself famously dubbed Kālidāsa "the Indian Shakespeare," inspiring continued research and translations.[29]

Postcolonial scholarship has shown how the colonial encounter with Sanskrit, Chinese, and Japanese classics shaped modern European practices of literary canonization and aesthetic theory.[30] *Śakuntalā* arrived in European readership circles in tandem and in conversation with the Romantic era's drawing of boundaries between "nature" and "culture." English, German, and French versions emphasized this binary. Thus, the tension in the original play between the realms of the forest and the settlement—a tension that scholars of Kālidāsa describe as between moral duty and sensual passions—prompted European translators to depict Śakuntalā as a "child of nature," primordial and unscathed: an ideal romantic that poets continually attempted to create and recreate in their writing. For example, act 4, in which Śakuntalā is bidding farewell to the hermitage, was read in Europe as the Christian fall from grace—a departure from paradise and the end of the age of innocence. In classical Sanskrit criticism, to the contrary, it has been read as an affirmation of the connection of man to nature.[31]

Śakuntalā's popularity in Europe was unprecedented by any previous translated work. Jones's translation served as the basis for further translations into almost all European languages during the nineteenth century—amounting to forty-six translations in twelve different languages.[32] In Germany, Georg Forster used Jones's translation to render the play into German in 1791. Forster's *Sakuntala Oder Der Entscheidende Ring* played a major role in contributing to the European popularization of the play. Forster touted *Śakuntalā* as a work that reveals the primordial, child-like relationship of "the Hindu" with nature—a relationship that could help German readers retrace their own lost connection to their origins. His translation became a favorite of both Goethe and Johann Gottfried von Herder.[33] Herder also wrote the forward to the second edition of Forster's translation, which came out in 1803 and noted that the character of Śakuntalā represents the child-like Indian who lives in the equivalent of paradise.[34] *Śakuntalā* has also been credited with sparking Goethe's early notion of Weltliteratur. After reading *Śakuntalā*, Goethe wrote a poem that famously climaxed with the verse: "Would you grasp at the earth and heaven itself in one sole name?/I name you, O Shakuntala, and everything is said"—a passage that has since become trite with repetition and been translated into dozens of languages.[35]

During the nineteenth century, circulation of *Śakuntalā* in Europe extended from book to stage. In 1858, it was adapted into a widely performed ballet by Théophile Gautier titled *Sacountala*. French and Russian symbolists were deeply inspired by the play and wrote many poems based on translations to Russian from French and English. The play's popularity in Russia continued into the twentieth century, and in 1914, Alexander Tairov produced a massively well-received *Śakuntalā* as the inaugural production of his experimental theater Kamerny, alongside Bertolt Brecht's *The Threepenny Opera* and plays by Oscar Wilde and Eugene O'Neill.[36] The international success of *Śakuntalā* modified the reading and performance of the nāṭaka in late nineteenth- and early twentieth-century India. The 1858 translation by Monier-Williams inspired in India a new wave of translations to regional languages with associated dance and drama productions. *Śakuntalā* was always regarded as an important classic by Sanskrit-reading intelligentsia, but it was the enthusiastic popularization of the play in Europe that cemented its status as an icon of Hindu culture and helped shape a budding discourse of

Hindu nationalism. As I show in chapter 1, the British crown—bolstered by British orientalists, many of whom were missionaries—endorsed and fueled the Aryan myth that the Hindu religion represented the "true" India, before it was conquered by the "foreign" Mughal Empire.[37] Symbolizing as it did the Sanskrit culture, Śakuntalā came to embody a symbolic value crucial for cementing the narrative of the Hindu origin of India. Śakuntalā remained the most popular nāṭaka in modern India into the twentieth century: the seminal Prithvi Theatre founded in 1944 in Mumbai opened with a production of Śakuntalā, and a 1954 Śakuntalā Sanskrit production inaugurated the first National Drama Festival in Delhi.[38]

Chinese intellectuals were not indifferent to the global influence of Śakuntalā in the late nineteenth and early twentieth centuries. Although the 1957 production was the first time that the play was staged in China, more than a half dozen different translations of the play into modern Chinese had appeared by the early fifties. Most of these were partial translations done by consulting French and English versions; consequently, the reception of Śakuntalā in China in the early twentieth century shows the markings of European readings of the play. The writer Su Manshu published a partial translation from Sanskrit (now lost) in 1907, and he incorporated the play in several of his stories and his literary criticism. In my discussion of Su's work in chapter 1, I highlighted how his reliance on British sources and translations for studying Sanskrit lodged strands of imperialist knowledge—specifically, the perception that human culture originated in India—in an otherwise thoroughly anticolonial discourse. As Shaden Tageldin's work on imperialist seduction reveals, orientalist adoration of cultures in Asia and the Middle East as gateway to a primordial past ultimately bolstered imperialism by fashioning "an affective economy that empowers the colonized to declare themselves 'equal to' or 'greater than' the European through the prism of an orientalist thesis itself attractive because it issues from the gaze of the colonizer."[39] Su Manshu's discussions of Śakuntalā reiterated British and German enthusiasm over the play's representation of a paradise lost to those who have fallen from grace. He introduced the plot of the drama as such, and reiterated William Jones's description of Kālidāsa as "India's Shakespeare."[40]

Such introductions of the play to a Chinese audience reinforced its position as a Western-certified masterpiece and persisted into the 1920s, as partial translations of the play, mostly from French, were published in literary supplements of Chinese language journals. In 1933, the first stand-alone full translation, again from the French, was completed by Wang Weike 王維克 (1900–1952). By 1957, Kālidāsa's Śakuntalā was translated in nine different translations, partial or full, from Esperanto, English, and French, and into several genres, including a short narrative and a Nanqu (南曲) opera version. Articles about Kālidāsa were consistently published in widely read journals such as *Jingbao* (京報), *Shenbao Monthly* (申報月刊) and *Xiandai Qingnian* (現代青年).[41]

The Indian Sources of Chinese Drama: Forging a Theory

Along with the first translations of Śakuntalā to Chinese from European languages, the 1920s and 1930s also witnessed the beginning of Chinese academic studies of Indian theater. Pioneered by scholarly works of Sino-Indian exchange that I discuss in this book—Xu Dishan's on religion and literary realism, and the literary critic Zheng Zhenduo's translations of Tagore's work—such studies tried to establish a theory by which classical Chinese drama emerged out of an encounter with Sanskrit theater. Two important archaeological findings precipitated the circulation of the theory. In 1893, in a small monastery in Tiantai Mountain in Zhejiang, a German archaeologist discovered, on a single palm-leaf manuscript dating to the thirteenth century, a short narrative of Kālidāsa's life. Because the vast majority of extant Sanskrit texts that traveled from India to China were Buddhist texts, the discovery of this brief biographical study of a Brahmin writer piqued the curiosity of German and French philologists.[42] Another important drama-related discovery was made in 1906 in Xinjiang by German archaeologists who discovered a manuscript of the canonical Buddhist nāṭaka *Maitreyasamiti*, in which the plot predicts the coming of Maitreya—Buddha of the future. These two discoveries prompted interest in the drama-related connections between China and India. The curiosity of scholars also underscored, as Ji Xianlin noted, the frustration with imperialist infrastructures enabling foreign, rather than Chinese, archaeologists to make such discoveries. A keen desire to build a research field dedicated to China and India's cultural exchange within China emerged from this burgeoning awareness of the dramatic forms circulating between the two countries.[43]

The archaeological discoveries of Indian dramatic texts in China and the emergence of conversation about China-India dramatic exchange also overlapped with the establishment of Chinese drama as a field of study. Much is known about the inspiration European and Japanese modernism held for writers of the first Chinese spoken-dramas (*huaju* 話劇) in the early years of the twentieth century, and about the emergence of drama as an independent field and an important part of national culture building.[44] Little remembered, however, is the fact that Wang Guowei 王國維 (1877–1927), whose 1913 study *A History of Song and Yuan Drama* (*Song yuan xiqu shi* 宋元戲曲史) is credited with launching the field of Chinese drama, mentioned the importance of music and song coming to China from Xinjiang, known as "the Western regions." Traveling through the Xinjiang area, at the heart of the Silk Roads, these forms of cultural exchange were recognized by Wang Guowei as central to the development of various genres in China, from the Five Dynasties period (907–960) to the Yuan dynasty (1279–1368).[45]

Xu Dishan and Zheng Zhenduo took up this argument with their own publications emphasizing the significance of India in the formation of Chinese drama. Between 1925 and 1930, Xu Dishan published several influential studies in which he traced the Indian and Iranian (Central Asian) origins of Chinese Song and Yuan dramas.[46] In one study—titled *The Style of Sanskrit Drama and its Gradual Diffusion into Chinese Drama* (*Fanju tili ji qi zai han ju shang dian di di* 梵劇體例及其在漢劇上的點點滴滴) and based on research he conducted during his stint at Oxford University with the well-known Sanskrit specialist A. A. Macdonell—Xu examined similarities in theatrical forms between southern China and India, and traced the etymologies of Chinese terms to Sanskrit. Echoing Wang Guowei, Xu Dishan traced the earliest bourgeoning of Chinese drama to new styles of music and dance that came into China via Xinjiang during the Six Dynasties period (222–589), which saw the disintegration of imperial unity and the flourishing of new religious formations such as Daoism, as well as a dramatic increase in the circulation of Buddhist scriptures and practices. According to Xu, circulation of new song and dance styles from "the Western regions" (*xiyu* 西域) ensued in the *zaxi* (雜戲) form: early folk theater involving music and acrobatics. As we know, Xinjiang served as an important connecting space between China and India during those times; Xu Dishan thus extended Wang Guowei's preliminary conclusions regarding the Western regions to include India. Xu then went on to explore another potential route for theatrical exchange with focus on India.

He locates significant similarities between Indian and Chinese puppetry (*guileixi* 傀儡戲) and shadow play (*piyingxi* 皮影戲), especially from Quanzhou and Chaozhou areas in Fujian and Guangdong, by comparing not only the etymologies of these terms in Sanskrit and Chinese but also the techniques and recurring plot lines across the two cultures.[47] Xu concluded with a lengthy comparative section on Song and Yuan drama plotlines, and on devices such as prologues that include benedictions given by the director (also seen in Yuan drama), epilogues, stock characters, and the use of off-stage dialogue to report actions not seen on stage. All of these are pervasive in Sanskrit theater, especially in nāṭakas.

Xu Dishan's work was cited and echoed in the writings of Zheng Zhenduo. Unlike Xu Dishan, Ji Xianlin, and other Indologists such as Jin Kemu, Zheng was neither trained in Sanskrit nor familiar with any Indian languages. Yet, since the early 1920s, Zheng Zhenduo had been a major figure in promoting the study of China-India exchange and was categorically more outspoken than Xu Dishan about India being the major source of world-literature and a major influence on China's theatrical culture. Between 1932 and 1934, Zheng published a seminal work consisting of six volumes and titled *Illustrated History of Chinese Literature* (*Chatuben: Zhongguo wenxue shi* 插圖本中國文學史). In a chapter titled "The Origins of Xiwen Drama" (Xiwen de qilai 戲文的起來), Zheng reiterated Xu Dishan's argument that drama developed in China through contact with India, describing it as a piecemeal that took place when new religious formations, which included ritualistic songs and dances, were introduced to China by merchants. Zheng focused on the development of the Chinese opera form *xiwen*, also known as *chuanqi* (傳奇)—a folk theater form from southern China based on song and dance (*nanqu* 南曲). For China to explore and understand the origins of its theater, Zheng argued, claims grounded only in examining the cultural practices in the Six Dynasties, Sui, and Tang eras had to be rejected. It was essential to examine theatrical forms in other countries with which China had been in contact. This was where India came in.

Zheng specifically brought up the Indian Ocean route and argued that it was through the maritime route and not the Silk Roads that such theatrical forms developed in South China. He excitedly mentions the discoveries of the nāṭaka *Maitreyasamiti* and the thirteenth-century manuscript that mentions Kālidāsa's life story. That this manuscript was found in a monastery not too far from the Chaozhou area, where *xiwen* theater originated, cannot be a mere coincidence, Zheng exclaimed.[48] Like Sanskrit dramas, Zheng continued, *xiwen* forms tend to assign different linguistic registers for characters based on their status, much like the distinction between Sanskrit-speaking characters and Prakrit-speaking characters in Kālidāsa's works. Zheng concluded by noting similarities in plotlines and characterization shared by Chinese and Sanskrit dramas. He discussed the plot of the oldest *nanxi* (南戲), now lost, and pointed out the recurring theme in many *nanxi* of the "besotted girl in love with a heartless man" (*chi xin nüzi fu xin han* 痴心女子負心漢). Here, Zheng mentioned *Śakuntalā*'s similarities with this trope and argued that Sanskrit dramas informed Chinese *nanxi* plays such as *Zhao the Chaste Maid and the Second Son Cai* (*Zhao zhen nü cai er lang* 趙貞女蔡二郎) and *Wang Kui* (王魁)—both revenge love stories. The first survived in dramatic form and the second as a short story with song and dance. Both feature the themes of China's southern theatrical tradition, which focused on love, disillusion, and betrayal.[49]

The idea that Xu Dishan and Zheng Zhenduo tried to promote— that Chinese drama emerged through historical connections with India—has been challenged by Chinese scholars since the 1950s and remains contested today. Opposition to the theory is mainly grounded in its sweeping argument that Chinese drama owes its very development to Sanskrit drama.[50] Nevertheless, the genesis of the theory itself in the 1920s and 1930s, and its support by China's leading literary critics at that time, remains an important moment in Chinese writers' envisioning of China-India cultural encounters in the first half of the twentieth century. More recently, the essays I discuss here by Zheng Zhenduo and Xu Dishan have seen renewed interest from scholars reconsidering the origins of Chinese drama and China-India connections.[51] A leading voice on China-India's historical connections and a former Ji Xianlin student, Xue Keqiao (薛克翹), in his recent monograph *A History of China-South Asia Cultural Exchange* (*Zhongguo yu nanya wenhua jiaoliu zhi* 中國與南亞文化交流志), has reiterated the idea that Chinese drama developed out of contact with India.[52]

In their writings about Indian themes, tropes, and terms that are etymologically similar in Chinese and Indian languages, the writers I have discussed here all pointed to the example of *Śakuntalā*. Often alluding to its global appeal, or locating its imagined traces in Chinese dramatic texts, the Republican-era writings about *Śakuntalā* that hypothesized an Indian origin for Chinese drama reflect an important shift in Chinese intellectuals' thinking about India. Between the 1910s and late 1940s, they imagined a mutual ground of shared culture between the two countries that facilitated a literary language of decolonization. Yet the mediating role of English-language translations of Indian texts and of Euro-American discursive constructs such as "civilization," "nation," even "the East" meant that even this idea of a China-India connection, which sought to challenge orientalist thinking, was itself often tinged by the imperial unconscious. With the work of Xu Dishan, as I show in chapter 3, efforts to envision a literary practice grounded in Chinese and Indian interactions emerged from a heightened awareness of the problems posed by orientalist epistemology. Continuing and developing this direction, Ji Xianlin's work, and especially his translation of Śakuntalā, was a critical stepping stone for an emergent Sino-Indology that paid critical attention to the Western legacies that informed it and was aware of the inability to completely disavow them.

"Nearer the Ideal": *Shagongdaluo* in Chinese Aesthetics Debates in the 1950s

Ji Xianlin began his studies as a German major at Tsinghua University. He graduated in 1934 from the Department of Western Literatures, where he wrote a senior thesis on the early poems of Friedrich Hölderlin. A student exchange program took Ji Xianlin in 1935 to Göttingen, where he began to study Sanskrit. As the Sino-Japanese War erupted in 1937, followed by World War II, Ji Xianlin ended up staying in Germany, which in the late nineteenth- and early twentieth-centuries was one of the most robust training environments for scholars of Indian languages, history, and literature outside India.[53] After a decade in Göttingen, Ji Xianlin received a PhD and formally trained as an Indologist, having studied with Wilhelm Siegling and Emil Sieg, the first scholars to analyze the grammar of Central Asian Tocharian languages, using manuscripts they excavated in the Turfan area of Xinjiang. In the 1890s, German expeditions to this area had excavated the first known Tocharian manuscripts. These were followed by British, French, Japanese, and Russian expeditions to the Tarim Basin north of the Taklamakan Desert.

Germany was the hub for the study of Tocharian. Research into Tocharian manuscripts aligned with the nineteenth-century taxonomy project of historical linguistics I discuss in chapter 1, by which the concept of linguistic families was created. The metanarrative of historical linguistics argued that all human languages evolved in an identical process, from monosyllabic words and pictographs to phonetic script. The study of language families foregrounded a new category of "Indo-European languages" and sought to excavate the universal origin of all human languages by tracing linguistic continuities between India and Europe. Tocharian was and still is understood to belong to the Indo-European language family.[54]

Unlike others studying Tocharian, however, Ji Xianlin's passion for the study of its languages—a field in which he was a well-known authority throughout his life—did not spring from a desire to celebrate the Indian roots of Europe or the universal singular source of all human languages.[55] To the contrary, Ji Xianlin was highly cognizant of the imperialist nature of linguistic universalism. Writing about his days in Germany, he noted that his mentors had told him many times that scholarship "recognizes no national boundaries." Of course, he wrote, I always knew this was wrong— that it was something that only my German professors, who traveled across the globe and even to China, could say.[56] Keenly aware of the imperialist privileges that enabled his mentors to conduct archaeological studies in the Taklamakan Desert and make sweeping pronouncements about language, Ji Xianlin's Tocharian research had other aims. He sought not to prove the Indo-European language theory, but to excavate historical interactions between China and India by situating Tocharian texts and the Xinjiang area as a critical connector of two cultures. Extant Tocharian manuscripts are Buddhist texts that consist, among other things, of translations and adaptations of Jātaka tales, such as the Buddhist nāṭaka *Maitreyasamiti* I mentioned earlier in the chapter. The critical role the Xinjiang area played in the formation and dissemination of Buddhism from India to China inspired Ji Xianlin to move away from the Indo-European focus of his mentors in Germany, to a transregional approach for the study of cultural exchange.

In an essay published during the China-India bonhomie of 1955, titled "The Discovery and Philological Study of Tocharian and its Use in Studying China-India Exchange" (Tuhuoluoyu de faxian yu kaoshi ji qi zai zhong yin wenhua jiaoliu zhong de zuoyong 吐火羅語的發現與考釋及其在中印文化交流中的作用), Ji urged his readers to remember the critical role of Central Asia's Tocharian peoples and languages in mediating historical encounters between China and India. The essay built an alternative history of the discovery and study of Tocharian. Ji related the first reports of Tocharian not to nineteenth-century German archaeologists, but to the famous Buddhist pilgrims from China to India in the fourth and seventh centuries, Faxian and Xuanzang, and pointed to Tocharian as the languages through which words from Sanskrit merged into Chinese.[57]

Beginning his career as a scholar of literature, and particularly enthralled by Sanskrit literature, Ji Xianlin realized that in order to secure a livelihood as an academic in the fledgling People's Republic of China in the late 1940s and early 1950s, he needed to focus his efforts on something that could prove useful for the national agenda.[58] Thus Ji Xianlin became China's foremost India specialist. As a philologist and historian of Sino-Indian linguistic, religious, scientific and cultural exchange, he played an important role in the tightening of the two countries' relationship prior to 1962. But his passion for literary studies, especially poetry, did not wane. He published studies that helped found the discipline of comparative literature (*bijiao wenxue* 比較文學) in China. His translations not only introduced critical renditions of Sanskrit classics to Chinese readership, but also, in a similar vein to how his work on Tocharian grammar strove to undo Indo-European universalism in favor of transregional contact, made an important intervention in contemporary debates on the role of literature in social life.

In recent years, studies have focused on socialist aesthetics in Chinese art and literature during what is often called the Seventeen Years Period—the years between the establishment of the People's Republic of China in 1949 and the launching of the Cultural Revolution in 1966.[59] Yet, unlike the robust scholarship we have on Republican China's practices of translation, discussions of post-1949 engagement with foreign literature in China are still few.[60] Ji Xianlin's translations, particularly his translation of *Śakuntalā*, open a window for us to another dimension of Chinese aesthetic culture during the Maoist era. *Shagongdaluo* engages one of the key concerns of Chinese socialist art: the problem of referentiality, understood as the relation between a text and the reality it depicts, or between the fictional world and nonfictional world.[61] *Shagongdaluo*, its accompanying paratexts, and its stage production, add an important layer to our understanding of 1950s literary dynamics in China and compel us to broaden our study of the period's aesthetics by examining translation alongside original work.

The 1950s literary scene in China was characterized by a duality. On the one hand, there was increasing openness to literature outside China, expressed by a deluge of translations of writers hailing from across Asia, Latin America, and the Middle East. On the other hand, the centralization of publishing presses and journals redrew the boundaries of interpretation of said translations, as editorials, prefaces, and footnotes that now accompanied the translations communicated the official stance on the translator's country and personal political inclination.[62] A similar dynamic shaped original work and literary criticism. Chinese writers experimented with and developed socialist literature and artforms while working within clearly demarcated priorities and censorial frameworks. Literature in the early 1950s, for the first time in Chinese history, was to be based on insights gained through interacting with the peasants in the countryside. Literature was to be written for the people and about the people—that is, written in a language that peasants, workers, and soldiers could understand and that would represent their experience.[63] The cultural turn toward massification (dazhonghua 大眾化) had begun in the early 1940s with discussions that took place at Yan'an, a Shaanxi Province rural area that served as the base for the Chinese Communist Party between 1937 and 1949 and was thus immortalized in the national memory as the birthplace of the Chinese revolution. These discussions resulted in the publication of several of the most widely read Chinese novels of the twentieth century, from Ding Ling's The Sun Shines Over the Sanggan River (Taiyang zhao zai sanggan he shang 太陽照在桑乾河上, 1948) to Zhou Libo's The Hurricane (Baofeng zhouyu 暴風驟雨, 1948) and Yang Mo's Song of Youth (Qing chun zhi ge 青春之歌, 1958). These works were made possible by literature's new status as critical fuel for the revolution. Writers and artists strove to produce work with high artistic merit that also enacted the directives given by Mao Zedong in lectures in Yan'an and later published as Talks at Yan'an Forum of Art and Literature (Yan'an yishu tanhui 延安藝術談會) in 1943.[64]

The Talks delineated an elaborate literary theory that essentially comprised Mao's pronouncements on what literature is, how to write it, and (most importantly) for whom is it meant. In these lectures Mao called on intellectuals to join the ranks of the revolution and inspired a generation of Chinese artists. Writers and artists were instructed not only on what themes they should engage, such as war of resistance with Japan and the Chinese rural sphere, but also on what methods they should use—namely, adapting language and representation from the experience of the masses while constantly striving to elevate the level of artistic merit of the works.

Beyond the prescriptive facets of the lectures, *Talks* is a work in artistic criticism that ponders the function of art in society and then develops specific directives based on these reflections. *Talks* expressed a firm belief that while art and artists are subordinated to the revolution, the success of the latter depends on the former because the people need art and literature; both are essential to communist society. What makes them so important? In *Talks*, Mao defined the life of the masses as art and literature in their natural form. The practice of artistic creation, Mao argued, moves art from this natural form (the raw materials of life) into a processed form (the artwork). In effecting the transformation from natural to processed, artists and writers take the raw materials shaping the life of the masses and organize, condense, and stylize them into the work of art. Revolutionary literature and art are, in this sense, life in a more concentrated form. People need art and literature because they depict and intensify life itself. Art, in other words, transforms reality into a heightened version of itself. As such, art gives the people a sense of truth about their lives that their everyday reality does not. As Mao put it in one of the most cited passages from *Talks*:

> Although man's Social life is the only source of literature and art and is incomparably livelier and richer in content, the people are not satisfied with life alone and demand literature and art as well. Why? Because, although both are beautiful, life as reflected in works of literature and art can and ought to be on a higher plane, more intense, more concentrated, more typical, nearer the ideal, and therefore more universal than actual everyday life.[65]

The publication and dissemination of *Talks*, a major milestone in modern Chinese literary theory, changed the aesthetics of Chinese art and literature for the next thirty years.

Mao's discussion of how art produces a concentrated reality dramatically rerouted decades-long debates over realism—the form privileged by the May Fourth fiction writers since the early 1920s; in chapter 3, I discussed Xu Dishan's work as a major intervention in that realist practice. Whereas the realist fiction composed by Lu Xun, Mao Dun, Ye Shaojun, and others was generally underscored by social Darwinist views of society that informed linear depictions of degeneration and decline, Xu Dishan, inspired by his work on Buddhism and Hinduism, introduced a structure I call "cyclical realism"—a literary portrayal of human life as a patchwork of repetitive rituals, like a spider's web. The variegation Xu contributed to the 1920s and 1930s critical realism was, nevertheless, informed as well by a mimetic logic that explored literary portrayal as an attempt to reflect social reality.

The idea of realism that Mao Zedong presented in *Talks* was different. Art and literature now had to not simply reflect reality, but actively produce a better version of it. Through the act of condensing, typifying, and enhancing the distinctions between good and bad, literature was tasked with conjuring a new and improved world. The new reality had to be simple rather than complex, clear rather than obscure, always beautiful and energizing. Its purpose was to show the ideal as possible, to embody utopian sensibilities, and to actually assist in producing that utopia. After the publication of *Talks*, the realism in socialist fiction came to be understood as *zhen* (真), which can be understood as "true," dismissing the earlier *shi* (實), which is closer in artistic representation to what we would understand as a mimetic reality.[66] The artistic process of producing *zhen* involved "discarding the dross and selecting the essential." Socialist art should focus on "eliminating the false and retaining the true."[67] The pivotal literary critic Zhou Yang 周揚 (1908–1989) defined the relation between *zhenshi* and reality in these words:

> As for "zhenshi" and "realism," we have a totally different understanding from the revisionists. Under the pretense of "zhenshi" and "realism," the revisionists usually oppose the tendentiousness (*qingxiang* 傾向) of socialist literature and art. . . . Their so-called realism is "realism" without progressive ideals, which is actually not realism but naturalism. . . . In class society, writers exclusively observe and describe reality with a certain class tendentiousness. It is only by keeping the progressive stand of class and people that writers can deeply understand and reflect upon *zhenshi* of the time. *Zhenshi* and revolutionary tendentiousness are a unity in our understanding.[68]

Infusing the portrayal of reality with tendentiousness was Zhou Yang's interpretation of a *zhen*-based portrayal—the depiction of a particular reality in the artwork, where the relation to the reality outside the text is not one of reflection but of augmentation. Studies of artistic representation of reality in Chinese socialist culture, from fiction and poetry to drama and film, have highlighted the paradigmatic status of *Talks* in informing a highly stylized representation of reality.[69] Yet, to my knowledge, few studies have examined how the aesthetic paradigm established in *Talks* informed practices of translation during the 1950s and early 1960s. This line of inquiry is challenging, since literature in foreign languages was a finished product and could not be commissioned to cover the themes directed by Mao Zedong or to employ methods of characterization that corresponded to the paradigms of *Talks*. Therefore, a study of the socialist aesthetics of translated literature does not necessarily focus on themes, characters, or narrative elements, but rather must direct its attention to things like the selection of texts, word choices, editorial decisions (such as omissions or additions), as well as paratexts—in particular, prefaces, that often explained the circumstances of translations and editorial decisions taken.

In *Shagongdaluo* as well as in essays he published on Kālidāsa's work, Ji Xianlin demonstrates a profound engagement with *zhenshi* aesthetics. *Shagongdaluo*, which was first published in 1956 and reissued in new editions in 1957 and 1959, is a full critical and annotated translation. Whereas translators to Western languages often glossed over Sanskrit terms for mountains, flowers, or deities, Ji Xianlin transcribed them in Chinese characters and added lengthy footnotes explaining to the Chinese reader allusions and concepts from Hindu religious traditions, such as the Hindu lunar calendar, or practices of asceticism. To further make the play accessible to a Chinese audience, Ji Xianlin used several Buddhist terms in translating concepts, referring for example to Śakuntalā as a *xiuxingren* (修行人)—a term meaning "religious practitioner" used to index Buddhist or Daoist practitioners in China.[70] He made certain additions to the original text, which suggest that he was already thinking about the stage production while translating from the text. Ji also added musical interludes (*chaqu* 插曲) in acts 3 and 4 to emphasize transitions to key scenes. Ji broke several of the poems recited by the characters in the original into shorter paragraphs and added connectives such as "and" (*erqie* 而且) between them, making it easier for the audience to follow and creating a more dynamic exchange in the dialogues. *Shagongdaluo* thus straddles a philological approach that aspires to elucidate terms and allusions and a vision of the text on stage. In a substantial preface appended to the translation, Ji balanced a historical study of Kālidāsa—whom he crowned the most illustrious poet in the history of world literature—with a theoretical discussion of the representation of reality in the drama. Combining a historical study of Kālidāsa's world with a literary theory that takes on the relationship between art and reality— one of the most critical concerns of the day—enabled Ji Xianlin to envision

Shagongdaluo, on paper and on stage, as the embodiment of a reality that is "nearer the ideal."

The preface to Ji Xianlin's translation begins with a detailed historical discussion. Ji situates the nāṭaka and its writer in the heyday of the Gupta Empire in the fifth century, and elaborates about the period's agriculture, economy, and culture as well as the development of Sanskrit-language literature, which peaked during the Gupta era. Throughout, Ji Xianlin mentions coterminous historical developments in China, highlighting similarities and differences, and adds information about Chinese travelers to India. Sensitive to the current political climate, Ji's tone is at times apologetic: for example, he notes that as a court poet, Kālidāsa had no choice but to praise the traditional system, the monarchy, gender inequality, and exploitation of the disenfranchised. Yet, Ji insists, Kālidāsa also challenged other social norms of his time and criticized the ruler. His depiction of the abandoned Śakuntalā, unrecognized by her husband, clearly presents her as the sympathetic character. It was in this way, Ji surmises, that Kālidāsa conveyed the inequality between the king and the peasants.[71] The contradictions in *Śakuntalā*, Ji argues—for example, a plot that glorifies the production of a male heir alongside genuine critique of social inequality—needed to be placed in historical context.

Importantly, this was no mere toeing of the party line. Earlier, Ji Xianlin used his research of China and India connections to critique and correct what he viewed as a historical error made by Marx. Ji noted that in *A Contribution to the Critique of Political Economy* (1859), Marx makes the point that the development of art does not correspond to the development of material conditions in a society. Marx is correct with regard to many Western societies, especially if we think of ancient Greece, Ji submits, but not in the cases of China and India, where instead the two processes often unfold at the same time. He cites the examples of the economic development and poetic revival during the Tang dynasty and the Gupta Empire eras. Judging old literature by today's standards, Ji argues, adopts an idealist rather than materialist approach to history.[72]

The timing of the publication of *Shagongdaluo* offers a clue to explain the otherwise puzzling question of how Ji Xianlin dared to so boldly critique Marx and develop, as I show below, a vision of *zhenshi* aesthetics that broadened the thematic terrain stipulated in Mao's *Talks*. Ji was writing during the Hundred Flowers Movement (*Baihua yudong* 百花運動, 1956–1957), a period during which the central government encouraged political tolerance and criticism. Mao Zedong had many reasons to feel optimistic: he was enjoying a high level of popularity after the Agrarian Reform and Marriage Laws of 1950, had made tremendous gains against the United States in the Korean War, had successfully reorganized industry and agriculture under state control, and was making strides toward a leadership position in Third Worldist movements. In 1956, Mao often addressed groups of intellectuals and solicited their opinions and critique of any aspect of Chinese social and political life. Invoking the slogan "Let a hundred flowers blossom, let a hundred schools of thought contend" (*baihua qifang, baijia zhengming* 百花齊放，百家爭鳴), Mao intended not only to solicit useful critiques and suggestions of the government function, but also to revive China's cultural scene, which he viewed as stifled by the initial revolutionary art forms promoted in the 1942 Rectification Movement (*Yanan zhengfeng yundong* 延安整風運動)—the pioneering attempt to produce art that would aid in recruiting the rural population to the War of Resistance and overthrowing the Guomindang. New blood was needed to speak to urbanites and intellectuals as well. Response to Mao's call was enthusiastic: intellectuals engaged in heated debates over, for example, the artistic merit of popular genres or the role foreign literature and music should take in the new China.[73] The pendulum of tolerance eventually swung back to suppressing dissenting voices in June and July 1957, with the launching of the Anti-Rightist Campaign (Fan you yundong 反右運動, 1957–1959). And yet, the legacy of the Hundred Flowers Movement—the opening of new possibilities for artistic and intellectual innovation during the height of Third World diplomatic efforts on China's end—adds important layers to our understanding of the ways in which exploring the cultural connections between India and China energized Chinese thinkers' literary practice. Ji's critique of Marx's cultural history as Eurocentric is emblematic of the possibilities of the period.

The remainder of the preface, consisting of more than half, moves on to discuss what Ji underscores as *Śakuntalā*'s particular grandeur. Ji notes the global success of the play and mentions, briefly, details about translations and stage productions in Europe, but this is not where his main interest lies. Instead, Ji Xianlin draws on his profound knowledge of Sanskrit and Indian history to frame the problem of literary referentiality as central to the aesthetic sphere. Ji asks: What makes *Śakuntalā* the ultimate masterpiece? Not the plot, which is not original but adapted from the *Mahabharata*. And not an exciting new theme: Kālidāsa's drama depicts romantic love between the king and Śakuntalā—all too common in practically every literary tradition in the world. The magnificence of Kālidāsa's contribution, Ji submits, lies in his particular ability to take up common themes and familiar stories and re-create them in poetry that breathes new life into the characters. In characterization, Ji argues, Kālidāsa has reached "an astonishing degree of truthfulness" (dadao jing ren de zhenshi de chengdu 達到驚人的真實程度). Here, Ji Xianlin draws directly from the Maoist artistic discourse on the relation between the artistic act and reality: when an artwork is successful, it reaches a high level of truthfulness (zhenshi), defined as a more intensified sense of reality. Kālidāsa's stage directions, Ji notes, detail the facial expressions of every character, their movements, their voices. In doing so, Kālidāsa makes the most insignificant characters, such as the attending palace girls, vibrate with life.[74] In Ji Xianlin's reading of Śakuntalā, the effect of truthfulness that distinguishes the piece is embedded in this sensibility of vivid depiction.

In Sanskrit nāṭakas, representation of the realm of the forest is shaped by a religious reading of correlative cosmology, the principle of which positions the realms of the human, the natural, and the supernatural, in relation and in constant interaction with one another. The natural world in Indian correlative cosmology is not still but vibrates with the divine presence of the gods—in the case of Śakuntalā, the presence of Śiva for whom a prayer is offered in the prologue. The religiously informed representation of nature as reverberating builds the romance between the hero and the heroine. The characters are connected not only to one another: their emotions interact with the natural world. The spring, the flowers in bloom, and the frolicking forest animals all resonate their emotions in sympathy. One of the hermitage disciples in act 4 makes the connection apparent when musing in verse: "The moon sets over the western mountain/as the sun rises in dawn's red trail—rising and setting, these two bright powers/portend the rise and fall of men."[75]

The notion of sympathetic resonance between humans and the natural world is the backbone of the cosmologies of both China and India.[76] The ideas of correlative cosmology had been pervasive in China since the Han era, extending from the Chinese medical understanding of the human body as responding in illness or health to the five phases and the cycle of seasons and to astronomy, government, and literature. In classical Chinese literary criticism, the poet composing on the bank of the river is an integral part of the cosmic pattern of spring, by which the poet and the natural elements of the poem, such as the moonlight or the budding lilies upon the river, are complementary and interdependent. The poetic act thus become a physical manifestation of a latent pattern in nature, "passing from world to mind to literature."[77] Ji points to this resonance between humans and nature in poetry as a shared tradition in both China and India. He invokes the luminary Du Fu's 杜甫 (712–770) poem "View in Spring" (Chun wang 春望), which depicts the spring lushness joining in mourning over the havoc wrought by the An Lushan rebellion ravaging the country at the time. Ji compares the verse "Stirred by the time, flowers, sprinkling tears splash/Hating parting, birds, alarm the heart"[78] to the fourth act in Śakuntalā, in which the heroine says her goodbyes to the forest hermitage, and the flora and fauna all respond to her feelings: flowers lower their head, animals sob in sympathy with her sadness.[79] Far from the orientalist reading of act 4 as a fall from grace, Ji Xianlin offers an interpretation grounded in the correlative cosmological vision shared by Chinese and Indian cultures. Like many of his contemporary readers, Ji was, of course, familiar with the translational history of the play into English, French, and German and its enthusiastic embrace in Europe. Indeed, he discusses both to bolster his statement that Kālidāsa is India's most renowned poet and one of the greatest writer in the history of world literature (shijie wenxue 世界文學).[80] But nowhere does Ji use the orientalist description of "India's Shakespeare," nor does he reiterate interpretations offered by translations to European languages. His explanation for the fourth act's status as "The Core" of the play in India points to the act's poetic depictions of resonance. Chinese poetry, he notes, employs a similar notion of referentiality, in which poetry does not simply reflect nature but resonates with it. Citing poems by Du Fu and Bai Juyi 白居易 (772–846) as examples, Ji Xianlin explains that in both Chinese and Indian traditions of poetic criticism, the way in which the poetic act takes part in the cosmological cycle extends from the poet aroused by nature to the reader whose emotions are stimulated by the poem's reading.[81]

In translating Śakuntalā, Ji Xianlin pays particular attention to two key scenes that make the interconnectedness between art and its reference—reality—apparent. These are also the only two scenes that he embellishes to reinforce his own reading of their original significance.[82] The first is a scene in act 3 in which Śakuntalā, struggling to verbally express her feelings to Duṣyanta, describes her passion in a verse that she etches on a lotus leaf with her fingernails. The leaf becomes an embodied testament of her emotion. As Śakuntalā reads the verse aloud, Duṣyanta, who was in hiding, emerges, having received proof that his love is reciprocated. And with that, the romance is launched. Ji Xianlin rephrases the suggestion one of Śakuntalā's maids makes, to inscribe the poem on a lotus leaf, as a question: Why don't you use your finger to engrave your poem on this lotus leaf that is as smooth as a parrot's crop? Ji also gives a new line to Śakuntalā when she responds to the king's declaration of love following her reading of the poem. Paired with a stage directive noting that Śakuntalā is embarrassed, Ji adds the following soliloquy: "My heart! surprisingly, you are too embarrassed to utter a word!"[83] Posing the maid's suggestion to etch the love declaration to the king with Śakuntalā's fingers as a question adds a sense of dynamism to the critical action that sets the love story in motion. By adding an exclamation soliloquy at the end of the scene, Ji Xianlin's translation extends the emotive terrain that the poem—etched by the loving body on a surface belonging to nature— is meant to invoke in the spectator of the drama. The visceral link between the writing body, the nature as canvas, and the emotional response that the actor is meant to extend to the audience is reiterated later in the play.

In act 6, the king, whose memory of his pregnant wife is renewed when the ring he gave her is found by a fisherman, feels deep longing and remorse as he searches for her and draws her portrait. The majority of the act takes place in front of the portrait, as the king and his companion gaze at the canvas, which has been brought on stage, and comment on its resemblance to Śakuntalā. Indeed, the portrait is a crucial element of the plot. Sānumatī, a forest nymph who is close with Śakuntalā's mother, remains in hiding to test the king's recollection by examining the portrait for resemblance.

In the course of act 6, the painting becomes more than a two-dimensional representation. The king's buffoon notes that the picture is so full of life that he has to stop himself from speaking to it. The king, unable to remove his gaze from the picture, calls attention to the stains that his perspiring fingers left on the canvas and a swelling in the paint caused by his tears. The artist's sweat and tears embellish the painting in a particular way: they embed the painter king's body with Śakuntalā's painted figure and augment a two-dimensional representation with the physical reality outside of it, as the bodily fluids change the surface of the canvas. Augmenting the two-dimensional representation with the body of its creator, the verisimilitude of the painting plays tricks on the observers as the boundaries between art and its referent are dissolved. Throughout the scene, Sānumatī observes the king's engagement with the portrait, which he plans to continue. Sānumatī approves the portrait's likeness to Śakuntalā, thus certifying the king's recollection of his beloved and lifting the curse. The blurring of the boundaries between painting and referent reaches a climax when a bee, mistaking the painted Śakuntalā for a real human, lands on the portrait and tries to sting its subject. Duṣyanta drives the bee away, worried that it will hurt his beloved, prompting the buffoon to exclaim, "But sir, it's just a picture!"[84] As the king wakes from the illusion that he is facing his beloved, his sorrow and remorse grow even stronger. In his translation of act 6, Ji Xianlin creates a dynamic sense of dialogue by sectioning the character's short monologues and verses, adding connectives such as "but" and "and" to create a more rapid exchange of words. He adds stage directives, such as emotive sighs, or renders the line in a high or low pitch, as well as specifies that characters move closer or farther away from the portrait to hold it or put it down. To emphasize the painted subject's vividness, Ji gives the king a new sentence: "She seems to be about to begin speaking!" The buffoon then affirms this sentiment: "I have such strong desire to chat with her!"[85]

The two artistic creations depicted in the play—a poem etched by the heroine's fingers on a lotus leaf and a portrait that literally includes the hero's sweat and tears—stand at critical plot junctures, launching and relaunching the romance. To Ji Xianlin, the power of poetry to emotionally stir its readers lies in its portrayal of a world grounded in *zhenshi*: a heightened and intensified depiction of reality that brings it to life. The most important aspect of *Śakuntalā* for Ji was its power to conjure a world that feels more alive than even the world its aims to represent. He writes:

The crux of the matter [in *Śakuntalā*] is the problem of the relation between art and reality (*Yishu yu xianshi de wenti* 藝術與現實的問題). The ability to reflect reality is not what transforms something into a work of art. That lies in the ability to elevate reality beyond itself. Chairman Mao said: "Life as reflected in works of literature and art, compared with ordinary actual life, can and ought to be on a higher plane, more intense, more concentrated, nearer the ideal, and therefore more universal." . . . An artist's creativity is expressed in his ability to elevate the real (*xianshixing* 現實性) to the true (*zhenshixing* 真實性). . . . the fact that readers in India and outside of it are deeply moved by this play, the play's very power of moving, lies in its truthfulness, and not in its realism.[86]

In rendering Ji Xianlin's translation to the stage, the creators of the 1957 stage production *Shagongdaluo* continued his efforts to engage the current discourse on *zhenshi* aesthetics. A cover of the popular *China Pictorial* (*Renmin huabao* 人民畫報) at the time featured a photograph of the actress Bai Shan (白珊) on stage as Śakuntalā (figure 4.1).

Fully adorned, with the king behind her, Śakuntalā is the focus of the photograph. With her gaze purposefully turned sideways and her fingers gesticulating, the actress is performing in accordance with the stylistic traditions of Sanskrit drama, using eyes and hands to accentuate emotional states. Four years after the production debuted, Bai Shan published an article in *Theater Journal* (*Xiju bao* 戲劇報) that explained the methodology she developed while portraying Śakuntalā. Titled "Stress, Intonation, Pause, and Breath" (Chongdu, yudiao, tingdun he huxi 重讀語調停頓和呼吸) Bai Shan instructs actors to break up and analyze text-lines—down to the word-by-word level—to determine where to breath, pause, or stress, and what intonation to affect. This was the only way, she relates, that she was able to activate the emotional subtext of Śakuntalā in a way that captured its complexity. Only by working this way, she concludes, did she manage to avoid formalism (*xingshizhuyi* 形式主義) and fill the texts she recited with action and life.[87] Indeed, Bai Shan's performance was key to the success of the production. The actors were wary of the pitfalls of characters becoming automatic—merely formulaic—as they performed traditional stylized acting. But using the technique described by Bai Shan and assisted by specialists in the style, the nonrealistic acting and dance conveyed a suppositional vividness that sought to produce *zhen*—a condensed ideal reality.

A short article published in the same issue of *China Pictorial* annotated five photos and color illustrations of the production. The author Wu Xue, the director of the production, articulates an appreciation of Kālidāsa similar to that of Ji Xianlin. He writes: "A well-known myth has been bestowed upon the world by the masterful pen of this writer. In his profound, truthful (*zhenshi* 真實) portrayal of characters, he immortalized this drama, which is an apex of world culture."[88] With these words as well as the production he directed, Wu Xue solidified the new Chinese understanding of Śakuntalā,

FIGURE 4.1 Cover of *Renmin huabao* 人民畫報 [*China pictorial*] 7 (1957).

inaugurated by Ji Xianlin's translation, as a canonical work of world literature. But whereas the nāṭaka garnered its global acclaim thanks to German,
British, and French scholars (mis)reading the lost Garden of Eden in its pages,
Chinese Indologists put their knowledge of Sanskrit philology to a different
use. Working to locate transregional connections, they had other reasons
to include Śakuntalā in the canon of world culture. In China, Śakuntalā was
celebrated for its brilliance in bringing characters to life, thus creating a
reality more intense and nearer the ideal. Kālidāsa was understood to be a
master in extracting the true from the real. Prompted by Ji Xianlin's translation and the China Youth Art Theater's performance, Chinese appreciation
of the play brought together traditional and transregional modes of criticism with contemporary paradigms of socialist culture.

Conclusion

The modern history of Śakuntalā in China captures the broader dynamics of
the China-India imagination I explore in this book. Translated into Chinese
from European versions, Śakuntalā was first introduced through the lens of
a specifically late nineteenth-century European view of world culture. The
play was deemed a masterpiece according to a universalist paradigm similar to that which identified India as the source of all human languages. In
the 1920s and 1930s, as more scholars began to study Indian languages and
thought, Śakuntalā played a role in founding the field of drama studies in
China, which sought in its early days to trace the origins of Chinese theater
to a Sanskrit antecedent. In the late 1940s and 1950s, as Chinese Indology
flourished alongside efforts to build a historic friendship between the two
nations, and as ideals of Third World solidarity animated cultural exchange
grounded in language learning and research, Shagongdaluo entered the scene,
in text and on stage, to help shape a new Chinese vision of world culture.
Supported by the political climate of China-India amity and the openness
encouraged by the Hundred Flowers Movement, Shagongdaluo ushered in a
new understanding of world culture that identified transregional exchange
as its engine. This perspective, promoted by Ji Xianlin and his generation,
did not suggest an exclusive focus on Asia and Africa that would reject Europe
and the United States. Goethe, William Jones, Monier Monier-Williams,
Herder, and Forster—their embrace of Kālidāsa was crucial in canonizing the

text, even for a Chinese audience. What Ji Xianlin's scholarship and translation popularized for the first time was a reading of the play that, while recognizing the clout of Śakuntalā in Europe as paving its position as a canon of world literature, anchored its interpretation in transregional knowledge and history. "World literature" could mean more than great masterpieces of the world outside Europe; it could unsettle the Eurocentric assumptions that defined the genre itself—even those of Marx—and dare to trace a history of mutual horizons and cultural exchange.[89] The exchange between China and India forged a particular type of referentiality—a mimesis based on resonance and heightened sensuality—exemplified in the translation and Chinese staging of Śakuntalā. Drawing from Mao's *Talks* as well as Du Fu, Ji Xianlin deepens our understanding of socialist art by adding historical layers to the notion of *zhenshi* and revealing, through his own work, how envisioning the China-India connection had a formative impact on China's literary culture in the 1950s.

The 1959 second theater production of *Shagongdaluo*, along with the third edition of Ji's translation, cemented the status of the nāṭaka as one of the most successful and beloved foreign literary works of the period. Yet, at the same time, 1959 also marked a dramatic transformation in the relationship between India and China, which began to openly unravel in the aftermath of the Tibet Uprising, and escalated in the 1962 Sino-Indian War, bringing an end to the regional friendship between the two nations. While realpolitik did not sever the study of China-India interactions or the translation of premodern Indian literature, the events that took place from 1959 to 1962 carried lasting ramifications for the multiple imaginaries of Chinese-Indian cultural horizons, which, after close to a decade of institutionalization via conferences, film festivals, and delegations of artists, writers and dancers, have receded into the background. Decolonization efforts through translation of Afro-Asian literatures continued in the early 1960s, but these no longer featured India prominently in the new directions of China's Third World culture building.

Epilogue

After 1962: The Ongoing Literary Work of Mourning

I would suspect that meaningful cultural meetings had taken place between India and China over the last two thousand years. But colonialism has now created a situation where we have to talk to each other through centres of knowledge which are located five thousand miles away. And that is something which is tragic too.

—ASHIS NANDY, FROM "OPEN PASTS, OPEN FUTURES," 2009

When a pen draws the horizon
you're awakened by a gong from the East
blooming in the echoes is
the rose of time

—BEI DAO, FROM "THE ROSE OF TIME," 2009

IN APRIL 1963, THE Chengdu Military Command's War Flag Literature and Art Collection Series, a division of the People's Liberation Army Publishing Press, published a slim volume of poems celebrating China's seizure of disputed territories in the Himalayan border during the war with India, which took place from October to November 1962. Titled *Songs of Salutation: In Dedication to the Hero Frontier Guards* (*Weiwen shicao: xiangei yingxiong de bianfangbudui* 慰問詩草：獻給英雄的邊防部隊), the twenty-five poems in the volume were composed by a soldier named Li Wei (李衛) upon his return home.[1] The poems are predictable. Published (and most likely) commissioned by a military propaganda bureau, they not only hail the heroism and dedication of the Peoples Liberation Army (PLA), as well as its compassion toward Indian captives and frontier populations, but also bolster a claim to disputed territories in the Plateau of Aksai Chin bordering Ladakh, Tibet, and Xinjiang, and in the Assam Himalaya Region to the northeast.

With the 1962 Sino-Indian War, a near decade of tightening diplomatic relations and thriving cultural and scientific exchange between China and India had come to a crashing halt. There were signs pointing to this outcome, as I explain in the following paragraphs, from multiple directions.

When Jawaharlal Nehru and Zhou Enlai signed the Panchsheel Treaty in 1954, they committed to its five principles: mutual respect for sovereignty, nonaggression, noninterference in another country's internal affairs, equal and mutual benefits, and peaceful coexistence. But they glossed over (and thus left unresolved) disagreements, especially pertaining to the position of Tibet and how it impacted the demarcation of boundaries between the two new nations.

Earlier still, when in the first decade of the twentieth century Su Man-shu envisioned a Buddhist utopia, the India he wrote into poetry and prose was a colonial space extending to Sri Lanka. By the 1950s and afterward, the most important venue in China for translating and publishing foreign literature, the journal *World Literature*, featured works hailing from decolonized nations in South Asia by clearly distinguishing India from Sri Lanka and Pakistan from Nepal. Yet, imperial era territorial logic nevertheless simmered within the language of decolonization in both China and India.

Between 1951, when Tibet was declared an autonomous region of the People's Republic of China, and 1959, when popular revolt flared up in Lhasa against the PRC's control, China and India managed to keep at bay disputes over Tibetan sovereignty and control over its borders.[2] With the March 1959 uprising resulting in the Dalai Lama's escape to Lhasa and his asylum in Dharamsala, bridging over barriers became increasingly more difficult, which culminated in the 1962 war. Ramifications of that war continue to manifest in periodical eruptions in the Galwan Valley's contested boundary line separating China and India.[3]

The ongoing clashes over territories on the Himalayan frontier are an inheritance from the imperial era. The 1914 Simla Convention Treaty, part of a broader British project of mapping and establishing borderlines in Central and South Asia, demarcated the borders between Tibet, China, and British India, while attaching a status of Chinese suzerainty with de facto autonomous administration to Tibet. The treaty was signed by Tibetan and British representatives of colonial India with the Republic of China in absentia. China never ratified the Sino-Tibetan-Indian border delineated in one of its annexes by what was known as the McMahon Line (after the administrator who drew it, Sir Henry McMahon). The PRC's claim to Tibet was likewise never recognized by India. Tensions amassed between the two recent allies, as Britain and the United States kept a close vigil on the happenings and lent support to India and Tibet in the late 1950s and during the 1962 war, which nevertheless ended when China, despite making significant inroads into Indian territory, announced a ceasefire and withdrew to what became known as the Line of Actual Control.[4]

The 1962 Sino-Indian War and its aftermath threw into sharp relief the enduring legacy of earlier regimes that seemed for over a decade, at least rhetorically, part of the past. India fought to sustain British imperial boundary drawing. China, seeing the war as an extension of the 1959 Tibet Uprising, upholds to this day the Qing's territorial pursuits.[5] The political project of Indian-Chinese brotherhood, of mutual leadership of the Third World, which some argue, was tenuous all along in light of its unwavering commitment to nationalism,[6] had decisively unraveled.

These are the fitful winds of change that affected Li Wei's 1963 poetry collection. Alongside glorifying tributes to the PLA, the poems are rife with derogatory depictions of the rival Indian troops. Repeatedly, Li depicts Indian troops in China as "bearded soldiers" (鬍子軍, huzi jun), resurrecting a colonial-era trope. The mid to late nineteenth century had seen the rising presence in China's port cities of Indian soldiers and guards who performed policing duties in the service of Britain and played a major role in quelling the Boxer Uprising (1899–1901) in service of Britain and other European powers. Highly visible in urban centers, especially Shanghai, the turban-donning, mustache- and beard-sporting soldiers were depicted in late Qing fiction and visual art, thus inscribing the "bearded soldier" into the Chinese collective memory as an enslaved executor of imperial greed and violence—traitor to his own people, and collaborator in the imperialization of Asia at large.[7] Yet, the beard and turban's metonymic value—standing for Indian aggression—did not originate in China. The provenance of the metonym is the British theory of "Martial Races," which argued that since certain groups in India (especially Punjabi and Jat Sikh soldiers) traditionally bore arms, they are the fittest to fight in service of the empire. As a result, almost exclusively, Sikhs were chosen to fill the ranks in China's treaty ports.[8] Indian soldiers thus became synonymous with a turban, a beard, and colonization. Singling out the bearded soldier as an extension of colonialism, Li Wei's poems are plagued by the imperial unconscious—reifying the British

Empire's race doctrine to voice resistance to British imperial boundaries. Lying dormant for the several decades that I investigate in this book, the bearded soldier reincarnates, again and again, in Li Wei's post-Sino-Indian War collection. Except in one place. The penultimate poem in the volume, titled "Tibetan Brothers Supporting the Troops" (*Zang bao zhiqian* 藏胞支前), concludes with the following vignette:

> Melting snow and ice provide for irrigation
> Sunlight radiates over highland barley crop
> China and India's people resonate in unison
> Whole-heartedly clasp hands and chant Mituo.[9]

The lines of verse preceding this one all celebrate the crushing of the Indian army, with lyrics such as "We greet the grand army who secured victory/Anti-Chinese songs and gongs are silenced!" Yet, here, with no transition, we read a conflicting image. The Lohit River flowing from Tibet to Arunachal Pradesh is depicted in hyperrealist tones: the white and blue of melting snow, the green of barley, the yellow sun, the smiling faces united in prayer—a harmony of humans and nature. Why conclude a series of admonitions of the bearded soldiers with a vision of Chinese and Indians resonating with a change of seasons, bringing forth a spring of friendship as they chant the name Mituo (Amitabha, one of the most widely worshipped Bodhisattvas in Mahayana Buddhism)?

Herein lies a certain quality of literary expression in which Ashis Nandy, a contemporary political theorist and postcolonial thinker, sees a powerful capacity to mourn despite forgetfulness. Nandy addressed Indian and Chinese writers who came together unofficially, not under the auspices of states or institutions, and spoke of the ethical imperative of mourning—in ways that deliberately eschew geopolitical perspectives—what has been lost, found, and lost again in the China-India modern encounter under the shadow of colonialism:

> We have forgotten the language of mourning. Our literature, our art, they do reflect this mourning of what we have lost. But that is by default. Because, while negotiating modernity, both these civilisations [China and India] have learnt to shed the language of mourning. They have learnt the language of accountancy, the gains and losses from different sectors of modernity as it enters different

sectors of our lives. So we are supposed to celebrate only what we have gained from modernity. And not lament the fact that there are crucial elements of ourselves which we have to jettison or reject or discard in accepting modernity. This rejection of the language of mourning is most pronounced in our social knowledge. As I have said in literature it can enter indirectly despite the writer or the artist. Even when the artist is proudly modern there can be that recognition of what we have lost.[10]

Can we read the incongruency of the final lines of "Tibetan Brothers Supporting the Troops" in relation to the rest of the poem, indeed, to the rest of the collection, as the ethical work of mourning that seeps in despite (perhaps) the poet himself—a mourning over a vision of mutuality drowned in the sounds of war? I submit that by inhabiting the same poetic space with bearded soldiers and the chants of Chinese and Indian people alike, the poet was likely performing an act of lamenting, longing for a sense of unity that could pierce through the celebration of national victory that this volume of poems set out to accomplish.[11]

Reading for the ethical work of mourning in literary expression is made possible because literature—whether fiction, poetry, or drama—is grounded in a suspension of disbelief that allows it to simultaneously engage more than one threshold of reality. Should we perform this reading to contemporary texts, we would be bound to reckon with a multidimensional answer to the question whether an era of China-India solidarity was an empty promise—a house of cards that collapsed after 1959 when imperial demarcation of borders forcefully pushed itself yet again, as it still does, to mediate the interaction between the two cultures.[12] Undeniably, 1962 changed the scale and nature of China-India connections. Until the mid-1980s, Indian literature in translation all but vanished from Chinese publishing presses and literary journals, although translation efforts of literatures from Asia and Africa continued, with prominence given to works hailing from Pakistan, Nepal, Sri Lanka, Myanmar, Vietnam, Algeria, Angola, Nigeria, Senegal, and Egypt.[13] Cultural delegations to India stopped altogether.

Even with the discontinuation of state-sponsored institutions of Hindi Chini Bhai Bhai, research and writing about India, especially on Sanskrit and Pāli literatures, still continued, albeit in the works of individuals. To state two examples, Ji Xianlin still published in *World Literature* a translation and interpretation of selected sections in the *Jataka* in 1963.[14] He continued to study and publish on the history of Buddhism and Sanskrit prose until the launch of the Cultural Revolution (1966–1976), during which, despite persecution, Ji managed to complete a celebrated translation of Valmiki's *Ramayana*, which was published in 1980. Ji Xianlin's long-time colleague, the esteemed Indolog Jin Kemu, published in 1964 the first Chinese-language history of Sanskrit literature.[15] And in 1965 his translations of treatises by the premodern musicologist Bharata-muni, the Sanskrit grammarian Daṇḍin, and the poet and rhetorician Vishvanatha Chakravarty Thakur were collected in the tenth volume of the *Collection of Classical Theory of Literature and Art in Translation* (*Gudian wenyi lilun yicong* 古典文藝理論譯叢).[16] Along with their ongoing work of translation and research, Ji Xianlin and Jin Kemu continued to build the field of Chinese Indology and the study of China-India historical interaction at the Department of Eastern Languages and Literatures (*Dongfang yuyan wenxue xi* 東方語言文學系) in Beijing University. Today, the department they founded boasts Sanskrit, Pāli, Hindi, and Urdu tracks as well as a track for the study of South Asian culture.

Indology remains a substantial field in Chinese academia; and Chinese literary markets circulate works by paragons of Indian literature—especially Tagore, whose collected works were translated from the original Bengali for the first time in 2016.[17] But after 1962, India no longer consistently inspired epistemic resistance to imperialism in Chinese literature, as it did from the late Qing until the late 1950s. The beginning and the end of this literary sphere compels us to recognize the power South-South thinking had for uncovering and rejecting the grasp of imperialist knowledge on the mind through literary practice, the limitations to this project posed by the mediation of the North, and its ongoing urgency today.

What is the long-term significance of the modern China-India oneness project? The question lays bare a broader concern: the viability of decolonialization, and the future potential of Global South collaborations—real and imagined—to achieve this goal. As I show in this book, a literary perspective refuses to polarize, to deem decolonization imaginaries a success or failure. The Chinese writers I examine here show that it has been, and remains impossible, to disavow the North, to simply extract it from the South-North-South equation. But literary acts of epistemic disobedience that writers perform open a space of grieving—for the past, and for a present that remains mired in fear-mongering rhetoric of the clash of Asian superpowers.

Where does contemporary literature of mourning for what we lose in the enduring condition of coloniality take us? I suggest that in the literary space of mourning we find a polyphonic history and a view of possible horizons that is aware of its limitations but continues to forge cracks in the "colonial matrix of power" from within. As such, literary decolonization is the ongoing project of writers who are committed to building bridges that coloniality-informed geopolitics are bent on taking apart. Poems such as those emerging from a contemporary China-India literary network—The China India Writers Dialogues collective (*Zhongyin zuojia duihua* 中印作家對話), and routinely published in the Hong Kong- and New Delhi–based journals, *Today* (*Jintian* 今天) and *Almost Island*—offer some examples of what I mean. I conclude with these.[18]

The writers in the China-India Dialogue collective are cognizant, as Nandy notes in the epigraph to this epilogue, of the enduring barriers established by the shared yet distinct experiences of colonialism.[19] They acknowledge the still necessary mediation of the English language in facilitating their encounters by recognizing the translators of poetry from Chinese to English (and the onsite interpreters working in the writers' workshops) as part of the collective. In the New Delhi–based poet Sharmistha Mohanty's "Editorial Sutras," she conveys a sense of what their workshops are like. Through the trope of a burnt ravine, her text laments the violence colonial mediation wreaked upon regional ties:

There *were* mountains and rivers, paper and ink, brushstrokes. There *were* caves with painted narratives. There *are* offices of glass, innumerable highways, the metro moving silently on its tracks. In between, an enormous ravine that our bodies cross at will, back and forth. In the ravine, no river, no stream, nothing moving. The fish that rest on the bottom are carved from blackened silver. The lightness of red sandstone in ruins and tombs. Its heaviness in poems that emerge from them.[20]

Portraying physical and textual sites of China-India interaction, Mohanty not only makes room for history to show itself (for there *were* mountains, there *were* painted caves), but also for poetry that, like fish carved from heavy blackened silver, simultaneously embodies death and the memory of water, which could flow once again in the ravine. The hope is there. In the works of Mohanty's Chinese collaborators, Asian connected history unfolds in multiple and fleeting temporalities that capture a sense of immanent loss; think of Bei Dao's rose of time, blooming in the echoes made by the gong that sounds each time a pen attempts to commit the East to paper, or Ouyang Jianghe's competing linear time and the truth of impermanence, conveyed in verse such as "The ancients and moderns look at each other with the eyes of a flower. And seen through Buddha's eyes, all are blind."[21] Shared in the texts emerging from this collective is an epistemic break with modern linear time that suggests a new direction for the work of decolonization in literary practice. These Chinese and Indian writers construe a manifold idea of history that is made apparent in such poetic gestures as the blooming and dying of flower petals and the red dust rising from the sandstone ruins only to sink deeper into the poems now written: poems that, like the paintings on caves, bear and convey more than "gains and losses from different sectors of modernity." Their literary work of mourning, inspired by their interactions, is deeply committed to opening up new radical imaginaries of shared pasts and futures in ways that look straight into the horizon that is never a single line drawn by a pen, as Bei Dao submits, but a resounding of echoes.

Notes

Introduction

1. Zheng Zhenduo notes in the preface to this study that he consulted and borrowed his title from John Drinkwater's *The Outline of Literature* (London: G. Newnes, 1923), and also drew structure and content from John Macy, *The Story of the World's Literature* (London: Peter Owen Limited, 1925).
2. Macy, *The Story of the World's Literature*, 23–39.
3. Drinkwater, *The Outline of Literature*, 92–106.
4. Zheng Zhenduo, "Wenxue dagang," in *Zheng Zhenduo quan ji* 鄭振鐸全集 [Collected works of Zheng Zhenduo] (Shijiazhangshi: Hua shan wenyi chubanshe, 1998), 131.
5. Jing Tsu offers a different reading of Zheng Zhenduo's *An Outline of Literature*, which she sees as a move to bolster national literature by incorporating Chinese classics into the emerging canon of world literature—what she calls "filling a 'China' gap in an intended global literary history." See Jing Tsu, "Getting Ideas About World Literature in China," *Comparative Literature Studies* 47, no. 3 (2010): 290. Certainly, the chapters on Chinese literature are the most comprehensive in Zheng's study, but the lengthy discussions he included of Indian literary works suggest a broader thinking of the meaning of a world canon beyond a nation-bound paradigm. In this sense, I suggest that we take seriously Zheng's opening claim in *An Outline of Literature* that "literature has no national boundaries." See Zheng Zhenduo, "Wenxue dagang," 1. Beyond the somewhat pompous and universalist inclination of this statement, Zheng was genuinely interested in pushing Chinese writers and readers to look beyond European and Russian literatures. Indian poetry, epics, and drama struck him as particularly significant for Chinese readers to explore given the history of China-India literary and dramatic exchange—a topic he elaborates on in *An*

Illustrated History of Chinese Literature (*Chatuben Zhongguo wenxue shi* 插圖本中國
文學史 [1932]. See Zheng Zhenduo, *Chatuben Zhongguo wenxue shi* (Beijing:
Wenxue guji kan xing she: Xinhua shudian faxing, 1959). I discuss Zheng
Zhengduo's study of Indian and Chinese drama exchange in chapter 4.

6. Johan Wolfgang von Goethe, *Conversations of Goethe with Johann Peter Eckermann*
[1836] , trans. John Oxenford (Boston: Da-Capo Press, 1998).

7 Maire and Edward Said, trans. "Philology and Weltliteratur by Erich Auerbach," *The Centennial Review* 13, no. 1 (1969): 1.

8. Zheng Zhenduo, "Wenxue dagang," 115.

9. It is likely that Zheng made this argument based on two of the sources he mentions in his works-cited list. John Drinkwater, in *The Outline of Literature* (91),
writes "The first of the Sacred Books in the order of antiquity are the Vedas of
the Brahmans"; and Arthur Anthony Macdonell, *A History of Sanskrit Literature*
(New York: D. Appleton, 1900), 280, notes, "It would be a mistake to suppose
that Sanskrit literature came into being only at the close of the Vedic period,
or that it merely forms its continuation and development. As a profane literature, it must, in its earliest phases, which are lost, have been contemporaneous with the religious literature of the Vedas." That the *Mahabharata* and
Ramayana are not the most ancient literary works was widely acknowledged
when Zheng Zhenduo wrote this chapter (the earlier Akkadian *Epic of Gilgamesh*,
for example, was discovered in 1853). But I am less interested here in Zheng
Zhenduo's faulty periodization than in the superlative he assigns to the Indian
epics as the earliest origins of human literary culture. I trace how British-
German nineteenth-century framings of Sanskrit literature as Ur-culture
came to inform Chinese literary circles in chapter 1.

10. Ngũgĩ wa Thiong'o, *Decolonising the Mind: The Politics of Language in African Literature* (London: J. Currey, 1986). Ngũgĩ writes: "English, like French and Portuguese, was assumed to be the natural language of literary and even political
mediation between African people in the same nation and between nations in
Africa and other continents. In some instances, these European languages were
seen as having the capacity to unite African peoples against divisive tenden-
cies inherent in the multiplicity of African languages within the same geographic state. Thus Ezekiel Mphahlele later could write in a letter to *Transition*
number 11, that English and French have become the common language with
which to present a nationalist front against white oppressors, and even 'where
the whiteman has already retreated' as in the Independent states, these two
languages are still a unifying force,' " 6–7.

11. See, for example, Leo Ou-fan Lee, *The Romantic Generation of Chinese Writers*
(Cambridge, MA: Harvard University Press, 1973); Merle Goldman, ed., *Modern
Chinese Literature in the May Fourth Era* (Cambridge, MA: Harvard University
Press, 1977); Lydia H. Liu, *Translingual Practice: Literature, National Culture, and
Translated Modernity China, 1900-1937* (Stanford, CA: Stanford University Press,
1995); Shu-Mei Shih, *The Lure of the Modern: Writing Modernism in Semicolonial
China, 1917-1937* (Berkeley: University of California Press, 2001).

12. Karen Thornber, *Empire of Texts in Motion: Chinese, Korean and Taiwanese Transculturations of Japanese Literature* (Cambridge, MA: Harvard Asia Center, 2009);

Satoru Hashimoto, *Afterlives of Letters: The Transnational Origins of Modern Chinese, Japanese and Korean Literatures* (forthcoming).

13. To state a few examples: Lydia H. Liu, *Translingual Practice*; Jing Tsu, *Failure, Nationalism and Literature: The Making of Modern Chinese Identity 1895-1937* (Stanford, CA: Stanford University Press, 2005); Haiyan Lee, *Revolution of the Heart: A Genealogy of Love in China, 1900-1950* (Stanford, CA: Stanford University Press, 2006); Tze-ki Hon, *Revolution as Restoration: Guocui xuebao and China's Path to Modernity, 1905-1911* (Leiden: Brill, 2013); Mingwei Song, *Young China: National Rejuvenation and the Bildungsroman, 1900-1959* (Cambridge, MA: Harvard University Asia Center, 2015); Jie Gao, *Saving the Nation through Culture: The Folklore Movement in Republican China* (Vancouver: University of British Columbia Press, 2019).

14. The most comprehensive English-language history of these exchanges, to date, is Tansen Sen, *India, China and the World: A Connected History* (Lanham, MD: Rowman & Littlefield, 2017).

15. See John Kieschnick and Meir Shahar, *India in the Chinese Imagination: Myth, Religion and Thought* (Philadelphia: University of Pennsylvania Press, 2013); Sheldon Pollock and Benjamin Elman, *What China and India Once Were: The Pasts That May Shape the Global Future* (New York: Columbia University Press, 2018).

16. See, for example, Yao Yuanmei, "Nanya guancha: Yindu bianjieguan ji 'lang wai po' zuofa" 南亞觀察：印度邊界觀及'狼外婆'做法 (South-Asia Survey: India's Concept of Borders and the Practice of 'The Wolf in Sheep's Skin'), *Pengpai xinwen* October 7, 2020, accessed February 11, 2022, https://www.thepaper.cn/newsDetail_forward_9458212.

17. Shishir Gupta, "Why is Sikh Soldier a Bogeyman for Chinese Army at Ladakh," *Hindustan Times*, September 17, 2020, accessed February 11, 2022, https://www.hindustantimes.com/india-news/why-is-sikh-soldier-a-bogeyman-for-chinese-army-at-ladakh/story-4FuLsEa991pKKEuafxmKcL.html.

18. Prasenjit Duara, "Introduction," in *Decolonization: Perspectives from Now and Then* ed. Prasenjit Duara (London: Routledge, 2003), 2.

19. Robert J. C. Young, *Postcolonialism: An Historical Introduction* (Oxford: Blackwell, 2001), 60–61; Kuan-Hsing Chen, *Asia as Method: Toward Deimperialization*, (Durham, NC: Duke University Press, 2010), 3, 66–113.

20. Eve Tuck and K. Wayne Yang, "Decolonization is Not a Metaphor," *Decolonization: Indigeneity, Education & Society* 1, no. 1 (2012): 3.

21. Patrick Wolfe, "Settler Colonialism and the Elimination of the Native," *Journal of Genocide Research* 8, no. 4 (2006): 387–409.

22. Nancy Shoemaker, "A Typology of Colonialism," *Perspectives on History*, October 1, 2–15, accessed February 11, 2022, https://www.historians.org/publications-and-directories/perspectives-on-history/october-2015/a-typology-of-colonialism. Elsewhere, Jeffrey Ostler and Nancy Shoemaker argue that, counter to Tuck and Yang's call cited above, "settler colonialism" has itself become such a powerful keyword that it now extends from the field of early American history to Native American and indigenous studies, as well as histories of the American West and the study of gender and sexuality, resulting in the obliteration of critical distinctions between different forms of colonialism in recent studies (see Ostler and Shoemaker, "Forum: Settler Colonialism in

Early American History: Introduction," *William and Mary Quarterly* 76, no. 3 (2019): 361–368. For a survey on the development of settler colonialism studies in North America and Australia-New Zealand over the last decade see also Jane Carey and Ben Silverstein, "Thinking With and Beyond Settler Colonial Studies: New Histories After the Postcolonial," *Postcolonial Studies*, 23, no. 1 (2020): 1–20.

23. Kuan-Hsing Chen, *Asia as Method*, 10.

24. The Japanese Empire, for example, employed settler-colonial practices in Taiwan and imperial and extractive colonialism in Korea, simultaneously. Arguably, Qing China practiced settler-colonialism in Taiwan, Inner Mongolia, and Dzungaria (Northern Xinjiang), all while being colonized via a series of unequal treaties with Western Empires as early as 1842 that ceded control over Hong Kong and granted foreign concessions in China's coastal cities to European countries and the United States. On settler-colonialism in East, West, and North Asia, see Edward Cavanagh and Lorenzo Veracini, eds., *The Routledge Handbook of the History of Settler Colonialism* (London: Routledge, 2017), 311–368. On disputes within the scholarly community in China and in the United States and Europe over whether or not Qing expansion and settler practices should be understood as colonialism, see Julia C. Schneider, "A Non-Western Colonial Power? The Qing Empire in Postcolonial Discourse," *Journal of Asian History* 54, no. 2 (2020): 311–342.

25. I am referring to the humanities-based field of postcolonial studies, the beginnings of which are generally attributed methodologically to poststructuralism and deconstruction, as they informed late 1970s and 1980s pioneering studies by Gayatri Chakravorty Spivak, the Subaltern Studies Group, and Edward Said. For an overview of some of the arguments that mark different directions taken in postcolonial studies and decoloniality studies in relation to questions of historicism, analytical methods, and geographies of research subjects, see Elleke Boehmer, *Empire, the National and the Postcolonial 1890-1920: Resistance in Interaction* (Oxford: Oxford University Press, 2002); Revathi Krishnaswamy and John C. Hawley, eds., *The Postcolonial and the Global* (Minneapolis: University of Minnesota Press, 2008); and Benjamin P. Davis and Jason Walsh, "The Politics of Positionality: The Difference Between Post-, Anti-, and De-colonial Methods," *Culture, Theory and Critique* 61, no 4, (2020): 374–388. Importantly, Walter Mignolo comments that it would be counter-productive to invest too much in differentiating one from the other: "I do not see decoloniality and postcoloniality campaigning for elections to win the voting competition that decides which is the best, but as complementary trajectories with similar goals of social transformation. Both projects strive to unveil colonial strategies promoting the reproduction of subjects whose aims and goals are to control and to possess." Walter D. Mignolo, *The Darker Side of Western Modernity: Global Futures, Decolonial Options* (Durham, NC: Duke University Press, 2011), xxvi.

26. Aníbal Quijano, "Coloniality of Power, Eurocentrism and Latin America," *Nepantla: Views from South* 1, no. 3 (2000): 533–580.

27. Walter D. Mignolo and Catherine E. Walsh, *On Decoloniality: Concepts, Analytics, Praxis* (Durham, NC: Duke University Press, 2018), 114. See also the work of

Enrique Dussel, a critical interlocutor for Mignolo and Walsh; especially Dussel's "Without Epistemic Decolonization, There is No Revolution," *Venezuelan Analysis*, October 21, 2016, accessed March 1, 2022, https://venezuelanalysis.com/analysis/12734.

28. Walter D. Mignolo and Catherine E. Walsh, *On Decoloniality* (116). I treat imperialism and colonialism as interrelated processes or two sides of the same historical process of European economic expansion as early as the fifteenth century (together with the United States during the nineteenth century, the collective ramifications of which are still evident in the neoliberal world order today). There is, however, a customary distinction between the two, which we can trace to Edward Said's distinction in *Culture and Imperialism* between imperialism as a logic and a theory of "a dominating metropolitan center ruling a distant territory," and colonialism as one possible consequence of imperialism, "the implanting of settlements on distant territory." See Edward Said, *Culture and Imperialism* (New York, NY.: Knopf, 1993,) 9.

29. Walter D. Mignolo and Catherine E. Walsh, *On Decoloniality*, 108.

30. Anne Garland Mahler, *From the Tricontinental to the Global South: Race, Radicalism, and Transnational Solidarity* (Durham NC: Duke University Press, 2018), 5–7.

31. Nour Dados and Raewyn Connell, "The Global South" *Contexts* 11, no. 1 (2012): 12.

32. Richard Wright, *The Color Curtain: A Report of the Bandung Conference* (Jackson: Banner Books, University of Mississippi/Jackson, 1956); Dipesh Chakrabarty, "Legacies of Bandung: Decolonization and the Politics of Culture" *Economic and Political Weekly* 40, no. 46 (2005): 4812–4818.

33. For a genealogy of the shift from 1960s "Third World" to "Global South" see Arif Dirlik, "Global South: Predicament and Promise," *The Global South* 1, nos. 1 and 2 (2007): 12–23.

34. South Commission, *The Report of the South Commission: The Challenge to the South* (New York: Oxford University Press, 1990), v.

35. For a comprehensively annotated summary of the spread of the concept "Global South" from development studies and international relations to the humanities, see Russel West-Pavlov, "Toward the Global South: Concept or Chimera, Paradigm or Panacea?" in *Global South and Literature*, ed. Russell West-Pavlov (Cambridge: Cambridge University Press, 2018), 1–11.

36. Duara dates decolonization in Asia to Japan's victory in the 1905 Russo-Japan War, "which was widely hailed as the first victory of dominated peoples against an imperial power." See Prasenjit Duara, *Decolonization: Perspectives from Now and Then* (London: Routledge, 2004), 2. See also, Rebecca E. Karl, *Staging the World: Chinese Nationalism at the Turn of the Twentieth Century* (Durham, NC: Duke University Press, 2001); Pankaj Mishra, *From the Ruins of Empire: The Revolt Against the West and the Remaking of Asia* (Harmondsworth, UK: Penguin, 2012); Sugata Bose and Kris Manjapra, eds., *Cosmopolitan Thought Zones: South Asia and the Global Circulation of Ideas* (Basingstoke, UK: Palgrave Macmillan, 2010).

37. Isabel Hofmeyr advocates this type of interrogation. See Isabel Hofmeyr, "Against the Global South." in *Global South and Literature*, Russel-West Pavlov, ed., 307–314.

38. I note some examples below. In English literature, Laura Chrisman points to the unconscious of imperial enterprises as the manifestation of internal contradictions, weaknesses, and anxiety over self-justification within the seemingly omnipotent metanarratives of empires. See Laura Chrisman, "The Imperial Unconscious? Representations of Imperial Discourse," in *Colonial Discourse and Postcolonial Theory: A Reader*, ed. Patrick Williams and Laura Chrisman (New York: Routledge, 1993), 498–516. Amy Kaplan similarly reads the figuration of Hawaii in the writings and lectures of Mark Twain as rife with imperial premises that unconsciously gloss over the link between American slavery and American expansion in solidifying national identity and Twain's position as a national author, in Amy Kaplan, "Imperial Triangles: Mark Twain's Foreign Affairs," *Modern Fictions Studies* 43, no. 1 (1997) 237–248. See also Camilla Fojas, *Islands of Empire: Pop Culture and US Power* (Austin: University of Texas, 2014), where she examines early American films in order to decode representations of what she terms the "American imperial unconscious." Other studies on cinema have employed similar approaches, such as Julianne Burton's early work. See Julianne Burton, "Don (Juanito) Duck and the Imperial-Patriarchal Unconscious: Disney Studios, the Good Neighbor Policy, and the Packaging of Latin America," in *Nationalism & Sexualities*, ed. Andrew Parker et al. (London: Routledge, 1992), 21–41. Studies on the formation and development of American sociology employ "the imperial unconscious" to expose imperial underpinnings that continue to inform scholarship, such as Julian Go, "Sociology's Imperial Unconscious: The Emergence of American Sociology in the Context of Empire," in *Sociology and Empire*, ed. George Steinmetz (Durham, NC: Duke University Press, 2013), 83–105; and Thomas M. Kemple and Renisa Mawani, "Global Public Life: The Sociological Imagination and Its Imperial Shadows," *Theory, Culture & Society* 26, no. 7–8 (2009): 228–249. The late critical geographer David Slater developed the idea of an imperial unconscious to demarcate the persistence of imperialist imperatives in hidden or indirect form in US-Latin geopolitics. For example see David Slater, "The Imperial Present and the Geopolitics of Power," *Geopolítica(s)* 1, no. 2 (2010): 191–205.

39. Kakuzō Okakura, *The Ideals of the East: With Special Reference to the Art of Japan*, second edition (New York: E. P. Dutton and Company, 1905), 1.

40. Peter van der Veer, "Spirituality in modern Society," *Social Research* 76, no. 4 (2009): 1097–1120; and Peter van der Veer, *The Modern Spirit of Asia: The Spiritual and the Secular in China and India* (Princeton, NJ: Princeton University Press, 2014).

41. See R. John Williams, *The Buddha in the Machine: Art, Technology and the Meeting of East and West* (New Haven, CT: Yale University Press, 2014), where he looks at aesthetic practices that the "Asia as remedy" perspective engendered in England and the United States, ranging from book design to narrative techniques, poetics, and cinema.

42. Rabindranath Tagore, *The Essential Tagore*, ed. Fakrul Alam and Radha Chakravarty (Cambridge, MA: Belknap Press, 2011), 186.

43. Partha Chatterjee, "Tagore, China, and the Critique of Nationalism," *Inter-Asia Cultural Studies* 12, no. 2 (2011): 271–283.

44. Jingkui Jiang and Yan Jia, "The History of the Production of India-Related Knowledge in Post-1950 China," *History Compass* 2 (April 18, 2018), https://doi.org/10.1111/hic3.12448.

45. On Liang Shuming's engagement with Bergson see An Yanming, "Liang Shuming and Henri Bergson on Intuition: Cultural Context and the Evolution of Terms," *Philosophy East and West* 47, no. 3 (1997): 337–362.

46. Donna V. Jones, *The Racial Discourse of Life Philosophy: Négritude, Vitalism and Modernity* (New York: Columbia University Press, 2010), 10. See also Souleymane Bachir Diagne, *African Art as Philosophy: Senghor, Bergson and the Idea of Negritude* (London: Seagall Books, 2012).

47. Naveeda Khan, *Muslim Becoming: Aspiration and Skepticism in Pakistan* (Durham, NC: Duke University Press, 2012); Souleymane Bachir Diagne *Islam and Open Society Fidelity and Movement in the Philosophy of Muhammad Iqbal* (Dakar: Codersia, 2011), 5–17.

48. On Barak, *On Time: Technology and Temporality in Modern Egypt* (Berkeley: University of California Press, 2013), 1–20.

49. Robert H. Sharf, "The Zen of Japanese Nationalism," *History of Religion* 33, no. 1 (1993): 1–43.

50. Prasenjit Duara's work on the transformation of the discourse of "civilization" from furnishing the European inter-state system to underscoring a new meaning of Asian civilization offers a different perspective on the rise of the "Asianness" episteme in China and Japan. To Duara, Asian-ness served to bolster Chinese nationalism in the first half of the twentieth century by foregrounding the great cultural achievements of Asian civilizations, such as China. Duara's insights are key for understanding important features of Pan-Asianism, especially the Japanese embrace of this ideology in its own empire building. Yet, to my mind, thinkers such as Liang Shuming, as well as Su Manshu and Wang Tongzhao (whom I examine in chapters 1 and 2), were more interested in dismantling the Western view of civilization enshrined in the colonial civilizing mission than in claiming "civilization" for Asia. See Prasenjit Duara, "The Discourse of Civilization and Pan-Asianism," *Journal of World History* 12, no. 1 (2001): 99–130; "Asia Redux: Conceptualizing a Region for Our Time," *The Journal of Asian Studies* 68, no. 4 (2010): 963–983.

51. Raewyn Connell, *Southern Theory: The Global Dynamics of Knowledge in Social Sciences* (Cambridge: Polity, 2007).

52. Gayatri Spivak recently noted: "I think the global South is a reverse racist term, one that ignores the daunting diversity outside Europe and the United States." For Spivak, the concept "Global South," as it is used in the humanities, denotes a center that produces counter-modernities or counter-universals that exercise a colonial violence of generalization, even with the best of intentions. As she puts it, "our definition of the global South ignores the largest sectors of the electorate in Asia, Africa, and Latin America, below the radar of nongovernmental organizations and below the class apartheid in education. The terms global and South must be shaken up in different ways—recognizing that empiricism is without guarantees." See Gayatri Chakravorty Spivak, "How do We Write, Now?," *PMLA* 133, no. 1 (2018): 166, 168.

53. Rachel Leow, "A Missing Peace: The Asia-Pacific Peace Conference in Beijing, 1952, and the Emotional Making of Third World Internationalism," *Journal of World History* 30, no. 1–2 (2019): 53. Arif Dirlik warned about the academic tendency to romanticize and idealize the 1950s concept of Third World alliance, which, despite its social power as a "mobilization myth" nevertheless "temporarily disguised the deep differences that divide these societies from one another." See Arif Dirlik, "'Specters of Third World:' Global Modernity and the End of the Three Worlds," *Third World Quarterly* 25, no. 1 (2004): 136. See also a study of 1950s Afro-Asian writers conferences, which decisively moves beyond the simplification of South-South exchange as a horizontal politics of friendship and offers a reading of the conferences as defying the tenets of diplomacy that organized them: Adhira Mangalagiri, "A Poetics of Writers' Conferences: Literary Relation in the Cold War World," *Comparative Literature Studies* 58, no. 3 (2021): 509–531.

54. See Adhira Mangalagiri, *States of Disconnect: The China-India Relation in the Twentieth Century*, forthcoming with Columbia University Press, and several recent articles by Yan Jia: for example, "Cultural Bandung or Writerly Cold War? Revisiting the 1956 Asian Writers' Conference from an India-China Perspective" in *The Cultural Cold War and the Global South: Sites of Contest and Communitas*, ed. Kerry Bystrom, (New York: Routledge, 2021), 29–44; and "Trans-popular Aesthetics: the Reception of Hindi Popular Fiction in 1980s China," *Journal of World Literature* 4 (2019): 530–551.

55. Aamir R. Mufti, *Forget English! Orientalisms and World Literature* (Cambridge, MA: Harvard University Press, 2016), 16, 31, 49. Though English is most relevant to this book's examination of the Chinese imagination of India, English was not the only language that linked Orientalist scholarship to literary production and circulation. For recent studies of German and Russian hegemonies in the nineteenth and twentieth centuries, see B. Venkat Mani, *Recoding World Literature: Libraries, Print Culture, and Germany's Pact with Books* (New York: Fordham University Press, 2017); Galin Tihanov, *The Birth and Death of Literary Theory: Regimes of Relevance in Russia and Beyond* (Stanford, CA: Stanford University Press, 2019).

56. It would take several decades during which Chinese study of Indian languages became a robust and thriving field of study, and China-India relations tightened, for competing definitions of world literature—the kind of definitions that turned to India to invent a new canon—were made possible by some of Zheng's contemporaries, such as Ji Xianlin, whose work is the subject of chapter 4.

57. See, for example, Lydia H. Liu, *The Clash of Empires: The Invention of China in Modern World Making* (Cambridge, MA: Harvard University Press, 2005); Rey Chow, *The Age of the World Target: Self Referentiality in War, Theory and Comparative Work* (Durham, NC: Duke University Press, 2006), 71–92; Ari Larissa Heinrich, *The Afterlife of Images: Translating the Pathological Body Between China and the West* (Durham, NC: Duke University Press, 2008).

58. Tageldin writes: "While most Egyptian literati of the nineteenth and early twentieth century decried the military, economic, and political violences that European imperialism wreaked on their land, many resisted the notion that

Europe also was doing cultural violence to the understandings of language and literature and to their broader ways of thinking and knowing. Often, they imagined their relationship to European aesthetics and epistemologies in terms of 'love,' not subjection." Shaden Tageldin, *Disarming Words: Empire and the Seduction of Translation in Egypt* (Berkeley: University of California Press, 2011), 6.

59. One of the late-Qing period's most widely read political thinkers, Kang Youwei 康有為 (1858–1927), spent 1901 to 1903 in exile in Darjeeling. Making every effort to structure his time in India as a pilgrimage, Kang's travelogue is rife with disappointed portrayals of unkempt ruins and the replacement of Buddhist scripture halls with Brahmin temples. Moved by a desire to rediscover the Buddhist sites he had read about, Kang also misidentified certain places in his writing. He confused, for example, Agra and the city of Shewei (Sravasti), which is mentioned in Chinese Buddhist scriptures. See Liu Xi, "Kang Youwei's Journey to India: Chinese Discourse on India During the Late Qing and Republican Periods," *China Report* 48: 1, no. 2 (2012): 171–185.

60. Jürgen Osterhammel defines the period between 1895 and 1905 as "the scramble for China" and distinguishes Germany, Russia, and Japan, which colonized territories within the Chinese sphere such as Taiwan, Shandong and Southern Manchuria, from European powers such as Britain, France, and Belgium, which managed, through a series of unequal treatises with China, to obtain railroad building privileges and mining concessions; as well as from the United States, which was most interested in forging commercial influence and decreed an open-door policy for all countries interested in engaging with the Chinese market. Jürgen Osterhammel, *The Transformation of the World: A Global History of the Nineteenth Century* (Princeton, NJ: Princeton University Press), 401.

61. Importantly, the colonial networks were used not only by the British for commercial, military mobilizing, and evangelical purposes, but also served Kashmiri and Parsi traders and Chinese migrants, as well as Indian travelers whose experiences in China were documented in several travelogues. See Tansen Sen, "China-India Studies: Emergence, Development, and State of the Field," *The Journal of Asian Studies* 80, no. 2 (2021): 368

62. Tansen Sen writes about several cases of Chinese travelers to India, mostly statemen sent on information gathering missions to provide the Qing court with information in *India, China, and the World: A Connected History*, 262–270. Most information about India during the late Qing, however, ranging from geography, to customs, religions, and economy was translated from English-language texts.

63. I discuss Su Manshu in chapter 1. On Zhang Taiyan's writings on India, by which the famed Buddhist philosopher critiqued a linear progressive understanding of history and placed Asia at the beginning of history, see Viren Murthy, "Rethinking Pan-Asianism through Zhang Taiyan: India as Method" in *Beyond Pan-Asianism: Connecting China and India, 1840s-1960s*, ed. Tansen Sen and Brian Tsui (New Delhi: Oxford University Press, 2021), 94–128.

64. Lyle Campbell, "Why Sir William Jones Got it All Wrong, or Jones' Role in How to Establish Language Families," *Anuario del Seminario de Filología Vasca 'Julio de*

Urquijo' 45 (2006): 245–264. The philologer passage begins: "The Sanskrit language, whatever be its antiquity, is of a wonderful structure; more perfect than the Greek, more copious than the Latin and more exquisitely refined than either; yet bearing to both of them a strong affinity, both in the roots of verbs and in the forms of grammar, than could possibly have been produced by accident; so strong indeed, that no philologer could examine them all three without believing them to have sprung from some common source, which perhaps no longer exists." See Sir William W. Jones, "The Third Anniversary Discourse, Delivered 2 February 1786," *Asiatick Researches, or, Transactions of the Society Instituted in Bengal, for Inquiring into the History and Antiquities, the Arts, Sciences, and Literature of Asia* 1 (1801): 422–423.

65. Max Müller developed the evolutionary theory of historical linguistics, which viewed Indo-European languages as the most developed given their elaborate structures of inflections. These languages were viewed as more developed than languages with non-inflected grammar, such as Chinese. See Tomoko Masuzawa, *The Invention of World Religions: Or, How European Universalism Was Preserved in the Language of Pluralism* (Chicago: University of Chicago Press, 2005), 221–228. Lydia H. Liu writes about the Chinese luminary linguist Ma Jianzhong, whose grappling with the Indo-European hypothesis underscored one of the milestones in modern Chinese linguistic. See Lydia H. Liu, *Ma's Universal Principles of Classical Chinese* (馬士文通 *Mashi wentong*, 1898) in *The Clash of Empires*, 181–209.

66. See Tansen Sen, "China-India Studies: Emergence, Development, and State of the Field," 366.

67. Serge Elisséeff, "Stael-Holstein's Contribution to Asiatic Studies" *Harvard Journal of Asiatic Studies* 3, no. 1 (1938): 6.

68. Jingkui Jiang and Yan Jia, "The History of the Production of India-Related Knowledge in Post-1950 China," 3.

69. James St. André, "Relay Translation" in *Routledge Encyclopedia of Translation Studies*, ed. Mona Baker and Saldanha (London: Routledge, 2019), 470. Current studies of mediated translations often assume commensurability between languages and focus on identifying the texts that mediated between the source and target language texts, or mapping mistakes and distortions from the original in an attempt to sketch a typology of potential errors and deduce from them commonalities that could pertain to the practice of translation broadly conceived, thus extending to the ways in which mediated translations fashion reading habits and circulation patterns. See, for example, the research essays as well as the annotated bibliography in a recent special issue in the journal *Translation Studies*, ed. Alexandra Assis Rosa, Hanna Pięta, and Rita Bueno Maia, *Theoretical, Methodological and Terminological Issues Regarding Indirect Translation: An Overview* 10, no. 2 (2017). See also Gideon Toury, "A Lesson from Indirect Translation" *Descriptive Translation Studies and Beyond*, revised edition (Amsterdam: John Benjamins), 161–178. Recent works in comparative literature have begun to focus on formal aspects of indirect translations, often discussing them as palimpsests that add layers of meaning and literary devices that are worth investigating, See Kelly Washbourne, "Nonlinear Narratives: Paths of Indirect and Relay Translation," *Meta* 58, no. 3 (2013): 607–625; Iris Fernández

Muñiz, "Tracking Sources in Indirect Translation Archaeology: A Case Study on a 1917 Spanish Translation of Ibsen's *Et Dukkehjem* (1879)," in *New Horizons in Translation Research and Education*, vol. 4, ed. T. Rautaoja et al. (Joensuu: University of Eastern Finland, 2016), 115–132; Özlem Berk Albachten and Şehnaz Tahir Gürçağlar, eds,, *Perspectives on Retranslation: Ideology, Paratexts, Methods* (New York: Routledge, 2019).

70. According to Schleiermacher, while domestication makes the act of translation transparent, foreignization maintains a sense of linguistic awkwardness, thus exposing the reader to less familiar cultures and languages. See Friedrich Schleiermacher, "On the Different Methods of Translating" in *Theories of Translation: An Anthology of Essays from Dryden to Derrida*, ed. Rainer Schulte and John Biguenet (Chicago: University of Chicago Press, 1992), 36–54. This model has been reiterated by Lawrence Venuti's more recent reviving of the foreignization method. Venuti argues that Schleiermacher's method of "foreignization" should be revisited today because registering difference in the source culture rather than "domesticating" it so the reader would feel at home could assuage some of the ethno-violence inherent in the practice of translation. See Lawrence Venuti, *The Translator's Invisibility: A History of Translation* (New York: Routledge, 2008), 15–16.

71. Walter Benjamin, "The Task of the Translator," in *Walter Benjamin: Selected Writings Vol 1 1913-1926*, ed. Marcus Bullock and Michael W. Jennings (Cambridge, MA: The Belknap Press of Harvard University Press, 1996), 253–263; Emily Apter, *Against World Literature: On the Politics of Untranslatability* (New York: Verso, 2014), 99–114.

72. Michael Gibbs Hill, *Lin Shu, Inc.: Translation and the Making of Modern Chinese Culture* (Oxford: Oxford University Press, 2013), 19.

73. Mu Mutian, "Lun chongyi ji qita xia" 論重譯及其它(下) (On Mediated Translation and Other Matters, Second Part), *Shenbao ziyoutan*, July 2, 1934.

74. Lu Xun "Zai lun chongyi" 再論重譯 (On Mediated Translation, Again), *Shenbao ziyoutan*, July 7, 1934.

1. Unsettling the Violence of Comparison

1. Translations from Chinese to English are mine unless stated otherwise.

2. Huang Yi, "Su Manshu yindu wenxue yi jielun" 蘇曼殊印度文學譯結論 [On Su Manshu's translation and introduction of Indian literature], *Zhongguo bijiao wenxue* 1, no. 66 (2007): 82.

3. Gregory Blue, "Opium for China: the British Connection," in *Opium Regimes: China, Britain and Japan 1839-1952*, ed. Timothy Brook, Patrick Carr, and Maria Kefalas (Berkeley: University of California Press, 2000), 31–48.

4. James Hevia, *English Lessons: The Pedagogy of Imperialism in Nineteenth-Century China* (Durham, NC: Duke University Press, 2003).

5. Tansen Sen and Brian Tsui note that China-India interactions to this day remain deeply informed by the legacies of imperialist world-ordering agendas

that introduced concepts such as sovereignty, jurisprudence, extraterritoriality, and the nation-state. See Tansen Sen and Brian Tsui, "Introduction," in *Beyond Pan-Asianism: Connecting China and India, 1840s*–1960, ed. Tansen Sen and Brian Tsui (New Delhi: Oxford University Press, 2021), 1.

6. Tansen Sen, "The Impact of Zhen He's Expeditions on Indian Ocean Interactions," *Bulletin of the School of Oriental and African Studies* 79, no. 3 (2016): 609–636.

7. Tansen Sen, *China, India and the World: A Connected History* (Lanham, MD: Rowman & Littlefield, 2017), 195–292.

8. Sunil Amrith, *Crossing the Bay of Bengal: The Furies of Nature and the Fortunes of Migrants* (Cambridge, MA: Harvard University Press, 2013), 2. Amrith estimates the number of migrants across the China-India route between 1840 and 1940 to be 28 million.

9. Mosca highlights that as early as 1800, as the capacities of the Qing court diminished, Chinese scholars began to challenge China's geographical knowledge of its frontiers and used various official and unofficial sources to create a new lexicon for world geography that introduced a new sense of world order with China as part of a global system. He writes: "In perhaps no other case was the need for integrated knowledge so great, the difficulties in constructing such a system so daunting and the consequences of success so profound as that of China's understanding of British activities in India." Matthew Mosca, *From Frontier Policy to Foreign Policy: The Question of India and the Transformation of Geopolitics in Qing China* (Stanford, CA: Stanford University Press, 2013), 3–4.

10. See Zhang Ke "Through the 'Indian Lens': Observations and Self-Reflections in Late Qing Chinese Travel Writing on India," in *Beyond Pan-Asianism: Connecting China and India*, ed. Tansen Sen and Brian Tsui, 131–154.

11. Tansen Sen, *India, China and the World*, 263, 266.

12. On the link between the discourse of sovereignty and a broader paradigm of civilizational progress see David Armitage, *Foundations of Modern International Thought*, ed. David Armitage (Cambridge, MA: Cambridge University Press, 2013); Brett Bowden, *The Empire of Civilization: The Evolution of an Imperial Idea* (Chicago: University of Chicago Press, 2009).

13. Ann Laura Stoler, "Considerations on Imperial Comparisons," in *Empire Speaks Out: Languages of Rationalization and Self-Description in the Russian Empire*, ed. Ilya Gerasimov, Jan Kusber, and Alexander Semyonov (Leiden: Brill, 2009), 40.

14. Liu He, "Xuyan: quanqiu shi yanjiu de xin lujing" 序言：全球史研究的新路徑 [Introduction: A new direction in the study of global history], in *Shijie zhixu yu wenming dengji: quanqiushi yanjiu de xin lujing* [World order and stages of civilization: A new direction in the study of global history], ed. Liu He (Beijing: Shenghuo, dushu, xinzhi sanlian shudian, 2016), 4–5.

15. On imperial benevolence see Helen Gilbert and Chris Tiffin, *Burden or Benefit? Imperial Benevolence and its Legacies* (Bloomington: Indiana University Press, 2008). I discuss "the woman question" in chapter 3.

16. Herbert Spencer, *Social Statics: The Conditions Essential to Human Happiness Specified, and the First of Them Developed* (New York: Robert Schalkenbach Foundation, 1954), 143, 390. In a study of John Stuart Mill's philosophy of civilization,

Michael Levin devotes a chapter to discussions by Mill and his father, James Mill, on India and China, and he summarizes other writings by Tocqueville and Hegel that position China and India within the binary of civilization and savagery. See Michael Levin, *J. S. Mill on Civilization and Barbarism* (London: Routledge, 2004), 35–37; 94–120.

17. On missionaries/diplomats and the critical role they assumed, as translators of the doctrine of international law, which pivoted negotiations between Qing China and the British Empire before and after the Opium Wars, see Lydia H. Liu, *The Clash of Empires: The Invention of China in Modern World Making* (Cambridge, MA: Harvard University Press, 2004), especially 88–139.

18. In the 1850s, American diplomats used the absence of legislation for freedom of religious belief in Japan as reason for refusing to renegotiate trade treaties with an "uncivilized nation." This motivated the Meiji state to include a provision for religious freedom in its 1890 constitution, after decades of deliberations and multiple drafts. The provision introduced a separation between private faith, which state subjects could choose from among recognized religions, and a public sphere of worship, in which state subjects would observe Shintō, a systematic doctrine propagated through a newly canonized body of scripture and rites by a state-appointed priesthood. See Helen Hardacre, *Shintō and the State 1868–1988* (Princeton, NJ: Princeton University Press, 1989), 115.

19. Liu He, "Xuyan: quanqiushi yanjiu de xin lujing," 61.

20. On the intersection of evangelization and oriental scholarship in nineteenth-century Bombay, see Mitch Numark, "Translating Dharma: Scottish Missionary Orientalists and the Politics of Religious Understanding in Nineteenth-Century Bombay," *Journal of Asian Studies* 70, no. 2 (2011): 471–500.

21. Paul Rule, "Goa-Macao-Beijing: The Jesuits and Portugal's China Connection," in *Vasco da Gama and the Linking of Europe and Asia*, ed. Anthony Disney and Emily Booth (New Delhi: Oxford University Press, 2000), 248–260.

22. Emily Conroy-Krutz, *Christian Imperialism and American Foreign Missions* (Ithaca, NY: Cornell University Press, 2015), 11.

23. Rachel Leow, *Taming Babel: Language in the Making of Malaya* (Cambridge: Cambridge University Press, 2016).

24. Jiang Qian, "Translation and the Development of Science Fiction in Twentieth-Century China," *Science Fiction Studies* 40, no. 1 (2013): 116.

25. Significantly, as an imperial technology, comparison was also employed by non-European empires, including the Qing, Russian, and Ottoman empires during the nineteenth century. All these different empires were underlined, argue Ann Laura Stoler and Carole McGranahan, by a simultaneity of declaring exceptionalism and overtly comparing: "Claiming exceptionalism and investing in strategic comparison are fundamental elements of an imperial formation's commanding grammar." See Ann Laura Stoler and Carole McGranahan, "Introduction: Refiguring Imperial Terrains," in *Imperial Formations*, School for Advanced Research Series, ed. Ann Laura Stoler, Carole McGranahan, and Peter C. Perdue (Oxford: James Currey, 2007), 12.

26. Joseph Errington, "Colonial Linguistics," *Annual Review of Anthropology* 30 (2001): 19–39; David Chidester, *Empire of Religion: Imperialism and Comparative*

Religion (Chicago: Chicago University Press, 2013). I discuss comparative folklore in relation to colonialism in chapter 3.

27. Cited in Anand N. Bosmia, et al., "Benjamin Hobson (1816–1873): His Work as a Medical Missionary and Influence on the Practice of Medicine and Knowledge of Anatomy in China and Japan," *Clinical Anatomy* 27 (2014): 158.

28. James Legge, *Graduated Reading: Comprising a Circle of Knowledge in 200 Lessons*, (Hong Kong: London Missionary Society Press, 1864), Lesson 156. The title of Legge's translation of the original work of the same title by Charles Baker (1850) is *Zhihuan qimeng shuke chubu* 知環啟蒙塾課初步. Originally a British primary school textbook, like many books that missionaries translated for Chinese readers, *Graduated Reading* is divided into two hundred short paragraphs that account for "lessons." Guo Shuanglin writes about Legge's translation in a comprehensive analysis of the most prominent geography textbooks circulating in China. See Guo Shuanglin, "Cong jindai bianyi kan xixue dong jian—yi xiang yi dili jiaoke shu wei zhongxin de kaocha" 從近代編譯看西學東漸——一項以地理教科書為中心的考察 [Examining the gradual Easternization of Western learning from the perspective of late Qing translation and editing: With a focus on geography textbooks], in *Shijie zhixu yu wenming dengji*, 243–244.

29. *The Chinese Recorder* published a review and recommendation of two works by John Murdoch: *Review of Colportage in India During 1873; with Suggestions for Its Improvement* (1874) and *Bible Colportage A Letter to the British and Foreign Bible Society* (1874). See "Notices of Recent Publications," *The Chinese Recorder* 6 (1875): 303. Patrick Hanan mentions several works that Murdoch composed about China specifically. See Patrick Hanan, "Missionary Novels of Nineteenth-Century China," *Harvard Journal of Asiatic Studies* 60, no. 2 (2000): 414, 438–439.

30. "New English and Chinese School Books," *The Chinese Recorder and Missionary Journal* 33, no. 2 (1902): 116.

31. Elijah Coleman Bridgman, "Introductory Remarks," *Chinese Repository* 2, no. 1 (1834): 2–3. Italics in the original.

32. "General Characteristics of the Native Newspapers," *The Calcutta Christian Observer* 1, no. 4 (1832): 209.

33. "Introduction to the Chinese Repository," *The Siam Repository* 2, no. 1 (1870): 145.

34. Jatindra Kumar Majumdar, *Raja Rahmon Roy and Progressive Movements in India* (Calcutta: Art Press, 1941), 333.

35. "The English literary text," Viswanathan notes, "functioning as a surrogate Englishman in his highest and most perfect state, becomes a mask for economic exploitation, successfully camouflaging the material activities of the colonizer." Gauri Viswanathan, *Masks of Conquest: Literary Study & British Rule in India*, 2nd edition (New York: Columbia University Press, 2015), 20.

36. See Isabel Hofmeyr, *The Portable Bunyan: A Transnational History of the Pilgrim's Progress* (Princeton, NJ: Princeton University Press, 2018); and Webb Keane, *Christian Moderns: Freedom & Fetish in the Mission Encounter* (Berkeley: University of California Press, 2004), 60–61.

37. Eddy to Baton, June 5, 1856. Cited in Fruma Zachs, "Toward a Proto-Nationalist Concept of Syria? Revisiting the American Presbyterian Missionaries in the Nineteenth-Century Levant," *Die Welt des Islams* 41, no. 2 (2001): 156.

38. Meenakshi Mukherjee, "Mrs. Mullens and Mrs. Collins: Christianity's Gift to Indian Fiction," *The Journal of Commonwealth Literature* 16, no. 1 (1981): 65–75.

39. Benjamin A. Elman, "The China Prize Essay Contest and the Late Qing Promotion of Modern Science," paper presented at 7th conference on "The New Significance of Chinese Culture in the 21st Century," National Taiwan University, December 28–31, 2003, 37.

40. The first to point this out were: Patrick Hanan, *Chinese Fiction of the Nineteenth and Early Twentieth Centuries* (New York: Columbia University Press, 2004), 124–143; and Theodore Huters, *Bringing the World Home: Appropriating the West in Late Qing and Early Republican China* (Honolulu: Hawai'i University Press, 2005), 103–108. For more recent work on John Fryer's new fiction competition and its impact on modern Chinese literature, see Yao Dadui, *Xiandai de xiansheng: wan qing hanyu jidujiao wenxue* 現代的先聲：晚清漢語基督教文學 [The harbinger of modernity: late Qing Chinese Christian literature] (Guangzhou: Zhongshan daxue chubanshe, 2016), 218–240.

41. Padma Anagol, "Languages of Injustice: The Culture of 'Prize-Giving' and Information Gathering on Female Infanticide in Nineteenth-Century India," *Cultural and Social History* 14, no. 4 (2017): 434.

42. Riho Isaka, "Language and Dominance: The Debates over the Gujarati Language in the Late Nineteenth Century," *South Asia: Journal of South Asian Studies* 25, no. 1 (April 2002): 5–6, 12–13. On similar competitions in Egypt and Cameroon, see Lawrence R. Murphy, *The American University in Cairo: 1919-1987* (Cairo: American University in Cairo Press, 1987), 51; Henry Efesoa Mokosso, *American Evangelical Enterprise in Africa: The Case of the United Presbyterian Mission in Cameroon* (New York: Peter Lang, 2007), 29.

43. John Fryer appears as a fictional character in two major late Qing political novels: *Nie hai hua* 孽海花 [A flower in the sea of retribution] by Zeng Pu, and *Ershi nian mudu zhi guai xianzhuang* 二十年目睹之怪現狀 [Bizarre happenings eyewitnessed over two decades]. Both novels were serialized in the early 1900s in Liang Qichao's Yokohama-based journal *Xin xiaoshuo*. See Yao Dadui, *Xiandai de xiansheng*, 116.

44. Dorothy Ko, *Cinderella's Sisters: A Revisionist History of Footbinding* (Berkeley: University of California Press, 2005), 14.

45. *Wanguo gongbao* [A review of the times] 77 (1895): 66; *Educational Review* 8, no. 4 October (1916): 365; *West China Missionary News* 9, no. 7 (1907): 14; *West China Missionary News* (1908): 10.

46. Patrick Hanan, *Chinese Fiction of the Nineteenth and Early Twentieth Centuries*, 78.

47. Conrad Malte-Brun, *Universal Geography: Or A Description of All Parts of the World On A New Plan*, vol. 1 (Philadelphia: Anthony Finley, 1827), 281–282.

48. "萬國之情形，分為四等：一生番，二少有禮儀，三大有禮儀，四文學技藝" wanguo zhi qingxing, fen wei si deng: yi shengfan, er shao you liyi, san da you liyi, si wenxue jishu. Cited in Guo Shuanglin, "Cong jindai bianyi kan xixue dong jian," 254.

49. This group of reformers, especially Kang Youwei and Tan Sitong, were closely associated with missionaries such as Young J. Allen and Timothy Richard, who was invited by the Qing emperor Guangxu's tutor Weng Tonghe to draft a

program for reforms to strengthen China after the Sino-Japanese War. Richard's report, according to Rudolph Wagner, deeply informed the 1898 reforms. Titled *Xin zheng ce* 新政策 [Policies for a reform of governance], Richard's report drew from an earlier study he composed in 1894, which compared China, India, Japan, and Russia, among other countries in terms of development, and argued that the British Crown taking governance of India enhanced education and infrastructure there. See Rudolph G. Wagner, "China and India pre-1939," in *Routledge Handbook of China-India Relations*, ed. Kanti Bajpai et al. (New York: Taylor and Francis, 2020), 47–48.

50. Zhang Ke, "Through the 'Indian Lens,'" 144–150.

51. Adhira Mangalagiri, "Slave of the Colonizer: The Indian Policeman in Chinese Literature," in *Beyond Pan-Asianism: Connecting China and India 1840s–1960s*, ed. Tansen Sen and Brian Tsui, 32–34.

52. For statistics of India-related publication in late Qing Chinese newspapers, see Rudolph G. Wagner, "China and India pre-1939," 55–56. On the portrayal of India as responsible for its own colonization in late Qing novels, see Catherine Vance Yeh, *The Chinese Political Novel: Migration of a World Genre* (Cambridge, MA: Harvard University Asia Center, 2015), 118–120; and Rebecca Karl, *Staging the World: Chinese Nationalism at the Turn of the Twentieth Century* (Durham, NC: Duke University Press, 2001), 161–163.

53. Liang Qichao, "Wen ye san jie zhi bie" [Distinctions between three groups of people from savage to civilized] in *Yinbingshi heji*, vol. 2 (Beijing: Zhonghua shuju, 1989), 8–9.

54. Chan Sin-wai, *Buddhism in Late Ch'ing Political Thought* (Hong Kong: The Chinese University Press, 1985); Viren Murthy, *The Political Philosophy of Zhang Taiyan: The Resistance of Consciousness* (Leiden: Brill, 2011).

55. On the making anew of Buddhism in light of the violent encounter of Asian thinkers with European imperialism (such as in the case of Buddhist revivalism in Sri Lanka and Myanmar) as well as on Japanese and Chinese intellectuals' reading and study of Yogachara in connection with Romanticism, European Enlightenment philosophy, and Protestant liberal theology, see David L. McMahan, *The Making of Buddhist Modernism* (New York: Oxford University Press, 2009). On page 5 McMahan notes: "This new form of Buddhism has been fashioned by modernizing Asian Buddhists and Western enthusiasts deeply engaged in creating Buddhist response to the dominant problems and questions of modernity, such as epistemic uncertainty, religious pluralism, the threat of nihilism, conflicts between science and religion, war, and environmental destruction."

56. "Zappō" [Various reports], *Ōsaka mainichi shinbun*, October 8, 1898, translated and cited in Mori Noriko, "Liang Qichao, Late-Qing Buddhism, and Modern Japan," in *The Role of Japan in Liang Qichao's Introduction of Modern Western Civilization to China*, ed. Joshua A. Fogel (Berkeley: Institute of Asian Studies, University of California, Berkeley, Center for Chinese Studies, 2004), 222.

57. Mori Noriko, "Liang Qichao, Late-Qing Buddhism, and Modern Japan," 230–232.

58. Liang Qichao, "Lun fojiao yu qunzhi zhi guanxi" [On the relationship between Buddhism and the Government of the People], in *Yinbing shi heji*, vol. 2 (Beijing: Zhong hua shu ju, 2003), 8.

59. By facilitating reader's identification with the characters in a text, Liang argues, readers transcend their worldly existence while reading: "If the protagonist of the novel is Washington, the reader will be transformed into an avatar of Washington; if it is Napoleon, he will feel himself an avatar of Napoleon; and if it is Buddha or Confucius, he will become an avatar of Buddha or Confucius. This is the one and only way to transcend worldly life. There is no better way than this." Liang Qichao, "Lun xiaoshuo yu qunzhi zhi guanxi," in *Yinbing shi heji*, vol, 2 (Beijing: Zhong hua shu ju, 2003), 8; cited here in translation by Kirk Denton in *Modern Chinese Literary Thought* (Stanford, CA: Stanford University Press, 1996), 74–78.

60. Cited in Liang's essay, "Yindu shiji yu fojiao zhi guanxi" 印度史跡與佛教之關係 [The connection between Indian relics and Buddhism], see Yu Kuizhan, "Liang Qichao yu yindu wenhua, yindu wenxue" [Liang Qichao and Indian culture and literature], *Wenhua wenxue* 1 (2003): 82.

61. For preliminary discussions of the role of the Buddhist revival in modern Chinese literature see Lydia H. Liu, "Life as Form: How Biomimesis Encountered Buddhism in Lu Xun," *Journal of Asian Studies* 68, no. 1 (2009): 21–54; and Ying Lei, "Lu Xun, the Critical Buddhist: A Monstrous Ekayāna," *The Journal of Chinese Literature and Culture* 3, no. 2 (2016): 400–428. This important subject still awaits a comprehensive study.

62. Feng Xinhua, "Su Manshu yu yindu wenhua 蘇曼殊與印度文化 [Su Manshu and Indian culture], *Huaihua xueyuan xuebao* 27, no. 8 (2008): 19.

63. On the Datong schools curricula, particularly on how Chinese and Japanese educators collaborated in creating curricular emphases on classical Confucian culture alongside modern nationalism and patriotism, see Craig A. Smith, "The Datong Schools and Late Qing Sino-Japanese Cooperation," *Twentieth-Century China* 42, no. 1 (2017): 3–25.

64. Su Manshu contributed to a series of essays titled *Notes on Fiction* (*Xiaoshuo conghua* 小說叢話), which were published in *Xin xiaoshuo* between 1903 and 1905; in them Su discussed the function of fictional works in terms of reader response, as well as the merit of existing works available in the Chinese market at the time. Su penned two articles in *Xin xiaoshuo* 1, no. 11 (1904): 182–187 and *Xin xiaoshuo* 2, no. 1 (1905): 169–180, where he emphasized the importance of learning foreign languages and elaborated on differences between Western novels, which, he argued, focus on one plot and one theme, and Chinese novels, which are more variegated.

65. In 1907, Su Manshu published several of his drawings and poems in the anarchist journal *Tianyi bao* 天義報 [Natural justice] edited by the anarchist-feminist He-Yin Zhen. See *Tianyi hengbao*, vol. 1, ed. Wan Shigo and Liu He (Beijing: Zhongguo renmin daxue chubanshe, 2016). Earlier studies tend to divide the late Qing intellectual milieu into factions, distinguishing between reformers (Kang Youwei, Liang Qichao, Tan Sitong, and others) and radicals or anarchists such as those mentioned above. In reality, there were many figures, including Liang Qichao and Su Manshu, who do not comfortably fit into any specific camp and often interacted with more than one faction. Su Manshu, for example, worked closely with Liang Qichao, Zhang Taiyan, and the Marxist Chen Duxiu around the same time.

66. Rebecca Karl, *Staging the World*, 168–174. I am following Karl's translation of *Yazhou heqin hui* as Asia Solidarity Society. In their own publications, the English name for the society was the "Asiatic Humanitarian Brotherhood." Notably, the definition of imperialism the society adopted was not limited to Western imperialism. In the rhetoric of the Chinese members of the society, Karl notes, ethnonationalism intersected with anti-imperialist solidarity, as they viewed the Manchu Qing dynasty as foreign conquerors of China, and thus a major reason for its current plight under imperialism.

67. Wang Xiangyuan, *Fanxinfoying: Zhongguo zuojia yu yindu wenhua* 梵心佛影：中國作家與印度文化 [The pure mind and the shadow of Buddha: Chinese writers and Indian culture] (Beijing: Beijing shifan daxue chubanshe, 2007): 160–163.

68. Su Manshu, "Fan wen dian zi xu" 《梵文典》自序；"Chu bu fan wen dian qishi" 《初步梵文典》啟事; "Fan wen dian qishi" 《梵文典》啟事, in *Su Manshu wenji*, vol. 1, ed. Ma Yijun (Guangzhou: Hua cheng chubanshe, 1991), 257–265.

69. B. R. Deepak concluded that the identity of Borohan, who features in several writings related to the Asia Solidarity Society cannot be ascertained. B. R. Deepak, "The Colonial Connections: Indian and Chinse Nationalists in Japan and China," *China Report* 48, no. 1–2 (2012): 149.

70. In 1908, between June and October, more than twelve essays in support of the Indian Anti-colonial Movement were published in *Minbao* alone; see Ding Fusheng and Gu Yufeng "Su Manshu xuanze yijie yindu wenxue de yuanyin" 蘇曼殊選擇譯介印度文學的原因 [On the reasons leading Su Manshu to translate and introduce Indian literature], *Feitian* 16 (2011): 29.

71. For the first commentary on this aspect of Su Manshu, see Leo Ou-fan Lee, *The Romantic Generation of Modern Chinese Writers* (Cambridge, MA: Harvard University Press, 1973), 58–80; for a more recent discussion on how Su Manshu appropriated Buddhism to offer a new view of a sentimental individual see Hung-yok Ip, "Buddhism, Literature and Chinese Modernity: Su Manshu's Imaginings of Love (1911–1916)," in *Beyond the May Fourth Paradigm: In Search of Chinese Modernity*, ed. Kai-Wing Chow, Tze-ki Hon, Hung-Yok Ip, and Don C. Price (Plymouth, UK: Lexington Books, 2008), 230; and Makiko Mori, "Unfinished Revolution: A Paradox of Mourning Subjectivity in Su Manshu's *The Lone Swan*," *Frontiers of Literary Studies in China* 9, no. 1 (2015): 104–130.

72. With the exception of Jane Qian Liu, "The Making of Transcultural Lyricism in Su Manshu's Fiction," *Modern Chinese Literature and Culture* 28, no. 2 (2016): 43–89.

73. Makiko Mori mentions Su's citing of his translation of Byron's *Childe Harold's Pilgrimage* (1812) in his most well-known novella *The Lone Swan* (*Duanhong ling-yan ji* 斷鴻零雁記). See Makiko Mori, "Unfinished Revolution," 117 and n. 41.

74. *The Middle Kingdom: A Survey of the Chinese Empire and Its Inhabitants* was composed by the American missionary and philologist Samuel Wells Williams and originally published in 1848.

75. Su Manshu, "Wenxue yinyuan zixu" 《文學因緣》自序 [Introduction to *Literary Relations*, 1908], in *Su Manshu wenji*, vol. 1, 294–299. The verse Su cites in the end is the opening of his poem "Sentence" (Ju 句).

76. Lord Byron, *The Island, or, Christian and His Comrades* (London: John Hunt, 1823), canto 2, verse 17, p. 38.
77. Sir Monier Monier-Williams, *Sakoontala or the Lost Ring: An Indian Drama* (New York: Dodd, Mead and Company, 1885), 15.
78. The term Su uses here for divine speech is *Shen hua* 神話. In the 1920s, a compound comprising the two characters *shen* and *hua* came to signify "mythology" and furnished a new field of study of Greek mythology among Chinese intelligentsia and an avid interest in modern concepts of myth. Here Su Manshu is using the two words separately to indicate the supernatural realm within the story and the Buddhist inflected language and premises that guide the plot and the development of its protagonist.
79. Jane Qian Liu, "The Making of Transcultural Lyricism in Su Manshu's Fiction."
80. Su Manshu, "Suoluo haibin dunji ji" [A record of seclusion on Sal Beach], in *Su Manshu wenji*, vol. 2, ed. Ma Yinzhu (Guangzhou: Hua cheng chubanshe, 1991), 754, 758, 761.
81. For example: "When Shakyamuni gave the First Sermon at Dear Park, he addressed the numbness that had ossified people's hearts. He abolished the caste system and peace and equality were thus boundless (translator notes: in the First Sermon at Deer Park, Buddha spoke of how cause and effect produce one another, not about the caste system)." Su Manshu, "Suoluo haibin dunji ji," 767.
82. Beatrijs Vanacker and Tom Toremans, "Pseudotranslation and Metafictionality," *Interférences Littéraires* 19 (2016): 25.
83. Gideon Toury, *Descriptive Translation Studies and Beyond*: revised edition, (Amsterdam/Philadelphia: John Benjamins Publishing Company, 2012), 47–60.
84. Thomas O. Beebee and Ikuho Amano, "Pseudotranslation in the Fiction of Aukutugawa Ryūnosuke," *Translation Studies* 3, no. 1 (2010): 17. Beebee and Amano coin "transmesis" to signify the portrayal of translation within a fictional text.
85. Şehnaz Tahir Gürçağlar, "Pseudotranslation on the Margin of Fact and Fiction," in *A Companion to Translation Studies*, ed. Sandra Berman and Catherine Porter, (Chichester: Wiley-Blackwell, 2014), 520.
86. Su Manshu, "Suoluo haibin dunji ji," 756.
87. Su Manshu, "Sauouo haibin dunji ji," 759.
88. Su Manshu, "Suoluo haibin dunji ji," 761–762.
89. Su Manshu, "Suoluo haibin dunji ji," 762.
90. M. M. Bakhtin, *The Dialogic Imagination* (Austin: University of Texas Press, 1981), 41–68.
91. Su Manshu, "Suoluo haibin dunji ji," 763.
92. Wang Xianming and Shu Wen, "Jindai Zhongguoren dui Lusuo de jieshi" 近代中國人對盧梭的解釋 [Modern Chinese understandings of Rousseau], *Jindaishi yanjiu* 2 (1995): 16–22.
93. Ann Laura Stoler, *Haunted by Empire: Geographies of Intimacy in North American History* (Durham, NC: Duke University Press, 2006), 1.
94. Su Manshu, "Suoluo haibin dunji ji," 759.
95. Thomas R. Trautmann, *Aryans and British India* (Berkeley: University of California Press, 1997), 2–13.

96. Tomoko Masuzawa, *The Invention of World Religions: Or, How European Universalism Was Preserved in the Language of Pluralism* (Chicago: University of Chicago Press, 2005), 147–158.

97. The Indo-European language model and the Aryan migration theory remain highly potent frameworks in scholarship and popular debates. The Aryan migration theory has recently seen renewed interest in light of developments in ancient DNA research. See David Reich, *Who We Are and How We Got Here* (New York: Oxford University Press, 2018); and Tony Joseph, *Early Indians: The Story of Our Ancestors and Where We Came From* (New Delhi: Juggernaut, 2018). Raising questions of genetic purity versus hybridity, these studies and others focus on the genetic map of settlers in the region, which shows the movement of pastoralists from the Pontic steppe grasslands in Eastern Europe into South Asia and indicates mixing with a population of hunter-gatherers and farmers. In India, scientific research that supports the theory that ancestors of today's Indians are genetically diverse is vehemently rejected by Hindu nationalists, including leading figures in the ruling Bharatiya Janata Party who argue that Indians and Vedic culture are completely indigenous to India proper.

98. Revathi Krishnaswamy, "Nineteenth-Century Language Ideology: A Postcolonial Perspective," *Interventions* 7, no. 1 (2005): 43–71.

99. In chapter 14 of *The Lone Swan*, the protagonist's cousin keeps a copy of Su Manshu's *Sanskrit Grammar* in her library. In a conversation, the protagonists' sister mentions that the Sanskrit sentence structure is so elegant and refined that it is incomparable with English and French. See Su Manshu, *Duanhong lingyan ji*, in *Su Manshu wenji*, vol. 1, 114.

100. Su Manshu, "Suoluo haibin dunji ji," 760.

101. Shengqing Wu, *Modern Archaics: Continuity and Innovation in the Chinese Lyric Tradition* (Cambridge, MA: Harvard University Asia Center, 2013), 364; Huang Yi, "Su Manshu Yindu yi wenxue jielun" (On Su Manshu's translation of Indian literature), *Zhongguo bijiao wenxue* 66 (2007): 86.

102. Su Manshu, (1908) "Wenxue yinyuan zixu," 294.

103. On the culmination of this process with the P. C Bagchi and Ji Xianlin's "contact philology" see Tamara Chin, "The Afro-Asian Silk Road: Chinese Experiments in Postcolonial Premodernity," *PMLA* 136, no. 1 (January 2021): 17–38. I discuss Ji Xianlin's work in chapter 4.

104. Franz Fanon, *Black Skin, White Masks* (London: Pluto, 2008). See also Cynthia R. Nielsen, "Frantz Fanon and the Négritude Movement: How Strategic Essentialism Subverts Manichean Binaries," *Callaloo* 36, no. 2 (2013): 342–352.

105. Homi K. Bhabha, *The Location of Culture* (London: Routledge, 1994). For recent critiques of the Bhabha's idea of mimicry as too celebratory of resistance and thus reinforcing the trite binary of "colonial domination" versus "native resistance," see Shaden Tageldin, *Disarming Words: Empire and the Seduction of Translation in Egypt* (Berkeley: University of California Press, 2011), 2–3; Leela Gandhi, *Postcolonial Theory: A Critical Introduction,* 2nd edition (New York: Columbia University Press, 2019), 149–153.

106. Elleke Boehmer, *Colonial and Postcolonial Literature* (Oxford: Oxford University Press, 1995).

2. What Is Rising There in the East?

1. To state a few examples: Chow Tse-tsung, *The May Fourth Movement: Intellectual Revolution in Modern China* (Stanford, CA: Stanford University Press, 1962); Merle Goldman, ed., *Modern Chinese Literature in the May Fourth Era*, (Cambridge, MA: Harvard University Press, 1977); Vera Schwarcz, *The Chinese Enlightenment: Intellectuals and the Legacy of the May Fourth Movement of 1919* (Berkeley: University of California Press, 1986); Marston Anderson, *The Limits of the Realism: Chinese Fiction in the Revolutionary Period* (Berkeley: University of California Press, 1990).

2. Recently, Tagore's foray to China to form an alliance of Eastern spirituality has resurfaced in a controversy over the publication of *Fei niao ji* (飛鳥集, 2015), a new translation of *Stray Birds* (Tagore's own 1916 selective English translation from the original Bengali) executed by the contemporary writer Feng Tang (published in Hangzhou by Zhejiang wenyi chubanshe). Heavily criticized for inaccuracies in both content and form, the translation invoked such fury that the Zhejiang Wenyi Publishing House eventually pulled it from the market in early 2016. Interestingly, the heated debates about the translation on both Indian and Chinese online media were infused with language that reinforced Tagore's status as a spiritual prophet—from Tansen Sen's denouncement of Feng Tang for making a "mockery of Tagore" by grossly deviating from the original's "essence" to using the term "blasphemous" (*xiedu* 褻瀆) in Zhou Huaizong's description of the translation as an offense against both Tagore's legacy and the history of translating Tagore in China. See Tansen Sen, "The Belittling of Tagore by a Chinese Novelist," *Times of India*, January 22, 2016; and Zhou Huaizong, "Feng Tang chongyi Taigeer shi ji bei ping shi dui Taigeer de 'xiedu'" 馮唐重譯泰戈爾詩集被評是對泰戈爾的褻瀆 [Feng Tang's retranslation of Tagore criticized as 'blasphemy'], *Beijing chenbao*, November 25, 2015, accessed October 22, 2021, http://www.chinanews.com/cul/2015/11-24/7638371.shtml. In an interview he gave to the *New York Times*, Dong Youchen, the chief editor of the first Chinese translation from Bengali of the complete works of Tagore, noted that the recent controversy involving Feng Tang's translation demonstrates the "special place Tagore holds in the hearts of Chinese readers," because "he wrote with an Eastern sensibility that Chinese people even today can connect with." See Amy Qin, "Tagore Translation Deemed Racy Is Pulled from Stores in China," *New York Times*, February 2, 2015.

3. Prasenjit Duara, "The Discourse of Civilization and Pan-Asianism," *Journal of World History* 12, no. 1 (2001): 99–130.

4. Partha Chatterjee, *The Nation and Its Fragments: Colonial and Postcolonial Histories* (New York: Oxford University Press, 1993).

5. Cemil Aydin, *The Politics of Anti-Westernism in Asia: Visions of World Order in Pan-Islamic and Pan-Asian Thought* (New York: Columbia University Press, 2008).

6. "For many Chinese and Indian activists," Tsui writes, "Japan was both an inspiration for and an impediment to nationalist aspirations and solidarity among Asians." See Brian Tsui, *China's Conservative Revolution: The Quest for a New Order, 1927–1949* (Cambridge: Cambridge University Press, 2018), 197.

7. For example, see Sven Saaler and Christopher W. A. Szpilman, eds., *Pan-Asianism: A Documentary History: Volumes 1 and 2* (Lanham, MD: Rowman & Littlefield, 2011) for several essays on how Buddhism and Islam informed Pan-Asian thought in Japan and China.

8. Hans Martin Krämer, "How 'Religion' Came to be Translated as 'Shūkyō': Shimaji Mokurai and the Appropriation of Religion in Early Meiji Japan," *Japan Review* 25 (2013): 89–111.

9. Studies generally concur that the modern notion of "religion" (宗教) was introduced to Japan by Protestant missionaries during the nineteenth century, and from there, exported to China (as *zongjiao*) and Korea (as *chonggyo*) in the first decade of the twentieth century. See Don Baker, "Introduction," in *Religions of Korea in Practice*, ed. Robert E. Buswell Jr., (Princeton, NJ: Princeton University Press, 2007), 1–34; Rebecca Nedostup, *Superstitious Regimes: Religion and the Politics of Chinese Modernity* (Cambridge, MA: Harvard Asia Center: Harvard East Asian Monographs, 2009). Scholars disagree, however, on how *shūkyō* 宗教 came to denote "religion" in Japan—a question that bears upon the shaping of a new distinction between religious faith and practice during the first three decades of the Meiji period (1868–1912). Some argue that Protestant missionaries introduced a discourse on *shūkyō*, for example, see: Jason Ānanda Josephson, *The Invention of Religion in Japan* (Chicago: University of Chicago Press, 2012); and Trent Elliott Maxey, *The "Greatest Problem:" Religion and State Formation in Meiji Japan* (Cambridge, MA: Harvard University Asia Center, 2014). Hans Martin Krämer argues that it was earlier, in the first half of the nineteenth century, that the term was coined in debates between Japanese Shintōists and Buddhist scholars over who would exert more influence on Meiji ideology. In these debates, *shūkyō* was designated as sectarian teaching, in opposition to *jikyō* 政教, or civic teaching. While civic teaching marked Shintō state ideology and ethics, *shūkyō* designated the realm of the human interior, also known as the Buddhist version of soul (*reiki*). Later, this separation between civic and sectarian teaching was adopted to refer to another separation, this time introduced by Protestant Christianity, between church and state ideologies, or *shūkyō* and *kokyō* 國教. See Hans Martin Krämer, "How 'Religion' Came to be Translated as 'Shūkyō.' "

10. Sisir Kumar Das, "The Controversial Guest—Tagore in China," *China Report* 29, no. 3 (1993): 237–273; Sun Yinxue, *Taigeer yu Zhongguo* 泰戈爾與中國 [Tagore and China] (Guilin: Guangxi shifan daxue chubanshe, 2005); Wei Liming, "Historical Significance of Tagore's 1924 China Visit," in *Tagore and China*, ed. Tan Chung et al. (New Delhi: Sage Publications India, 2011), 13–43; Zhang Guanglin, *Zhongguo mingjia lun Taigeer* 中國名家論泰戈爾 [Famous Chinese writers on Tagore] (Beijing: Zhongguo huaqiao chubanshe, 1994).

11. Rabindrath Tagore, quoted in Fakrul Alam and Radha Chakravarty, eds., *The Essential Tagore* (Cambridge, MA: Belknap Press, 2011), 186.

12. Variations on this argument—extending to examinations of writers' hopes and disappointments with the potential of literature to truly mold a nation, have informed many scholarly works on modern Chinese literature since the

publication of C. T. Hsia's seminal discussion of Chinese authors: C. T. Hsia, "Obsession with China," in *A History of Modern Chinese Fiction* (New Haven, CT: Yale University Press, 1971). I discuss and contextualize Liang Qichao's dictum, "if one intends to renovate the people of a nation, one must first renovate its fiction," in chapter 1.

13. Michael Collins, *Empire, Nationalism, and the Postcolonial World: Rabindranath Tagore's Writings on History, Politics, and Society* (New York: Routledge, 2012).

14. Partha Chatterjee, "Tagore, China, and the Critique of Nationalism," *Inter-Asia Cultural Studies* 12, no. 2 (2011): 271–283.

15. Fakrul Alam and Radha Chakravarty, eds., *The Essential Tagore*, 186.

16. Fakrul Alam and Radha Chakravarty, eds., *The Essential Tagore*, xx.

17. Peter van der Veer, "Spirituality in Modern Society," *Social Research* 76, no. 4 (2009): 1097–1120.

18. Lakshmi Niwas Jhunjhunwala, *The World Parliament of Religions, 1893* (Kolkata: Advaita Ashrama, 2010), 102.

19. Stephen N. Hay, *Asian Ideals of East and West: Tagore and His Critics in Japan, China, and India* (Cambridge, MA: Harvard University Press. 2013); David Kopf, *British Orientalism and the Bengal Renaissance: The Dynamics of Indian Modernization, 1773–1835* (Calcutta: Firma K. L. Mukhopadhyay, 1969); Brian K. Pennington, *Was Hinduism Invented? Britons, Indians, and the Colonial Construction of Religion* (New York: Oxford University Press, 2005).

20. Kathi Kern, "Spiritual Border-Crossing in the US Women's Rights Movement," in *American Religious Liberalism*, ed. Leigh E. Schmidt and Sally M. Promey (Bloomington: Indiana University Press, 2012), 165.

21. William O. Shepard, "Christianity and the New Orient," *Methodist Review* (September 1914): 718.

22. Frank Crane, "The Works of Rabindranath Tagore," *New York Globe*, December 18, 1913, cited here from Rabindranath Tagore, *Chitra* (New York: Macmillan, 1914), 89.

23. W. B. Yeats, "Introduction," in *Gitanjali* (London: Macmillan, 1912), xx.

24. Chen Duxiu, "Zan ge" 讚歌 [Song offerings], *Xin qingnian* 1, no. 2 (1915): 2.

25. These figures are mentioned in Yang Mengya, "Taigeer fanghua yu ershi jishi Zhongguo wentan" 泰戈爾訪華與二世紀十中國文壇 [Tagore's Visit to China and the Chinese literary circle in the 1920s], *Zhongzhou xuekan* 154, no. 4 (2006): 212–216. For a detailed list of translations of Tagore's work into Chinese including translations and publication venues see Zhang Guanglin, *Zhongguo ming jia lun Taigeer*, 205–230.

26. Amartya Sen elaborates on the Western media's suppression of Tagore's politics. Amartya Sen, "Tagore and His India," in *The Argumentative Indian: Writings on Indian History, Culture and Identity* (London: Allen Lane, 2005), 89–120.

27. On the translation of the term "philosophy" (*zhexue* 哲學) into Chinese in the early twentieth century, and on Feng Youlan's key role in the interpretation process of early Chinese thought as a philosophy that is structurally compatible with Western philosophical tradition, see Xiaoqing Diana Lin, "Creating Modern Metaphysics: Feng Youlan and Chinese Realism," *Modern China* 40, no. 1 (2014): 40–73.

28. Tagore is referring to Caroline Augusta Foley Rhys Davids (1857–1942), a Pāli language scholar and president of the Pāli Text Society, which was founded by her husband Thomas William Rhys Davids.

29. Feng Youlan, "Yu yindu Taigeer tanhua" 與印度泰戈爾談話 [Conversation with Tagore of India], in *Wusi qianhou dongxi wenhua wenti lunzhan wenxuan*, ed. Chen Song (Beijing: Zhongguo shehui kexue chubanshe, 1989), 404.

30. Feng Youlan, "Yu yindu Taigeer tanhua," 407.

31. On Chinese understanding of Tagore's Eastern spirituality as another form of *zhong ti xi yong* see Zhang Guanglin, *Zhongguo ming jia lun Taigeer*, 187–204.

32. Rabindranath Tagore, *Nationalism/Rabindranath Tagore & Manabendranath Roy* (Kolkata: Renaissance, 2004), 41.

33. Ding Wenjiang, "Xuanxue yu kexue" 玄學與科學 [Metaphysics and science], in *Kexue yu renshengguan lunzhan*, vol 1, ed. Hu Shi (Taipei: Wenxue chubanshe), 42.

34. Rabindranath Tagore, *Nationalism/Rabindranath Tagore & Manabendranath Roy*, 18, 31.

35. Cited in Rabindranath Tagore, *Talks in China: Lectures Delivered in April and May 1924* (Calcutta: Visva Bharati, 1925), 5, 21.

36. I discussed in chapter 1 how an imagined precolonial past of uninterrupted Buddhist exchange deeply informed the Chinese members of the late Qing Asia Solidarity Society's inclination for studying Sanskrit. For Liang Qichao, writing in the early 1920s, nostalgia for precolonial connections was tied to the present vision of an East rising to counter Western avarice. Nostalgic longing for an imagined unscathed past continued to thrive in Pan-Asian writings, culminating in the 1950s Bandung moment that I examine in chapter 4. For an interrogation of the notion of precolonial nostalgia in the Bandung Conference and its persistence today in Global South Studies see Duncan M. Yoon "Bandung Nostalgia and the Global South" in *Global South and Literature*, ed. Russell West-Pavlov (Cambridge: Cambridge University Press, 2018), 23–33.

37. Rabindranath Tagore, *Talks in China*, 33.

38. Chen Duxiu, "Taiggeer yu dongfang wenhua" 泰戈爾與東方文化 [Tagore and Eastern culture], in *Wusi qianhou dongxi wenhua wenti lunzhan wenxuan*, 627.

39. Qu Qiubai, "Taigeer de guojia guannian yu dong fang" 泰戈爾的國家觀念與東方 [Tagore's view of the nation-state and the East], in *Wusi qianhou dongxi wenhua wenti lunzhan wenxuan*, 635.

40. Sisir Kumar Das, "The Controversial Guest—Tagore in China," 242.

41. Rabindranath Tagore, *Talks in China*, 119–120.

42. Partha Chatterjee, "Tagore, China, and the Critique of Nationalism," 277.

43. As I mention in the beginning to this chapter, while an ideal of China-India unity did not directly shape nation-building political programs, it did have a lasting impact on China's GMD Party (Guomindang) in the 1930s. See Brian Tsui, *China's Conservative Revolution: The Quest for a New Order 1927–1949*, 195–204.

44. With members trained in England and the United States, the Crescent Moon Society, led by Xu Zhimo and Wen Yiduo (聞一多1899–1946), represented a formalist trend in Chinese poetry—a reputation gained after Wen Yiduo published the essay "Shi de gelü" 詩的格律 [The form of poetry, 1926] in the

Crescent Moon publication *Shijuan*, a poetry supplement to the *Beijing Morning Post*. On the name "Crescent Moon" and the history of the society, particularly its members' precarious institutional position in relation to the Japan-trained symbolists of the Creation Society and the leftist Chinese League of Left-Wing Writers, see Lawrence Wang-chi Wong, "Lions and Tigers in Groups: The Crescent Moon School in Modern Chinese Literary History," in *Literary Societies of Republican China*, ed. Kirk A. Denton and Michel Hockx (Lanham, MD: Lexington Books, 2008), 279–312.

45. Xu Zhimo, "Tai shan ri chu," *Xiaoshuo yuebao* 14, no. 9 (1923): 1–2.
46. Zheng Zhenduo, "Huanying Taigeer" 歡迎泰戈爾 [Welcome Tagore], *Xiaoshuo Yuebao* 14, no. 9 (1923): 2.
47. Rabindranath Tagore, trans., *Gitanjali* [Song offerings] (London: Macmillan, 1913).
48. In one of his more famous essays, "Art and Life," originally written in English in 1923, Xu opposed art to science but did not link this opposition to a concrete criticism of nationalism or colonialism: "As for the cock-sure rationalism and baldheaded materialism that originated from the eighteenth and grew rampant in the nineteenth century, they have made their charming turn and ended in contradicting themselves to disaster, leaving a few pseudo-scientists clinging to their experimental tools in fury and the sanguine-colored Bolshevists worshipping their infallible God Karl Marx against a general awakening of a new idealism embracing humanity as its creed and art as its religion." See Xu Xhimo, "Art and Life," in *Xu Zhimo quanji bu bian* [The complete works of Xu Zhimo supplemented] (Xianggang: Shangwu yinshuguan, 1993), 451.
49. For example in Rabindranath Tagore, *Talks in China*, 30–31, 49–50.
50. Zhang Guanglin, *Zhongguo mingjia lun Taigeer*, 224.
51. Rabindranath Tagore, *Personality* (London: Macmillan, 1917), 29.
52. Rabindranath Tagore, *Talks in China*, 157.
53. Wang Tongzhao, "Taigeer de sixiang yu qi shige de biaoxiang" 泰戈爾的思想與其詩歌的表象 [The thought and poetics of Tagore] *Xiaoshuo yuebao* 14, no. 9 (1923): 14.
54. Wang Tongzhao, "Taigeer de sixiang yu qi shige de biaoxaing," 4.
55. Rabindranath Tagore, *Nationalism/Rabindranath Tagore & Manabendranath Roy*, 84–85.
56. Somewhat ironically, the religion that Tagore practiced and his father founded, Brahmo Samaj, was actually born out of exchanges between Bengali bhadralok elites and British missionaries and statesmen. Brahmo Samaj reformed Hinduism by drawing from unitarian Christianity and Bengali popular religion in a first of its kind attempt to offer universal Hinduism that does not recognize caste and denounces polytheism and idol worship. Brahmo Samaj started as a closed elite religion in Bengal but eventually had a significant impact on Indian intellectual circles and the reforms that led to the founding of the Republic of India. Despite the fact that Tagore's actual religion was monotheistic, Wang Tongzhao, who was likely more familiar with the poetry and plays of Tagore, saw him as hailing from a culture that offered a broader and less

restricted notion of religion than the Judeo-Christian framework introduced in China as "religion."

57. Rabindranath Tagore, *Talks in China*, 45.

58. Wang Tongzhao, "Taigeer de sixiang yu qi shige de biaoxaing," 7.

59. Vera Schwarcz, *The Chinese Enlightenment: Intellectuals and the Legacy of the May 4th Movement of 1919* (Berkeley: University of California Press, 1986).

60. Rabindranath Tagore, *Creative Unity* (London: Macmillan, 1922), 5.

61. Taigeer, "Shiren de zongjiao," Yu Zhi yi [The poet's religion, trans. Yu Zhi], *Xiaoshuo Yuebao* 9, no. 14 (1923): 2–3. Italics in the original.

62. Mao Dun, "Bing Xin lun" 冰心論 [Comments on Bing Xin], in *Bing Xin yanjiu ziliao* (Beijing: Beijing chubanshe, 1984), 244.

63. For a detailed list of the numerous instances in which Bing Xin commented on Tagore's work, see Zeng Qiong "Tagore's Influence on the Chinese Writer Bing Xin," *Tagore and China*, ed. Tan Chung et al. (New Delhi: Sage Publications India, 2011), 255–272.

64. In English, particularly thorough, is Liu Xiaoqing, "Writing as Translating: Modern Chinese Women's Writing in the Early Twentieth Century," PhD diss., University of South Carolina, 2009, 21–91.

65. Mao Chen, "In and Out of Home: Bing Xin Recontextualized," in *Asian Literary Voices: From Marginal to Mainstream*, ed. Philip F. Williams (Amsterdam: Amsterdam University Press, 2010), 63.

66. Bing Xin, *Bing Xin sanwen quanbian* 冰心散文全編 [Bing Xin's complete prose] (Hangzhou: Zhejiang wenyi chubanshe, 1995), 16.

67. Huang Ying [A. Ying] *Xiandai zhongguo nü zuojia* 現代中國女作家 [Women writers in modern China] (Shanghai: Beixin shuju chuban, 1931).

68. Lü Jin, *Xinshi de chuangzao yu jianshang* 新詩的創造與鑑賞 [On creation and appreciation of new poetry] (Chongqing: Chongqing chubanshe, 1982), 303.

69. Fu Zonghong, "Xiaoshi xin lun" 小詩新論 [New comments on the short poem] *Qinghai shifan daxue xuebao* 3 (1991): 108–113.

70. For an illuminating analysis of how the cultural discourse on Asianness traveled to Europe and the United States and was embraced by Pound and others as means to cope with the aftermath of the Industrial Revolution and the ensuing urban and technological alienation, see R. John Williams, *The Buddha in the Machine: Art, Technology, and the Meeting of East and West* (New Haven, CT: Yale University Press, 2014), especially 100–126. On modern Chinese writers' "rediscovery" of classical Chinese culture after Western, especially American poets acknowledged it as valuable, see Shu-Mei Shih, *The Lure of the Modern: Writing Modernism in Semicolonial China, 1917-1937* (Berkeley: University of California Press, 2011), especially 1–45, 190–203.

71. Bing Xin, *Bing Xin shi quanbian* 冰心詩全編 [Bing Xin's complete poems] (Hangzhou: Zhejiang wenyi chubanshe, 1994), 16–17.

72. Bing Xin, *Bing Xin shi quanbian*, 45.

73. Reading this poem, John Cayley has compared it to Tagore's final poem in *Stray Birds*, "Let this be my last word that I trust in thy love," and suggested that Tagore's words could be read as "directed towards or at least centered on the

poet," while "Bing Xin's gesture is unambiguously outward moving, humble, challenging, drawing the reader into her enterprise." John Cayley, "Birds and Stars: Tagore's Influence on Bing Xin's Early Poetry," *Renditions* 32 (1989): 118–124, 122. This important insight diverts us from a one-way influence paradigm and should be considered in conjunction with Bing Xin's attempt to tap into the interpersonal via Tagore's notion of a poet's religion.

74. Bing Xin, *Bing Xin shi quanbian*, 87.

75. Bing Xin, *Bing Xin shi quanbian*, 199.

76. Siddhartha Deb, "The New Face of India is the Anti-Gandhian: The Violence, Insecurity and Rage of Narendra Modi," *The New Republic*, May 3, 2016, accessed October 25, 2021, https://newrepublic.com/article/133014/new-face-india-anti -gandhi; Ian Hall, *Modi and the Reinvention of Indian Foreign Policy* (Bristol, UK: Bristol University Press, 2019), 81–104.

77. In 1937, Tagore instructed the Buddhist scholar Tan Yunshan (1898–1983) to establish in Visva Bharati an Institute for Chinese Studies, which came to be known as Cheena Bhavana. On the role Cheena Bhavana assumed in promoting Tagore's appeal to a China-India Pan-Asianism via exchanges and collaborations between Indian and Chinese intellectuals, see Brian Tsui, "When Culture Meets State Diplomacy: The Case of Cheena Bhavana," in *Beyond Pan-Asianism: Connecting China and India 1840s–1960s*, ed. Tansen Sen and Brian Tsui (New Delhi: Oxford University Press. 2021), 236–255.

78. Cited in Xue Keqiao, "Xu Dishan de xueshu chengjiu yu yindu wenhua de lianxi" 許地山的學術成就與印度文化的聯繫 [The relation between Indian culture and Xu Dishan's scholarly achievements], *Wen shi zhe* 4 (2003): 126.

3. Folklore, (Il)literacy, and Cyclical Realism

1. In 1930, Xu published a short volume, the first literary history of the literatures of India in China, with the prestigious Commercial Press: Xu Dishan, *Yindu wenxue* 印度文學 [*Indian Literature*] (Beijing: Shangwu yinshuguan, 1930). Between 1927 and 1930, Xu published several influential studies in which he examined a cultural history of contact between premodern Chinese drama and Indian and Persian literatures, including: "Zhongguo wenxue suoshou de Yindu Yilan wenxue de yingxiang" 中國文學所受的印度義蘭文學的影響 On the impact of Indian and Persian Literatures on Chinese Literature], *Xiaoshuo yuebao* 16, no. 7 (1925): 10; "Jin san bai nian lai Yindu wenxue gaiguan" 近三百年來印度文學概觀 [A general survey of Indian literature of the last three hundred years), *Tianjin yi shi bao* [in vols.] 12, 13, 16, 17, 18, 19, 20, 23; "Fanju tili ji qi zai hanju shang de dian-dian didi" 梵劇體例及其在漢劇上的點點滴滴 [The stylistic rules of Sanskrit drama and their gradual diffusion into Chinese drama], *Xiaoshuo yuebao* 17 (1927): 1–36. I elaborate on some of these studies in chapter 4.

2. Reverend Lal Behari Day, *Folk-Tales of Bengal* (London: Macmillan, 1912), viii. The author's name is sometimes transcribed as Dey.

3. Xu Dishan, *Mengjiala minjian gushi* 孟加拉民間故事 [Folk-tales of Bengal] (Shanghai: Shangwu yinshu guan, 1929), 3.

4. Xu Dishan, *Mengjiala minjian gushi*, 6.

5. Xu translated two other volumes of Indian folktales from English, which were published in the journal *Literature* (*Wenxue* 文學) in the mid-1930s as *Taiyang de xiajiang* 太陽的下降; and *Ershi ye wen* 二十夜, respectively translated from the English original titles *The Sunset* and *Digit of the Moon*. These folktale collections were composed and published by Francis William Bain, a British writer who spent a stint as a history professor at Deccan College of Poonah; he became immensely famous in England and the United States thanks to the publications of more than thirteen volumes of stories that he claimed were translations of Sanskrit manuscripts given to him by an old Brahmin. Bain's work garnered a substantial readership, as well as scathing criticism from British and American Indologists and philologists who deemed him a fraud. I find it highly unplausible that Xu Dishan was unaware of the controversy surrounding Bain's books. Why then, would a scholar of his stature translate fabricated folktales is a question I am still pondering. Indeed, even the career of a writer who, as I show in this chapter, developed an astute critique of the very core of imperial knowledge, was to a certain extent inscribed by the unconscious authority of English language writings about India.

6. I have modified Elsie Choy's translation in He Shuangqing, *Leaves of Prayer*, trans. Elsie Choy (Hong Kong: Chinese University Press, 2003), 111–112, to reflect the text more accurately. For the sake of clarity, I omitted one allusion from my translation but render it here. For 姜曰：舅氏徒陳仲子。恐未能學匍匐。思與萬章公孫丑為窗友乎 the literal translation would be: "I said, Uncle is following Chen Zhongzi. I'm afraid he hasn't managed to learn how to submit himself [to the teaching] so how is it that he sees himself as one among [such students] as Wan Zhang and Gong Sunchou?" Wan Zhang and Gong Sunchou were disciples appreciated by Mencius. Here, He Shuangqing is referencing a famous quote from Mencius (3B10), where the master criticizes Chen Zhongzi, a hermit who had famously declined material benefits, fearing that that he would be abusing the concept of *yi* 義, or "righteousness." Mencius deemed his behavior extreme and admonished Chen for neglecting his responsibilities to his father and brother, blaming it on his narrow view of moral behavior. He Shuangqing is mounting a similar critique of her uncle (who views the Dao as strict) and would have censored any textual evidence that negates his narrow understanding of the Dao.

7. Xu Dishan, "Shang ren fu," in *Xu Dishan ling yi xiaoshuo* 許地山靈異小說 (Shanghai: Shanghai wenyi chubanshe, 1996), 23.

8. Xu Dishan, "Shang ren fu," 27.

9. With some important exceptions. On modern Chinese writers' whose fiction pivoted South East Asia, including a chapter on Xu Dishan's time in and depiction of Myanmar in one of his first short stories "Birds of the Same Fate" [Ming ming niao 命命鳥, 1921], see Brian Bernards, *Writing the South Seas: Imagining the Nanyang in Chinese and Southeast Asian Postcolonial Literature* (Seattle: University of Washington Press, 2015).

10. Xu Dishan, "Shang ren fu," 30. According to William Nienhasuer's translation of this story, *Kurta* is an upper garment, *ma-la-mu* is a bodice, and *ai-san* are trousers. Xu Dishan, "The Merchant's Wife," trans. William Nienhauser, in *Columbia Anthology of Modern Chinese Literature*, ed. H. Goldblatt and Joseph Lau (New York: Columbia University Press, 1995), 21–34. Xu had a particular interest in religious attire and female bodily practices. A year before he published "The Merchant's Wife," Xu wrote a piece titled "On Women's Attire" (Nüzi di fushi 女子底服飾), which appeared in the Marxist-leaning journal *New Society* (*Xin shehui* 新社會). In the article, he argued that traditional women's clothing, hairstyle, and jewelry originated as forms of bondage, marking the female body as a possession and limiting its mobility. The function of jewelry in modern times is not so different, he argued, only now, these forms of oppression have been completely internalized by women: young brides take pride in their dowry, which always was and still is a form of capital given to them since they cannot have claims of inheritance or ownership over the family property. Cited here from Xu Dishan, *Xu Dishan sanwen jingdian quanji* 許地山散文精典全集 (Jilin: Shidai wenyi chubanshe, 2003), 237–240.

11. Xu Dishan, "Shang ren fu," 38.

12. Xu Dishan, "Yuguan," in Xu Dishan, *Wu you hua* 無憂花 [Flowers of no sorrow] (Nanjing: Jiangsu wenyi chubanshe, 2008), 238. I'm citing the English translation of Cecile Chu-chin Sun, while slightly modifying the romanization of Yü-Kuan to the pinyin Yuguan. See C. T. Hsia, Leo Ou-fan Lee, and Joseph S. M. Lau, eds., *Modern Chinese Stories and Novellas, 1919-1949* (New York: Columbia University Press, 1981), 53.

13. A follow-up question would be: How do we reconcile the fact that in both "Yuguan" and "The Merchant's Wife" subaltern women learn how to read alphabetic scripts, rather than Chinese characters? Yurou Zhong takes up this question in *Chinese Grammatology: Script Revolution and Literary Modernity 1916-1958* (New York: Columbia University Press, 2019), especially 88–99, where Zhong reads "Yuguan" in the context of Xu Dishan's participation in the Latinization Movement, which was committed to representing spoken Chinese dialects in literary writing.

14. Two quintessential examples are the wretched widow Xiangling's wife in Lu Xun's "The New Year's Sacrifice" [*Zhu fu* 祝福, 1924], who accosts the male intellectual upon his returning to his hometown and asks him if, after people die, they turn into ghosts, and Ming Feng, the bondmaid in Ba Jin's *Family* [*Jia* 家, 1933]—a character who is consistently invoked to contrast the well-read Gao family brothers.

15. Xu Dishan, "Shang ren fu," 31.

16. Quran, Sura 7: 11–35.

17. Xu Dishan, "Shang ren fu," 36.

18. In life, Xu Dishan practiced both Christianity and Buddhism. See Yang Jianlong. *Kuangye de husheng: Zhongguo xiandai zuojia yu jidujiao wenhua* 曠野的呼聲：中國現代作家與基督教文化 [A cry in the wilderness: Modern Chinese writers and Christian culture] (Shanghai: Shanghai jiaoyu chubanshe, 1998), 53–66.

19. Xu Dishan uses a similar strategy in the aforementioned "Yuguan." The protagonist, a Bible Woman, carries with her, and firmly believes, in the magic power of both the Bible and the *Yijing*. She remains unwavering in her personalized religious practice that would have been perceived as heretic by the foreign missionaries.

20. Xu Dishan, "Shang ren fu," 37.

21. Christina Crosby, *The Ends of History: Victorians and the Woman Question* (New York, London: Routledge, 1991).

22. Ann Towns, *Women and States: Norms and Hierarchies in International Societies* (Cambridge: Cambridge University Press, 2010).

23. Dorothy Ko, *Cinderella's Sisters: A Revisionist History of Footbinding*, (Berkeley: University of California Press, 2005), 9–37; Lydia H. Liu, Rebecca E. Karl, and Dorothy Ko, *The Birth of Chinese Feminism: Essential Texts in Transnational Theory* (New York: Columbia University Press, 2013), 27–50; Sanjay Seth, "Nationalism, Modernity and the 'Woman Question' in India and China," *The Journal of Asian Studies* 72, no. 2 (2013): 273–297.

24. Song Shaopeng, "'Xi yang jing' li de zhongguo nüxing" 西洋鏡裏的中國女性 [Chinese women in the Western mirror], in *Shijie zhixu yu wenming dengji*, ed. Lydia H. Liu (Beijing: Sheng huo du shu xin zhi san lian shu dian, 2016), 309.

25. Isabel Hofmeyr, *The Portable Bunyan: A Transnational History of* The Pilgrim's Progress (Princeton, NJ: Princeton University Press, 2003).

26. Xu Dishan, "Shang ren fu," 39.

27. Lal Behari Day, "Preface," in *Bengal Peasant Life, Folk-Tales of Bengal, Recollections of My School Days* (Calcutta: Editions Indian, 1969), 1. In 1871, Day competed in a missionary competition for new novels held in Bengal and was awarded first prize. His submission to the contest was one of the first novels about life of the rural classes in Bengal. Titled *Govinda Samantha*, this novel was published in 1874 by MacMillan to much acclaim. It became a bestseller in England and preceded the publication of *Folk-Tales of Bengal*.

28. Timothy Weston, *The Power of Position: Beijing University, Intellectuals, and Chinese Political Culture* (Berkeley: University of California Press, 2004); Vera Schwarcz, *The Chinese Enlightenment: Intellectuals and the Legacy of the May 4th Movement of 1919* (Berkeley: University of California Press, 1986).

29. Philip West *Yenching University and Sino-Western Relations* (Cambridge, MA: Harvard University Press, 1976); Daniel H. Bays and Ellen Widmer, eds., *China's Christian Colleges: Cross Cultural Connections, 1900-1950* (Stanford, CA: Stanford University Press, 2009).

30. Partha Chatterjee, *Texts of Power: Emerging Disciplines in Colonial Bengal* (Minneapolis: University of Minnesota Press, 1995).

31. Partha Chatterjee, *Texts of Power*, 10.

32. Rebecca E. Karl, "Creating Asia: China in the World at the Beginning of the Twentieth Century," *The American Historical Review* 103, no. 4 (1998): 1096–1118.

33. Sadhana Naithani, *The Story-Time of the British Empire: Colonial and Postcolonial Folkloristics* (Jackson: University Press of Mississippi, 2010).

34. Sadhana Naithani, "The Colonizer-Folklorist," *Journal of Folklore Research* 34, no. 1 (1997): 1–14.

35. On how British Orientalists' writing on cultural and linguistic affinities between Indians and Englishmen appealed to Bengali literati see Thomas R. Trautmann, *Aryans and British India* (Berkeley: University of California Press, 1997), 1–27.

36. Roma Chatterji, "Scripting the Folk: History, Folklore, and the Imagination of Place in Bengal," *Annual Review of Anthropology* 45, no. 1 (2016): 377–394.

37. Lydia H. Liu, "Translingual Folklore and Folklorics in China," in *A Companion to Folklore*, ed. Regina F. Bendix and Galit Hasan-Rokem (Malden, MA: Wiley Blackwell, 2012), 190–210.

38. Chang-tai Hung, *Going to the People: Chinese Intellectuals and Folk Literature, 1918–1937* (Cambridge, MA: Council on East Asian Studies, Harvard University, 1985).

39. Zhou Zuoren, "Zhongguo minge de jiazhi," 中國民歌的價值 [The value of Chinese folksongs], *Geyao zhoukan* 4, no. 6 (1923): 2.

40. Course bulletins with information on courses Xu Dishan offered in folklore studies at Yenching can be found in Yenching University bulletins from 1929–1932. Yenching Archives, Beijing China, files: Yj 1929022, Yj 1930023, Yj 1931022.

41. Ti-Shan Hsü, *A Study of Certain Chinese Texts Relating to Manichaeism*, Master's thesis, Columbia University, 1924.

42. Particularly, Chinese Christian revivalists such as T. C. Chao (Zhao Zichen 趙紫宸, 1888–1979) and Wu Leichuan 吳雷川 (1870–1944).

43. These are: "Qiang jian" 強奸 [Rape]; "Nüzi di fushi" 女子底服飾 [On women's attire]; and "Shijiu shiji liang da shehuixuejia di nüzi guan" 十九世紀兩大社會學家低女子觀 [Two 19th-century sociologists' views on women]," both published in 1920. See also: "Yue ou zai wenxue shang di diwei" 粵謳在文學上底地位 [The literary value of Yue ballads] (1922), originally published in *Min Duo Zazhi* 3, no. 3. All cited here from Xu Dishan, *San wen jingdian quanji*, 散文精典全集 [Completed collection of prose] (Jilin: Shidai wenyi chubanshe, 2003), 134–137; 237–240; 184–187.

44. I explore the key role missionaries played in introducing the concept of *mixin* to Chinese culture as predecessor to *zongjiao* (religion) in Gal Gvili, "Gender and Superstition in Modern Chinese Literature," *Religions* 10 (2019): 588.

45. Xu Zhuzhen, "Wo souji mixin minge hou de yidian ganxiang" 我搜集迷信民歌後的一點感想 [My thoughts after collecting superstitious folksongs], *Geyao zhoukan* 34 (1924): 2.

46. Xu Dishan's view on superstitions was made clear in 1941, when he published the pioneering academic study of the practice of spirit writing in China, titled *Fuji mixin di yanjiu* 扶箕迷信底研究 [A study of spirit writing superstition]. In the introduction, Xu attributes his inspiration for writing this work to the increasing popularity of spirit writing in China during his time, allegedly touted as an era of science and rationality. See Xu Dishan, *Fuji mixin di yanjiu* (Taiwan: Shangwu yinshuguan, 1945 [1941]).

47. The call for papers is cited in Yuan Hongming, "Bianzuan 'yeman shenghuo shi' zhengqiu tonggong de xiaoxi" [Information regarding soliciting skilled collaborators for the compilation of a history of barbarian life], *Minsu* 1, no. 3 (1932): 28.

48. Yuan Hongming, "Bianzuan 'yeman shenghuo shi' zhengqiu tonggong de xia-oxi," 32.
49. Xu Dishan. "Zongjiao de shengzhang yu miewang" 宗教的生長與滅亡 [The rise and fall of religions], *Dongfang zazhi* 19, no. 10 (1922): 27–42.
50. Xu Dishan. "Zongjiao de shengzhang yu miewang," 29–30.
51. F. Max Müller, *Introduction to the Science of Religion: Four Lectures Delivered at the Royal Institution in February and May 1870* (London: Longmans, Green, and Co., 1893), 14.
52. Richard King, *Orientalism and Religion* (New York: Routledge, 1999), 122. On Mül-ler's writings on the Vedānta school see Thomas J. Greene, *Religion for a Secular Age: Max Müller, Swami Vivekananda and Vedānta* (Surrey, UK: Ashgate, 2016).
53. Tracy Fessenden, *Culture and Redemption: Religion, the Secular and American Litera-ture* (Princeton, NJ: Princeton University Press, 2006).
54. Max Müller, *The Sacred Books of the East Vol 1: The Upanishads* (London: Routledge, 2013), xv, xix, xxxvii–xxxviii.
55. I discuss Xu Dishan's time in Myanmar in relation to his engagement of Hindu and Buddhist tropes in his short story "Goddess of Supreme Essence" [Tihu tiannü 醍醐天女]. See Gal Gvili, "China-India Myths in Xu Dishan's 'Goddess of Supreme Essence,'" in *Beyond Pan-Asianism: Connecting China and India, 1840s-1960s*, ed. Tansen Sen and Brian Tsui (New Delhi: Oxford University Press, 2021), 67–93.
56. Xu Dishan, "Zongjiao de shengzhang yu miewang," 29–30.
57. Xu Dishan, "Zhui wang lao zhu," in *Xu Dishan ling yi xiao shuo*, 78.
58. Shen Yangbing, "Zuihou yiye" 最後一頁 [The final page], *Xiaoshuo yuebao* 13, no. 2 (1922).
59. Chen Duxiu, "Jin ri de jiaoyu fangzhen" 今日的教育方針 [Today's educational policy] *Xin Qingnian* 1, no, 2 (1915).
60. Zhou Zuoren, "Ren de wenxue" 人的文學 [Literature of humans], *Xin Qingnian* 5, no. 6 (1918): 575–584.
61. Andrew F. Jones, *Developmental Fairy Tales: Evolutionary Thinking and Modern Chinese Culture* (Cambridge, MA: Harvard University Press, 2011), 10. On realism in Chi-nese literature of the first half of the twentieth century see also the field-making study by Marston Anderson, *The Limits of Realism: Chinese Fiction in the Revolution-ary Period* (Berkeley: University of California Press, 1990). Anderson argues, via eye-opening close readings that link classical Chinese literary criticism to twentieth-century fiction, that Chinese realist novelists saw the relation between their fiction and the social reality it portrayed with scientific accuracy not as mimetic, but as effective. More recent studies are calling attention to other discursive constructs which have also shaped realism in modern China. See Roy Bing Chan's *The Edge of Knowing: Dreams, History and Realism in Modern Chi-nese Literature* (Seattle: University of Washington Press, 2017), which demon-strates how the figuration of dreams in realist literature ruptured the domi-nance of a scientific framework in Chinese literary discourse.
62. Xu Dishan, "Chun Tao," in *Ling yi xiao shuo*, 153.
63. Xu Dishan, "Chun Tao," 152.

64. "If I then, your lord and teacher, have washed your feet, you also have to wash one another's feet" (John 13:14).
65. On wastepaper collectors as critical component of the cultural transformation in 1930s Beijing see Madeleine Dong Yue, *Republican Beijing: The City and Its Histories* (Berkeley: University of California Press, 2003).
66. Xu Dishan, "Chun Tao," 156.
67. Ruifuxiang Silk Store [Ruifuxiang chou bu dian 瑞蚨祥綢布店] is a famous silk and garments shop in Beijing, in business since 1862.
68. Xu Dishan. "Chun Tao," 154–155, 158.
69. Xu Dishan. "Chun Tao," 163.
70. Xu Dishan. "Chun Tao," 167.
71. Susan Glosser, *Chinese Visions of Family and State, 1915-1953* (Berkeley: University of California Press, 2003).
72. Xu Dishan, "Chun Tao," 174–175.
73. In 1919, after almost thirty years of collaborative work, British and American missionaries working with Chinese assistants published the first complete Mandarin *baihua* translation of the Bible into Chinese: *Old and New Testament of the Bible: Mandarin Union Version* [*Jiu xin yue quanshu Guanhua hehe yiben* 舊新約全書冠華和合譯本]. Concurrent with the May Fourth Movement in 1919, the publication of the *Union Version* Bible translation marked a moment of particular significance for the emergence of modern Chinese literature, as the first long work in Chinese modern vernacular. The widely circulated *Union Version* provided many neologisms for the fledgling Chinese vernacular, such as "repentance" (*chanhui* 懺悔), "sinking" (*chenlun* 沈淪), "revival" (*fuhuo* 復活) and "baptism" (*xili* 洗禮). See Jost Oliver Zetzsche, *The Bible in China: The History of the Union Version or the Culmination of Protestant Missionary Bible Translation in China* (London: Taylor and Francis, 1999); Wang Benchao, "Shengjing yu zhongguo xiandai wenxue de wenti jiangou" 聖經與中國現代文學的文體建構 [The Bible and modern Chinese literature's stylistic development], *Guizhou shehui wenxue* 1 (2001): 49–56; Liu Lixia, "Guanyu hehe ben shengjing de chenggong fanyi ji qi dui zhongguo xin wenxue de yingxiang" 關於和合本聖經的成功翻譯及其對中國新文學的影響 [On the Success of the Union Version translation and its impact on modern Chinese literature], *Nanjing shifan daxue wenxueyuan xuebao* 3 (2005): 89–95.
74. Two representative examples are Mao Dun's *Spring Silkworms* [*Chuncan* 春蠶, 1932] and Lao She's *Camel xiangzi* [*Luotuo xiangzi* 駱駝祥子, 1936].
75. Xu Dishan, "Bu poyi de lao furen" [The Old Lady Mending Clothes], cited here from *Kong shan ling yu: Xu Dishan suibi* (Beijing: Beijing daxue chubanshe, 2006), 56.
76. Xu Dishan, "Bu poyi de lao furen," 57.
77. Xu Dishan, *Mengjiala minjian gushi*, 10.
78. See, for example, Chen Pingyuan, "Lun Su Manshu Xu Dishan xiaoshuo de zongjiao secai" 論蘇曼殊許地山小說的宗教色彩 [On the religious sensibility in the fiction of Su Manshu and Xu Dishan], *Zhongguo xiandai wenxue yanjiu congkan* 3 (1984): 1–26.

79. A few examples of many are Rey Chow, *Woman and Chinese Modernity: The Politics of Reading Between East and West* (Minneapolis: University of Minnesota Press, 1991); Tani Barlow, ed., *Gender Politics in Modern China: Writing and Feminism* (Durham, NC: Duke University Press, 1993); and Tani Barlow, *The Question of Women in Chinese Feminisms* (Durham, NC: Duke University Press, 2004).

80. Haiyan Lee, "Tears That Crumbled the Great Wall: The Archaeology of Feeling in the May Fourth Folklore Movement," *Journal of Asian Studies* 64, no. 1 (2005): 35–65. Lee focuses on one myth which drew much attention from folklorists: the story of the widow Meng Jiang Nü whose tears of grief over her husband's death crumbled a section of the Great Wall, according to the legend. Lee explains the folklorists' attachment to the figure of the wailing woman: "Weeping for them is expression par excellence, for the heart, in its uncontrollable grief, has dispensed with the clumsy medium of language, and has 'spoken' directly, spontaneously" (51).

4. *Śakuntalā* in China

1. Liu Jianshu, "Zhongguo jieshou yindu fanju de lishi yanjiu: zhishi, sikao yu duihua, yi Shagongdaluo wei shijiao" 中國接受印度梵劇的歷史研究：知識，思考與對話以沙恭達羅為視角 [A study of the Chinese reception of Sanskrit drama: knowledge, thought and dialog with a focus on Śakuntalā], *Dongfang luntan* 4 (2017): 93–99.

2. Ji Xianlin, *Niupeng zaji* 牛棚雜憶 [Memories of the cowshed] (Beijing: Zhonggong zhongyang dang shi chubanshe, 2005). The memoir was recently translated into English by Chenxin Jiang as *The Cowshed: Memories of the Chinese Cultural Revolution* (New York: New York Review of Books, 2016).

3. Another press that published book-length translations of foreign literature between 1949 and 1966 was Zuojia chubanshe 作家出版社. I thank Michael Gibbs Hill for bringing this to my attention.

4. On the official policy in China toward translation in the 1950s, including preferred methods, languages, and texts, see Paola Iovene, *Tales of Futures Past: Anticipation and the Ends of Literature* (Stanford, CA: Stanford University Press, 2014), 51–80. On the importance of translations for China's participation in pan-socialist discourses in the 1950s, see Nicolai Volland, *Socialist Cosmopolitanism: The Chinese Literary Universe 1945-1965* (New York: Columbia University Press, 2017), 153–186.

5. "Beijing ge jie jinian san wei shijie wenhua mingren: Mao Dun jieshao Jialituo-sha, Hainie, Tuosituoyefusiji de shengping he zhuzuo" 北京各界紀念三位世界文化名人茅盾介紹迦梨陀裟，海涅，陀思妥也夫斯基的生平和著作 [All walks of life in Beijing commemorate three paragons of world culture: Mao Dun introduces the life and works of Kālidāsa, Heine and Dostoevsky], *Renmin ribao* [China Daily], May 27, 1956.

6. Wu Xue, "Shagongdaluo", *Renmin huabao* [China Pictorial] 7 (1957): 20–22. Wu Xue also met with Hindu cinema superstar Kamalabai Gokhale and with a Sanskrit theater specialist Kupate 庫帕特 (possibly Gupta).

7. K. Natwar Singh, *My China Diary 1956-88* (New Delhi: Rupa Publications, 2009). See March 30 through April 6, 1957, entries where Singh, then cultural consular at the Indian Embassy in Beijing, describes the enthusiastic response to Laxman's performance, as well as Premier Zhou Enlai's personal request that she returns to perform in China as soon as possible.

8. *Renmin ribao* provides extensive coverage of Laxman's visit, on which she was accompanied by her sister Radha and their mother, a well-known artist, in March and April 1957.

9. Zhang Fuji, "'Shagongdaluo' pailian chang shang de yi duan duihua" "沙恭達羅" 排練場上的一段對話 [A conversation during the stage rehearsals of *Śakuntalā*], *Renmin ribao*, May 13, 1957.

10. K. Natwar Singh, *My China Diary 1956-88*, entry for May 7, 1957.

11. "Yazhou dianyingzhou zai Beijing deng di jieshu: ge guo dianying daibiao guankan 'Shagongdaluo' '亞洲電影周'在北京等地結束 各國電影代表觀看'沙恭達羅'[Asia Film Week has concluded in Beijing and elsewhere: Delegates of all countries watched *Shagongdaluo*], *Renmin ribao*, August 9, 1957.

12. Vijay Prashad, *The Darker Nations: A People's History of the Third World* (London: The New Press, 2008), 39.

13. Emily Wilcox, "Performing Bandung: China's Dance Diplomacy with India, Indonesia, and Burma, 1953–1962," *Intra Asian Cultural Studies* 18, no. 4 (2017): 530.

14. Much of this activity was housed under the auspices of the India China Friendship Association established in Calcutta on February 12, 1951, and the China India Friendship Association established in Beijing in May 1952. China established several Friendship Associations in the 1950s (including with Sri Lanka, Myanmar, France, Switzerland and elsewhere). These were official state-backed organs established to promote people-to-people exchanges with other countries. The India China Friendship Association was an informal organization with eighteen branches across India. It aimed to increase learning of Chinese culture, promote exchange of films between the two countries, and improve trade and commerce. See Arunabh Ghosh, "Before 1962: The Case for 1950s China-India History," *Journal of Asian Studies* 76, no. 3 (2017): 697–727.

15. Jingkui Jiang and Yan Jia, "The History of the Production of India-Related Knowledge in Post-1950 China," *History Compass* 16, no. 4 (2018) 16, https://doi.org/10.1111/hic3.12448.

16. Arunabh Ghosh, "Before 1962: The Case for 1950s China-India History," 698.

17. Krista Van-Fleit, "'The Law Has No Conscience:' The Cultural Construction of Justice and the Reception of Awara in China," *Asian Cinema* 24, no. 2 (2013): 144.

18. Ji Xianlin, "Yindu wenxue zai zhongguo" 印度文學在中國 [Indian literature in China) [1958], in *Ji Xianlin quanji* [Collected works of Ji Xianlin], vol. 13 (Beijing: waiyu jiaoxue yu yanjiu chubanshe, 2009), 195.

19. Wang Bangwei et al., "Ji Xianlin nianpu jianbian" [A short chronology of the life of Ji Xianlin], in *Ji Xianlin quanji*, vol. 30, 137–138.

20. Tansen Sen, "Introduction: Ji Xianlin and Sino-Indology," *China Report* 48, no. 1–2 (2012): 1–10.
21. Jingkui Jiang and Yan Ji, "The History of the Production of India-Related Knowledge in Post-1950 China," 3.
22. Edwin Gerow, "Sanskrit Dramatic Theory and Kālidāsa's Plays," in *Theater of Memory: The Plays of Kālidāsa*, ed. Barbara Stoller Miller (New York: Columbia University Press, 1984), 44.
23. Edwin Gerow, "Sanskrit Dramatic Theory and Kālidāsa's Plays," 50–51.
24. Barbara Stoler Miller, ed. "Introduction," in *Theater of Memory*, 7–8.
25. Barbara Stoler Miller, ed. "Introduction," 18.
26. Romila Thapar, Śakuntalā: *Texts, Readings, Histories* (New Delhi: Kali for Women, 2010), 36.
27. Romila Thapar, Śakuntalā: *Texts, Readings, Histories*, 44.
28. Dorothy Matilda Figueira, *Translating the Orient: The Reception of* Śākuntala *in Nineteenth-Century Europe* (Albany: State University of New York Press, 1991), 24.
29. Sir William Jones, "Preface," in *Sacontala: or, The Fatal Ring* (London: Charleton Tucker, 1870), 8–9.
30. Gauri Viswanathan, *Masks of Conquest: Literary Study and British Rule in India* (New York: Columbia University Press, 1989); Norman J. Girardot, *The Victorian Translation of China: James Legge's Oriental Pilgrimage* (Berkeley: University of California Press, 2002).
31. Romila Thapar, Śakuntalā: *Texts, Readings, Histories*, 197–217.
32. Dorothy Matilda Figueira, *Translating the Orient*, 12.
33. Nicholas A. Germana provides a substantial discussion of how Jones's and Forster's translations shaped a mythical image of India for Herder and his contemporaries in *The Orient of Europe: The Mythical Image of India and Competing Images of German National Identity* (New Castle, UK: Cambridge Scholars, 2009), 50–57.
34. A. Leslie Wilson, *A Mythical Image: The Idea of India in German Romanticism* (Durham, NC: Duke University Press, 1964), 221.
35. David Damrosch, *World Literature in Theory* (Malden, MA: Wiley Blackwell, 2014), 15.
36. Felicia Hardison Londré, *World Theater: From the English Restoration to the Present* (New York: Continuum, 1999), 426.
37. Namrata Chaturvedi, "Introduction," in *Memory, Metaphor, and Mysticism in Kalidasa's* AbhijñānaŚākuntalam (London: Anthem Press, 2020), 1–7.
38. Amanda Culp, "Searching for Shakuntala: Sanskrit Drama and Theatrical Modernity in Europe and India, 1789–Present," PhD dissertation, Columbia University (2018), 35.
39. Shaden Tageldin, *Disarming Words: Empire and the Seduction of Translation in Egypt* (Berkeley: University of California Press, 2011), 9.
40. For a summary regarding Su Manshu's mention of *Śakuntalā* in his writings, see Wang Xiangyuan, *Fanxin foying: Zhongguo zuojia yu yindu wenhua* 梵心佛影：中國作家與印度文化 [The noble mind and the shadow of Buddha: Chinese writers and Indian culture] (Beijing: Beijing shifan daxue chubanshe, 2007), 170–171.

41. Liu Jianshu, "Zhongguo jieshou yindu fanju de lishi yanjiu: zhishi, sikao, yu duihua" 中國接受印度梵劇的歷史研究：知識，思考，與對話 [A study of the history of China's reception of Indian drama: Knowledge, thought and dialog], *Dongfang luntan* 4 (2017): 94.

42. Louis Finot, "Kālidāsa in China," *The Indian Historical Quarterly* 9, no. 4 (December 1933): 829–833.

43. Ji Xianlin, [1955] "Tuhuoluoyu [Tocharian] de faxian yu kaoshi ji qi zai Zhong yin wenhua jiaoliu Zhong de zuoyong" 吐火羅語的發現與考釋及其在中印文化交流中的作用 [The discovery and philological study of Tocharian and its use in studying China-India exchange], in *Ji Xianlin quanji*, vol. 13, 145–162.

44. Chen Xiaomei, "Introduction," in *Reading the Right Text: Anthology of Contemporary Chinese Drama* (Honolulu: University of Hawai'i Press, 2003), 1–65; Chen Xiaomei, ed., *The Columbia Anthology of Modern Chinese Drama* (New York: Columbia University Press, 2014), 4–15.

45. Wang Guowei, *Song Yuan xiqu shi*, chapters 1 and 16, accessed November 25, 2021, https://ctext.org/wiki.pl?if=gb&res=228945&remap=gb.

46. For example, as mentioned in chapter 3, Xu Dishan, "Zhongguo wenxue suo shou de yindu yilan wenxue de yingxiang" 中國文學所受的印度義蘭文學的影響 [On the impact of Indian and Persian literatures on Chinese literature], *Xiaoshuo yuebao* 16, no. 7 (1925).

47. Xu notes, for example, the similar pronunciation of Kathputli—a form of Indian puppetry native to Rajasthan and the southern Chinese pronunciation of *guileixi*. He hypothesizes that the Chinese terms for theatrical roles *se* (色) and *jue se* (角色) draw etymologically from Sanskrit. He also makes a link between the Yatra—an Indian folk theater procession and the Song-Yuan folk theater Yagu (訝鼓) processions. See Xu Dishan, "Fanju tili ji qi zai hanju shang di diandian didi," in *Zhongguo xiju qiyuan* 中國戲劇起源 [The origins of Chinese drama], ed. Li Xiaobing et al. (Shanghai: Zhishi chubanshe, 1990), 86–118.

48. Zheng Zhenduo, "Xiwen de qilai" [The rise of Western culture], in *Zhongguo xiju qiyuan*, 123.

49. Regina Llamas, "Retribution, Revenge and the Ungrateful Scholar in Early Chinese Southern Drama," *Asia Major* 20, no. 2 (2007): 75–101.

50. Ji Xianlin in 1958 argued that while Yuan drama did show some traces of Sanskrit drama, the theory promoted by Chinese scholars such as Xu Dishan and Zheng Zhenduo—that Sanskrit drama shaped Chinese drama—was too sweeping and lacked substantial evidence regarding the contact that supposedly enabled this one-way influence. In "Yindu wenxue zai zhongguo" [Indian literature in China], *Ji Xianlin quanji*, vol. 13, 188. For a more recent critique of Zheng Zhenduo and Xu Dishan's studies of China-India dramatic exchange, see Sun Mei, "Zhongguo xiqu yuan yu yindu fanju shuo zai tantao" 中國戲曲源於印度梵劇説在探討 [Renewed discussion of the theory that Chinese drama originated in Sanskrit drama], *Wenxue yichan* 2 (2006): 75–83.

51. See Li Xiaobing et al., eds., *Zhongguo xiju qiyuan*; and Wang Xiangyuan, *Fanxin foying: Zhongguo zuojia yu yindu wenhua*.

52. Xue Keqiao traces in *zaju* theater texts themes of pilgrimage and other Buddhist tropes, which he reads as evidence of China-India exchange in the Tang, Song, and Yuan eras. He also cites, at length, Xu Dishan's comparative work on Chinese and Indian puppetry. See Xue Keqiao, *Zhongguo yu nanya wenhua jiaoliu* (Beijing: Zhongguo da baike quanshu chubanshe, 2018), 388–397.

53. Douglas T. McGetchin, *Indology, Indomania, and Orientalism: India's Rebirth in Modern Germany* (Madison, NJ: Fairleigh Dickinson University Press, 2009).

54. More recent research argues that Tocharian languages are a subgroup of the Indo-European language family. See Colin Renfrew, *Archaeology and Language: The Puzzle of Indo-European Origins* (Cambridge: Cambridge University Press, 1987), 67.

55. On the late nineteenth-century universal claim that all languages evolved in a singular process that foregrounds Indo-European languages, see Tomoko Masuzawa, *The Invention of World Religions or, How European Universalism Was Preserved in the Language of Pluralism* (Chicago: University of Chicago Press, 2005), 225–226; and Lydia H. Liu, *The Clash of Empires: The Invention of China in Modern World Making* (Cambridge, MA: Harvard University Press, 2004), 181–209.

56. Ji Xianlin, "Deguo xuexi shenghuo huiyi" 德國學習生活回憶 [Memories of my student life in Germany], in *Ji Xianlin quanji*, vol. 1, 406–407.

57. Ji Xianlin gives as an example the Chinese term for the sacred mountain of Sumeru: *xumi* 須彌. Ji notes that the Sanskrit term "Sumeru" was not transcribed in Chinese characters to something more similar-sounding to Sanskrit because the term was not directly translated from Sanskrit but from the Tocharian Sumīra. Ji Xianlin, "Tuhuoluoyu de faxian yu kaoshi ji qi zai zhongyin wenhua jiaoliu zhong de zuoyong," *Ji Xianlin quanji*, vol. 13, 158.

58. Ji Xianlin, "Tang shi" 糖史 [A History of Sugar], *Ji Xianlin quanji*, vol. 18, 15.

59. Peter Button, *Configurations of the Real in Chinese Literary and Aesthetic Modernity* (Leiden: Brill, 2009); Krista Van Fleit, *Literature the People Love: Reading Chinese Texts from the Early Maoist Period (1949-1966)* (London: Palgrave Macmillan, 2013); Richard King, *Milestones on a Golden Road: Writing for Chinese Socialism 1945-1980* (Vancouver: University of British Columbia Press, 2013).

60. See Nicolai Volland, *Socialist Cosmopolitanism: The Chinese Literary Universe 1945-1965* (New York: Columbia University Press, 2017), 153–186; and Paola Iovene, *Tales of Futures Past: Anticipation and the Ends of Literature in Contemporary China* (Stanford, CA: Stanford University Press, 2014), 51–80.

61. Wolfgang Iser's work, especially in *The Act of Reading: A Theory of Aesthetic Response* (Baltimore: Johns Hopkins University Press, 1978) describes literary referentiality as a readerly construction. For the reader, he notes, "the plot is not an end in itself—it always serves a meaning, for stories are not told for their own sake but for the demonstration of something that extends beyond themselves" (123). In that sense, the nonfictional reality is inherently bound to the fictional reality in the experience of reading. I find the notion of the reader's construction of a referential relationship between the world in and outside the text very useful for understanding the paradigm that animates critical debates over socialist artworks, and which I explain further into the chapter—that art not only represents, but actively constructs reality.

62. Adhira Mangalagiri, "Ellipses of Cultural Diplomacy: The 1957 Chinese Literary Sphere in Hindi," *Journal of World Literature* 4 (2019): 509.

63. Krista Van Fliet, *Literature the People Love.*

64. Cai Xiang, *Revolution and Its Narratives: China's Socialist Literary and Cultural Imaginaries, 1949-1966,* trans. Rebecca E. Karl and Xueping Zhong (Durham, NC: Duke University Press, 2016).

65. Cited here from Kirk A. Denton, ed., *Modern Chinese Literary Thought: Writings on Literature 1893-1945* (Stanford, CA: Stanford University Press, 1996), 470.

66. On the oft used term "socialist realism" in the context of China see Krista Van Fliet, *Literature the People Love,* 13–14. Van Fliet argues that, despite the Soviet Union's role in shaping the formation of socialist culture in China, the Soviet version of "socialist realism" is not an apt framework to think through Chinese socialist literature's representation of reality, especially because the Soviet theory of socialist realism developed from the particular historical experience and material conditions of communism within the Soviet Union.

67. Jiang Kongyang, "Guanyu shehuizhuyi xianshizhuyi" 關於社會主義現實主義 [About Socialist Realism (1958): 64–78], translated and cited in Yang Lan, "'Socialist Realism versus 'Revolutionary Realism plus Revolutionary Romanticism,'" in *In the Party Spirit: Socialist Realism and Literary Practice in the Soviet Union, East Germany and China,* ed. Hilary Chung et al. (Amsterdam: Rodopi, 1996), 96.

68. Zhou Yang, "Wenxue de zhenshixing" 文學的真實性 [The Truthfulness of Literature, 1933], translated in Yang Lan, "'Socialist Realism versus 'Revolutionary Realism plus Revolutionary Romanticism.'"

69. Peter Button, *Configurations of the Real in Chinese Literary and Aesthetic Modernity,* 201–233. On drama, see Xiaomei Chen, *Acting the Right Part: Political Theater and Popular Drama in Contemporary China* (Honolulu: Hawai'i University Press, 2002), 123–158; and Shiao-ling Yu, "Politics and Theater in the PRC: Fifty Years of *Teahouse* on the Chinese Stage," *Asian Theater Journal* 30, no. 1 (2013): 90–121. On film, see Jason McGrath, "Cultural Revolution Model Opera Films and the Realist Tradition in Chinese Cinema," *The Opera Quarterly* 26, no. 2–3 (2010): 343–376.

70. The original *Śakuntalā* is considered to be part of the Hindu canon and does not consist of Buddhist elements, writes Romila Thapar, in Sakuntala: *Texts, Readings, Histories,* 46. Ji Xianlin relates *Śakuntalā* to Brahmin tradition—a term that was used in China interchangeably with Hinduism.

71. Elsewhere, Ji has written in praise of Kālidāsa's accurate characterization of the working classes' plight—pointing as an example to the character of the fisherman who finds the ring and is afraid to be punished by the king. Ji Xianlin, "Jinian yindu gudai weida de shiren jialituosuo" 紀念印度古代偉大的詩人迦梨陀娑, *Renmin ribao,* May 26, 1956.

72. Ji Xianlin, "Jinian Makesi de 'Bu lie dian zai yindu de tongzhi' zhu cheng yi bai zhounian" 紀念馬克思的《不列顛在印度的統治》著成一百周年 [Remembering Marx's *The British Rule in India* On Its Centenary], in *Ji Xianlin quanji,* vol. 10, 6. Ji Xianlin also translated Marx's *Notes on Indian History 664-1858* in 1951 as *Yindu*

dashi nianbiao 印度大事年表 and between 1951 and 1953 composed short essays covering Marx's writings on India. See *Ji Xianlin quanji*, vol. 10, 1–10.

73. Richard Kraus, "Let a Hundred Flowers Blossom, Let a Hundred Schools of Thought Contend," in *Words and Their Stories: Essays on the Language of the Chinese Revolution*, ed. Ban Wang (Leiden: Brill, 2010), 249–253.

74. Ji Xianlin, *Shagongdaluo*, in *Ji Xianlin quanji*, vol. 20, 15.

75. Barbara Stoler Miller, ed. and trans., *Theater of Memory*, 123.

76. Sympathetic resonance concepts were also exchanged between China and India, especially during the Buddhist revival in sixth-century China, during which a stimulus response model of sympathetic resonance was used to describe the Buddha's true body, which responds to believer's prayers. See Robert Sharf, *Coming to Terms with Chinese Buddhism* (Honolulu: University of Hawai'i Press, 2002), 81–83.

77. Stephen Owen, "Omen of the World: Meaning in the Chinese Lyric," in Corinne H. Dale, *Chinese Aesthetics and Literature: A Reader* (Albany: State University of New York Press, 2004), 78–79.

78. The second and third lines of Du Fu's poem "Chun wang," 感時花濺淚/恨別鳴驚心 (gan shi hua jianlei/hen bie wu jing xin); see Du Fu, *The Poetry of Du Fu*, trans. Stephen Owen (Boston: De Gruyter, 2016), 4.25, 258–259.

79. Ji Xianlin, *Shagongdaluo*, 18.

80. Ji Xianlin, *Shagongdaluo*, 11.

81. Ji Xianlin, , *Shagongdaluo*, 18.

82. Ji Xianlin used the Bengali recension of *Śākuntalā*. I rely here on the translation by Barbara Stoler Miller of the same recension, and I have also consulted the early translations by Sir William Jones and Sir Monier Monier-Williams (who used the Devanagari recension) to examine Ji Xianlin's treatment of the *nāṭaka*.

83. *Wo de xin ya! Ni xianzai jingran jiongde mei hua ke shuo le!* 我的心呀！你現在竟然窘得沒話可說了！(in Ji Xianlin, *Shagongdaluo*, 63).

84. Barbara Stoler Miller, *Theater of Memory*, 157.

85. *Ta zai hua shang fangfu jiu yao shuohua* 她在畫上彷彿就要說話; *Wo zhen ke wang tong ta shuo hua ya* 我真渴望同她說話呀, in Ji Xianlin, *Shagongdaluo*, 107–108.

86. Ji Xianlin, *Shagongdaluo*, 19–21. Significantly, right after citing from Mao Zedong, Ji also cites from Johann Peter Eckermann's *Conversations with Goethe*. Noting Goethe's distinction between "actuality" (Wirklichkeit) and "truth" (Wahrheit), Ji then paraphrases Goethe within the language of Mao Zedong thought: "'*zhenshixing*' (Wahrheit) is higher than *xianshixing*, more profound, more of an essence."

87. Bai Shan, "Chongdu, yudiao, tingdun he huxi" *Xiju bao* 5 (1961): 34–37.

88. Wu Xue, Shagongdaluo, *Renmin huabao* 7 (1957): 22.

89. On competing ideas of "world literature" in the 1950s see Duncan M. Yoon, "'Our Forces Have Redoubled:' World Literature Postcolonialism, and the Afro-Asian Writers' Bureau," *Cambridge Journal of Postcolonial Literary Inquiry* 2, no. 2 (2015): 233–252. Yoon writes on the work coming out of the Afro-Asian Writers' Bureau, in which Ji Xianlin was active, as an intervention in the

European conceptualization of Weltliteratur, epitomized in redefining world literature as "a cultural embodiment of a third world postcolonialism" by upholding "national culture movements as a means through which to rehabilitate the category of humanism on a global scale" (241). See also Pieter Vanhove, "'A World to Win:' China, the Afro-Asian Writers' Bureau, and the Reinvention of World Literature," *Critical Asian Studies* 51, no. 2 (2019): 144–165. In the writings that I examine in this chapter, Ji Xianlin opens up the notions of world literature enunciated by the European theory and those promoted by the Afro-Asian Writers' Bureau, by employing a longer durée of history than in the Goethean focus on the global circulation of translations, and a method of investigating transregional contact rather than placing the nation state as foundation for a solidarity imaginary.

Epilogue: After 1962: The Ongoing Literary Work of Mourning

1. Li Wei, *Weiwen shicao: xiangei yingxiong de bianfangbudui* [Songs of Salutation: In Dedication to the Hero Frontier Guards] (Chengdu: Chengdu junqu zhengzhibu wenhuabu yin, 1963).

2. Chen Jian, "The Tibetan Rebellion of 1959 and China's Changing Relations with India and the Soviet Union," *Journal of Cold War Studies* 8, no. 3 (2006): 80–89. For a detailed portrayal of Tibet's role in structuring tensions between China and India from the mid-1940s and until the 1962 war see John W. Garver, *Protracted Contest: Sino-Indian Rivalry in the Twentieth Century* (Seattle: University of Washington Press, 2001), 32–78.

3. Skirmishes on the China-India border had flared up to face offs most recently in June 2020. As this book goes to press in February 2022, relations between China and India remain tense as the two countries closely monitor each other's actions on the mutual border and initiate trade limitations and hostile coverage in their respective government-controlled media outlets. For ongoing journalistic coverage of the recent border clashes in English language media in China and India see Ananth Krishnan, *The India China Newsletter* (blog), accessed February 28, 2022, https://indiachina.substack.com.

4. On the American perspective on the 1962 war as a point of crisis in the Cold War see Bruce Riedel, *JFK's Forgotten Crisis: Tibet, the CIA, and the Sino-Indian War*, (Washington, DC: Brookings Institution Press, 2015).

5. Arunabh Ghosh, "Why India & China See Any Border Breach as a 'Threat' to Identity," *The Quint*, June 20, 2020, accessed February 10, 2022, https://www.thequint.com/voices/opinion/india-china-border-history-relationship-military-rise-of-ethno-nationalism-modi-govt-xi-jinping. Writing on the 1962 war, Manjari Chatterjee Miller argues that the trauma of colonialism, despite distinct differences between the two countries' experiences, has installed in China and India a sense of victimhood that fuels a particular idea of

nationalism that is underscored by what she calls: "Post-Imperial Ideology"—an ongoing search for redress over the atrocities and suffering inflicted by colonialism and imperialism. Victimhood powers a nationalism in China and India, she argues, in which "the memories of suffering and the sense of entitlement and recovery drive these states to maximize territorial sovereignty and status. The goal of maximizing territorial sovereignty is synonymous with an insistence on maintaining the traditional borders that were redrawn by colonialism and effort to regain 'lost' territory, often at the expense of material security." Manjari Chatterjee Miller, *Wronged by Empire: Post-Imperial Ideology and Foreign Policy in India and China* (Stanford, CA: Stanford University Press, 2013), 28.

6. I mentioned a study by Prasenjit Duara in endnote 4 of the introduction. More specifically about the limitations of the 1950s moment of decolonization, see Christopher J. Lee, "Between a Moment and an Era: The Origins and Afterlives of Bandung" and Julian Go, "Modeling States and Sovereignty: Postcolonial Constitutions in Asia and Africa," in Christopher J. Lee, ed., *Making A World After Empire: The Bandung Moment and Its Political Afterlives* (Athens: Ohio University Press, 2010), 1–44; 107–143.

7. Cao Yin's recent revisionist history of Sikh diaspora in Hong Kong and Shanghai demonstrates just how one-sided these literary depictions were by shedding important new light on the history of Sikh soldiers in China. Cao shows that far from a mere tool in service of European empires, Sikh policemen became deeply involved with the Chinese nationalist revolution, the international communist movement and the Ghadhar Party's struggle for armed overthrow of British rule in India. See *From Policemen to Revolutionaries: A Sikh Diaspora in Global Shanghai, 1885-1945* (Leiden, Boston: Brill, 2017). On the figure of the Indian policeman in late Qing fiction see Adhira Mangalagiri, "Slave of the Colonizer: The Indian Policeman in Chinese Literature," in *Beyond Pan-Asianism: Connecting China and India 1840s-1960s*, ed. Tansen Sen and Brian Tsui (New Delhi: Oxford University Press. 2021), 29–66.

8. Madhavi Thampi, "Indian Soldiers, Policemen and Watchmen in China in the Nineteenth and Early Twentieth Centuries," *China Report* 35, no. 4 (1999): 404–408.

9. Li Wei, "Zang bao zhiqian" [Tibetan Brothers Supporting the Troops], *Weiwen shicao*, 43.

10. Ashis Nandy, "Open Pasts, Open Futures," an address given at the inaugural India-China Writers Dialogue Collective meeting, cited in *Almost Island* (Monsoon 2009): 3, accessed February 10, 2022, https://static1.squarespace.com/static/612b5c38a84af13ad0a05fe2/t/6198e09d49dabd2b10dcf097/1637408925938/china.pdf.

11. Addressing writings about the 1962 war in India, Adhira Mangalagiri reads Krishnan Chander's 1964 novel *A Donkey in NEFA* as a scathing critique of the violent practice of border drawing on both sides. Through the protagonist, a talking donkey that experiences first-hand the atrocities of war, argues Mangalagiri, the text evinces a sense of mourning for lives lost that moves beyond national identity to reveal the violence inherent to the act of

drawing and protecting national boundaries. See Adhira Mangalagiri, "A Donkey Wisdom: Can Literature Help Us Respond to the China-India Border Clash?" *Economic & Political Weekly* 55, no. 34 (August 22, 2020), accessed November 30, 2021, https://www.epw.in/journal/2020/34/commentary/don keys-wisdom.html accessed.

12. Recent onslaughts India and China are hurling at each other in national and international media are deeply shaped by imperial taxonomy. For example, Hu Xijin, editor of the English language *People's Daily* subsidiary, *Global Times*, recently invoked in a tweet in response to a permanent ban India imposed on fifty-nine Chinese apps, the very logic of the imperial discourse on civilization, noting: "India is like a bandit in the world that advocates civilized trade. These Chinese apps have been legally registered in India. Their market shares now are barbarically robbed by New Delhi. India only has a layman's understanding of the international rules." Hu Xijin, Twitter Post, January 26, 2021, 8:16 a.m., https://twitter.com/HuXijin_GT/status/1354055650679033857.

13. Karen Laura Thornber, "Breaking Discipline, Integrating Literature: Africa-China Relationship Reconsidered," *Comparative Literature Studies* 53, no. 4 (2016): 706.

14. Ji Xianlin, *Guanyu baliwen fo bensheng gushi* 關於巴利文《佛本生故事》 [On the Pāli Jataka], *Shijie wenxue* 5 (1963): 61–77.

15. Jin Kemu, *Fanyu wenxue shi* 梵語文學史 [A History of Sanskrit Literature] (Beijing: renmin wenxue chubanshe, 1964). See Wang xiangyuan, *Fanxin fo ying*, 274–278 for a discussion of this work.

16. Bharata-muni "Wulun" 舞論 [On Dance], Daṇḍin, "Shi jing" 詩鏡 [Mirror of Poetry], Visvanatha "Wen jing" 文鏡 [Mirror of Literature], trans. Jin Kemu, *Gudian wenyi lilun cong shu* no. 10 (Beijing: Renmin chubanshe, 1965).

17. Dong Youchen et al., eds., *Taigeer zuopin quanji* 《泰戈爾作品全集》 [The Collected Works of Tagore] (Beijing: Renmin chubanshe, 2016). A team of eighteen Chinese scholars of Bengali worked for six years to complete this monumental translation, numbering thirty-three volumes.

18. The collective was established in 2009 and continues to meet every few years in locations in China and India. The core group, which was initiated by the poets Bei Dao and Sharmistha Mohanty, includes: Li Tuo, Ouyang Jianghe, Zhai Yongming, Xi Chuan, Ge Fei, Lydia H. Liu, Shuang Shen, Han Shaogong, Kunwar Narain, Irwin Allan Sealy, Joy Goswami, Vinod Kumar Shukla, Rukmini Bhaya Nair, Vivek Narayanan, and Ashis Nandy.

19. For the epigraph see Ashis Nandy, "Open Pasts, Open Futures," 2. See also Lydia H. Liu, "The Gift of a Living Past," in *Ashis Nandy: A Life in Dissent*, ed. Ramin Jahanbegloo and Ananya Vajpeyi (New Delhi: Oxford University Press, 2018). "The good news," Liu writes in relation to the barriers facing China and India today in light of the colonial past, "is that the tragedy has not stopped us from listening to each other and exploring what might open up and become possible again" (126).

20. Sharmistha Mohanty, "Editorial Sutras" *Almost Island* (Monsoon 2009): 3.

21. Bei Dao, "The Rose of Time" [Shijian de meigui 時間的玫瑰], trans. Eliot Weinberger, *Almost Island* (Monsoon 2009), accessed February 10, 2022, https://static1

.squarespace.com/static/612b5c38a84af13ad0a05fe2/t/619a6f961060bd48b
abf29b2/1637511068336/poems.pdf. I have modified Weinberger's translation
slightly: he translates 回聲中開放的是/時間的玫瑰 as "To bloom in the echoes is
the rose of time." Ouyang Jianghe, "Huojin huayuan" 霍金花園 [Hopkins Gar-
den], trans. Lucas Klein, *Almost Island* (Monsoon 2019): 7.

Bibliography

Amrith, Sunil. *Crossing the Bay of Bengal: The Furies of Nature and the Fortunes of Migrants*. Cambridge, MA: Harvard University Press, 2013.

An, Yanming. "Liang Shuming and Henri Bergson on Intuition: Cultural Context and the Evolution of Terms." *Philosophy East and West* 47, no. 3 (1997): 337–362.

Anagol, Padma. "Languages of Injustice: The Culture of 'Prize-Giving' and Information Gathering on Female Infanticide in Nineteenth-Century India." *Cultural and Social History* 14, no. 4 (2017): 429–445.

Anderson, Marston. *The Limits of Realism: Chinese Fiction in the Revolutionary Period*. Berkeley: University of California Press, 1990.

Apter, Emily. *Against World Literature: On the Politics of Untranslatability*. New York: Verso, 2014.

Armitage, David, ed. *Foundations of Modern International Thought*. Cambridge: Cambridge University Press, 2013.

Aydin, Cemil. *The Politics of Anti-Westernism in Asia: Visions of World Order in Pan-Islamic and Pan-Asian Thought*. New York: Columbia University Press, 2008.

Ba Jin. *Jia* 家 [Family]. Beijing: Renmin xuewen chubanshe, 2003.

Bai Shan. "Chongdu, yudiao, tingdun he huxi" 重讀語調停頓和呼吸 [Stress, intonation, pause, and breath]. *Xiju bao* 5 (1961): 34–37.

Baker, Don. "Introduction." In *Religions of Korea in Practice*, ed. Robert E. Buswell Jr., 1–34. Princeton, NJ: Princeton University Press, 2007.

Bakhtin, Mikhail. *The Dialogic Imagination*. Austin: University of Texas Press, 1981.

Barlow, Tani, ed. *Gender Politics in Modern China: Writing and Feminism*. Durham, NC: Duke University Press, 1993.

——. *The Question of Women in Chinese Feminisms*. Durham, NC: Duke University Press, 2004.

Bays, Daniel H., and Ellen Widmer, eds. *China's Christian Colleges: Cross Cultural Connections, 1900–1950*. Stanford, CA: Stanford University Press, 2009.

Beebee, Thomas O., and Ikuho Amano. "Pseudotranslation in the Fiction of Auku-tugawa Ryūnosuke." *Translation Studies* 3, no. 1 (2010): 17–32.

Bei Dao. "The Rose of Time" [Shijian de meigui 時間的玫瑰], trans. Eliot Weinberger. *Almost Island* (Monsoon 2009), accessed February 10, 2022, https://static1.square space.com/static/612b5c38a84af13ad0a05fe2/t/619a6f961060bd48babf29b2/1637 511068336/poems.pdf.

"Beijing ge jie jinian san wei shijie wenhua mingren: Mao Dun jieshao Jialituosha, Hainie, Tuosituoyefusiji de shengping he zhuzuo" "北京各界纪念三位世界文化名人茅盾介绍迦梨陀裟，海涅，陀思妥也夫斯基的生平和著作 [All walks of life in Beijing commemorate three paragons of world culture: Mao Dun introduces the life and works of Kālidāsa, Heine and Dostoevsky]. *Renmin ribao*, May 27, 1956.

Benjamin, Walter. "The Task of the Translator" In *Walter Benjamin: Selected Writings Vol. 1 1913-1926*, ed. Marcus Bullock and Michael W. Jennings. Cambridge, MA: The Belknap Press of Harvard University Press, 1996.

Berk, Özlem Albachten, and Şehnaz Tahir Gürçağlar, eds. *Perspectives on Retranslation: Ideology, Paratexts, Methods*. London: Routledge, 2019.

Bernards, Brian. *Writing the South Seas: Imagining the Nanyang in Chinese and Southeast Asian Postcolonial Literature*. Seattle: University of Washington Press, 2015.

Bhabha, Homi K. *The Location of Culture*. London: Routledge, 1994.

"Bible Colportage: A Letter to the British and Foreign Bible Society." *The Chinese Recorder and Missionary Journal*, 1874.

Bing Xin. *Bing Xin san wen quan bian* 冰心散文全編 [Bing Xin's complete prose]. Hangzhou: Zhejiang wenyi chubanshe, 1995.

——. *Bing Xin shi quan bian* 冰心詩全編 [Bing Xin's complete poems]. Hangzhou: Zhejiang wenyi chubanshe, 1994.

Blue, Gregory. "Opium for China: The British Connection." In *Opium Regimes: China, Britain and Japan 1839-1952*, ed. Timothy Brook, Patrick Carr, and Maria Kefalas, 31–48. Berkeley: University of California Press, 2000.

Boehmer, Elleke. *Colonial and Postcolonial Literature*. Oxford: Oxford University Press, 1995.

——. *Empire, the National and the Postcolonial 1890-1920: Resistance in Interaction*. Oxford: Oxford University Press, 2002.

Bose, Sugata, and Kris Manjapra, eds. *Cosmopolitan Thought Zones: South Asia and the Global Circulation of Ideas*. Basingstoke, UK: Palgrave Macmillan, 2010.

Bosmia, Anand, et al. "Benjamin Hobson (1816–1873): His Work as a Medical Missionary and Influence on the Practice of Medicine and Knowledge of Anatomy in China and Japan." *Clinical Anatomy* 27 (2014): 154–161.

Bowden, Brett. *The Empire of Civilization: The Evolution of an Imperial Idea*. Chicago: University of Chicago Press, 2009.

Burton, Julianne. "Don (Juanito) Duck and the Imperial-Patriarchal Unconscious: Disney Studios, the Good Neighbor Policy, and the Packaging of Latin America." In *Nationalism and Sexualities*, ed. Andrew Parker, Mary Russo, Doris Sommer, and Patricia Yaeger, 21–41. New York: Routledge, 1992.

Button, Peter. *Configurations of the Real in Chinese Literary and Aesthetic Modernity*. Leiden: Brill, 2009.

Byron, George G. *The Island or Christian and his Comrades.* Canto 2, verse 17, 38. London: John Hunt, 1823.

Cai Xiang. *Revolution and Its Narratives: China's Socialist Literary and Cultural Imaginaries, 1949–1966,* trans. Rebecca E. Karl and Xueping Zhong. Durham, NC: Duke University Press, 2016.

Campbell, Lyle. "Why Sir William Jones Got it All Wrong, or Jones' Role in How to Establish Language Families." *Anuario del Seminario de Filología Vasca 'Julio de Urquijo'* 45 (2006): 245–264.

Cao Yin. *From Policemen to Revolutionaries: A Sikh Diaspora in Global Shanghai, 1885–1945.* Leiden: Brill, 2017.

Carey, Jane, and Ben Silverstein. "Thinking With and Beyond Settler Colonial Studies: New Histories After the Postcolonial." *Postcolonial Studies* 23, no. 1 (2020): 1–20.

Cavanagh, Edward, and Lorenzo Veracini, eds. *The Routledge Handbook of the History of Settler Colonialism.* London: Routledge, 2017.

Cayley, John. "Birds and Stars: Tagore's Influence on Bing Xin's Early Poetry." *Renditions* 32 (1989): 118–124.

Chakrabarty, Dipesh. "Legacies of Bandung: Decolonization and the Politics of Culture." *Economic and Political Weekly* 40, no. 46 (2005): 4812–4818.

Chan, Roy Bing. *The Edge of Knowing: Dreams, History and Realism in Modern Chinese Literature.* Seattle: University of Washington Press, 2017.

Chan Sin-wai. *Buddhism in Late Ch'ing Political Thought.* Hong Kong: The Chinese University Press, 1985.

Chatterjee, Partha. "Tagore, China, and the Critique of Nationalism." *Inter-Asia Cultural Studies* 12, no. 2 (2011): 271–283.

——. *Texts of Power: Emerging Disciplines in Colonial Bengal.* Minneapolis: University of Minnesota Press, 1995.

——. *The Nation and Its Fragments: Colonial and Postcolonial Histories.* New York: Oxford University Press, 1993.

Chatterji, Roma. "Scripting the Folk: History, Folklore, and the Imagination of Place in Bengal." *Annual Review of Anthropology* 45, no. 1 (2016): 377–394.

Chatterjee Miller, Manjari. *Wronged by Empire: Post-imperial Ideology and Foreign Policy in India and China.* Stanford, CA: Stanford University Press, 2013.

Chaturvedi, Namrata. "Introduction." In *Memory, Metaphor, and Mysticism in Kalidasa's* AbhijñānaŚākuntalam. London: Anthem Press, 2020.

Chen Duxiu. "Jin ri de jiaoyu fangzhen" 今日的教育方針 [Today's educational policy] *Xin Qingnian* 1, no. 2 (1915).

——. "Zan ge" 讚歌 [Song offerings]. *Xin Qingnian* 1, no. 2 (1915): 1–2.

Chen Jian. "The Tibetan Rebellion of 1959 and China's Changing Relations with India and the Soviet Union." *Journal of Cold War Studies* 8, no. 3 (2006): 80–89.

Chen, Kuan-Hsing. *Asia as Method: Toward Deimperialization.* Durham, NC: Duke University Press. 2010.

Chen Pingyuan. "Lun Su Manshu Xu Dishan xiaoshuo de zongjiao secai." 論蘇曼殊許地山的小說宗教色彩 [On the religious sensibility in the fiction of Su Manshu and Xu Dishan] *Zhongguo xiandai wenxue yanjiu congkan* 3 (1984): 1–26.

Chen Xiaomei. *Acting the Right Part: Political Theater and Popular Drama in Contemporary China*. Honolulu: Hawai'i University Press, 2002.

——, ed. *The Columbia Anthology of Modern Chinese Drama*. New York: Columbia University Press, 2014.

——. "Introduction." In *Reading the Right Text: Anthology of Contemporary Chinese Drama*. Honolulu: University of Hawai'i Press, 2003.

Chidester, David. *Empire of Religion: Imperialism and Comparative Religion*. Chicago: Chicago University Press, 2013.

Chin, Tamara. "The Afro-Asian Silk Road: Chinese Experiments in Postcolonial Premodernity." *PMLA* 136, no. 1 (January 2021): 17–38.

Chow, Rey. *The Age of the World Target: Self Referentiality in War, Theory and Comparative Work*. Durham, NC: Duke University Press, 2006.

——. *Woman and Chinese Modernity: The Politics of Reading Between East and West*. Minneapolis: University of Minnesota Press, 1991.

Chow Tse-tsung, *The May Fourth Movement: Intellectual Revolution in Modern China*. Stanford, CA: Stanford University Press, 1962.

Chrisman, Laura. "The Imperial Unconscious? Representations of Imperial Discourse." In *Colonial Discourse and Postcolonial Theory: A Reader,* ed. Patrick Williams and Laura Chrisman, 498–516. New York: Routledge, 1993.

Collins, Michael. *Empire, Nationalism and the Postcolonial World: Rabindranath Tagore's Writings on History, Politics and Society*. New York: Routledge, 2012.

Connell, Raewyn. *Southern Theory: The Global Dynamics of Knowledge in Social Sciences*. Cambridge: Polity, 2007.

Conroy-Krutz, Emily. *Christian Imperialism and American Foreign Missions*. Ithaca, NY: Cornell University Press, 2015.

Course bulletins with information on courses Xu Dishan offered in Folklore Studies at Yenching University, 1929–1932, Files: Yj 1929022; Yj 1930023; Yj 1931022, Yenching University Bulletins Archives, Beijing, China.

Crane, Frank. "The Works of Rabindranath Tagore." *New York Globe*, December 18, 1913.

Crosby, Christina. *The Ends of History: Victorians and the Woman Question*. New York: Routledge, 1991.

Culp, Amanda. "Searching for Shakuntala: Sanskrit Drama and Theatrical Modernity in Europe and India, 1789–Present." PhD dissertation, Columbia University, 2018.

Dados, Nour, and Raewyn Connell. "The Global South." *Contexts* 11, no. 1 (2012): 12–13.

Damrosch, David. *World Literature in Theory*. Malden MA: Wiley Blackwell, 2014.

Das, Sisir Kumar. "The Controversial Guest—Tagore in China." *China Report* 29, no. 3 (1993): 237–273.

Davis, Benjamin P., and Jason Walsh. "The Politics of Positionality: The Difference Between Post-, Anti-, and De-colonial Methods." *Culture, Theory and Critique* 61, no 4 (2020): 374–388.

Day, Lal Behari. *Folk-Tales of Bengal*. London: Macmillan, 1912.

——. *Govinda Samantha*. London: MacMillan, 1874.

——. "Preface." In *Bengal Peasant Life, Folk-Tales of Bengal, Recollections of My School Days*. Calcutta: Editions Indian, 1969.

Deb, Siddhartha. "The New Face of India is the Anti-Gandhian: The Violence, Insecurity, and Rage of Narendra Modi." *The New Republic*, May 3, 2016.

Deepak, B. R. "The Colonial Connections: Indian and Chinse Nationalists in Japan and China." *China Report* 48, no. 1–2 (2012): 147–170.

Denton, Kirk A., ed. *Modern Chinese Literary Thought: Writings on Literature 1893–1945*. Stanford, CA: Stanford University Press, 1996.

Diagne, Souleymane Bachir. *African Art as Philosophy: Senghor, Bergson and the Idea of Negritude*. London: Seagall Books, 2012.

——. *Islam and Open Society Fidelity and Movement in the Philosophy of Muhammad Iqbal*. Dakar, Senegal: Codersia, 2011.

Ding Fusheng, and Gu Yufeng. "Su Manshu xuanze yijie yindu wenxue de yuanyin" 蘇曼殊選擇譯介印度文學的原因 [On the reasons leading Su Manshu to translate and introduce Indian literature]. *Feitian* 16 (2011).

Ding Wenjiang. "Xuanxue yu kexue" 玄學與科學 [Metaphysics and Science]. In *Kexue yu renshengguan lunzhan Vol. 1*, ed. Hu Shi. Taipei, Taiwan: Wenxue chubanshe, 1977.

Dirlik, Arif. "Global South: Predicament and Promise." *The Global South* 1, no. 1–2 (2007): 12–23.

——. " 'Specters of the Third World': Global Modernity and the End of the Three Worlds." *Third World Quarterly* 25, no. 1 (2004): 131–149.

Dong, Madeleine Yue. *Republican Beijing: The City and Its Histories*. Berkeley: University of California Press, 2003.

Dong, Youchen et al., eds. *Taigeer zuopin quanji* 泰戈爾作品全集 [The collected works of Tagore]. Beijing: Renmin chubanshe, 2016.

Drinkwater, John. *The Outline of Literature*. London: G. Newnes, 1923.

Duara, Prasenjit. "Asia Redux: Conceptualizing a Region for Our Time." *The Journal of Asian Studies* 68, no. 4 (2010): 963–983.

——. "The Discourse of Civilization and Pan-Asianism." *Journal of World History* 12, no. 1 (2001): 99–130.

——. *Decolonization: Perspectives from Now and Then*. London: Routledge, 2004.

Dussel, Enrique. "Without Epistemic Decolonization, There Is No Revolution." *Venezuelan Analysis*. October 21, 2016. Accessed March 1, 2022, https://venezuelanalysis.com/analysis/12734.

Educational Review 8, no. 4 (October 1916).

Elisséeff, Serge. "Stael-Holstein's Contribution to Asiatic Studies." *Harvard Journal of Asiatic Studies* 3, no. 1 (1938): 1–8.

Elman, Benjamin A. "The China Prize Essay Contest and the Late Qing Promotion of Modern Science," 37. Prepared for the 7th Conference on "The New Significance of Chinese Culture in the 21st Century" held at National Taiwan University, December 28–31, 2003.

Errington, Joseph. "Colonial Linguistics." *Annual Review of Anthropology* 30 (2001): 19–39.

Fanon, Franz. *Black Skin, White Masks*. London: Pluto, 2008.

Feng Xinhua. "Su Manshu yu yindu wenhua" 蘇曼殊與印度文化 [Su Manshu and Indian culture]. *Huaihua xueyuan xuebao* 27, no. 8 (2008).

Feng Youlan. "Yu Yindu Taigeer Tanhua" 與印度泰戈爾談話 [Conversation with Tagore of India]. In *Wu si qian hou dong xi wenhua wenti lun zhan wen xuan*, ed. Chen Song. Beijing: Zhongguo shehui kexue chubanshe, 1989.

Fessenden, Tracy. *Culture and Redemption: Religion, the Secular and American Literature.* Princeton, NJ: Princeton University Press, 2006.

Figueira, Dorothy Matilda. *Translating the Orient: The Reception of* Sakuntala *in Nineteenth-Century Europe.* Albany: State University of New York Press, 1991.

Finot, Louis. "Kālidāsa in China." *The Indian Historical Quarterly* 9, no. 4 (December 1933): 829–833.

Fojas, Camilla. *Islands of Empire: Pop Culture and US Power.* Austin: University of Texas, 2014.

Fu Zonghong. "Xiaoshi xin lun" 小詩新論 [New comments on the short poem]. *Qinghai shifan daxue xuebao* 3 (1991): 108–113.

Gandhi, Leela. *Postcolonial Theory: A Critical Introduction.* Second Edition. New York: Columbia University Press, 2019.

Gange, David. *On Barak, On Time: Technology and Temporality in Modern Egypt.* Berkeley: University of California Press, 2013.

Gao, Jie. *Saving the Nation through Culture: The Folklore Movement in Republican China.* Vancouver: University of British Columbia Press, 2019.

Garver, John W. *Protracted Contest: Sino-Indian Rivalry in the Twentieth Century.* Seattle: University of Washington Press, 2001.

"General Characteristics of the Native Newspapers." *The Calcutta Christian Observer* 1, no. 4 (1832): 209.

Germana, Nicholas A. *The Orient of Europe: The Mythical Image of India and Competing Images of German National Identity.* New Castle, UK: Cambridge Scholars, 2009.

Gerow, Edwin. "Sanskrit Dramatic Theory and Kālidāsa's Plays." In *Theater of Memory: The Plays of Kālidāsa*, ed. Barbara Stoler Miller. New York: Columbia University Press, 1984.

Ghosh, Arunabh. "Before 1962: The Case for 1950s China-India History." *Journal of Asian Studies* 76, no. 3 (2017): 697–727.

——. "Why India & China See Any Border Breach As A 'Threat' to Identity." *The Quint,* June 20, 2020. Accessed January 28, 2021, https://www.thequint.com/voices/opinion/india-china-border-history-relationship-military-rise-of-ethno-nationalism-modi-govt-xi-jinping.

Gilbert, Helen, and Chris Tiffin. *Burden or Benefit? Imperial Benevolence and Its Legacies.* Bloomington: Indiana University Press, 2008.

Girardot, Norman J. *The Victorian Translation of China.* Berkeley: University of California Press, 2002.

Glosser, Susan. *Chinese Visions of Family and State, 1915-1953.* Berkeley: University of California Press, 2003.

Go, Julian. "Modeling States and Sovereignty: Postcolonial Constitutions in Asia and Africa." In *Making A World After Empire: The Bandung Moment and Its Political Afterlives,* ed. Christopher J. Lee, 107–143. Athens: Ohio University Press, 2010.

——. "Sociology's Imperial Unconscious: The Emergence of American Sociology in the Context of Empire." In *Sociology and Empire* ed. George Steinmetz, 83–105. Durham, NC: Duke University Press. 2016.

Goldman, Merle, ed. *Modern Chinese Literature in the May Fourth Era*. Cambridge, MA: Harvard University Press, 1977.

Greene, Thomas J. *Religion for a Secular Age: Max Müller, Swami Vivekananda and Vedānta*. Surrey, UK: Ashgate, 2016.

Guo Shuanglin. "Cong jindai bianyi kan xixue dong jian—yi xiang yi dili jiaoke shu wei zhongxin de kaocha" 從近代編譯看西學東漸——一項以地理教科書為中心的考察 [Examining the gradual Easternization of Western learning from the perspective of late Qing translation and editing: With a focus on geography textbooks]. In *Shijie zhixu yu wenming dengji: quanqiushi yanjiu de xin lujing*, ed. Liu He, 243–244. Beijing: Shenghuo, dushu, xinzhi sanlian shudian, 2016.

Gupta, Shishir. "Why is Sikh Soldier a Bogeyman for Chinese Army at Ladakh." *Hindustan Times*, September 17, 2020.

Gürçağlar, Şehnaz Tahir. "Pseudotranslation on the Margin of Fact and Fiction." In *A Companion to Translation Studies,* ed. Sandra Berman and Catherine Porter, 516–527. Chichester, UK: Wiley-Blackwell, 2014.

Gvili, Gal. "China-India Myths in Xu Dishan's 'Goddess of Supreme Essence.'" In *Beyond Pan-Asianism: Connecting China and India, 1840s-1960s,* ed. Tansen Sen and Brian Tsui, 67–93. New Delhi: Oxford University Press, 2021.

——. "Gender and Superstition in Modern Chinese Literature." *Religions* 10 (2019): 588.

Hall, Ian. *Modi and the Reinvention of Indian Foreign Policy*. Bristol, UK: Bristol University Press, 2019.

Hanan, Patrick. *Chinese Fiction of the Nineteenth and Early Twentieth Centuries*. New York: Columbia University Press, 2004.

——. "Missionary Novels of Nineteenth Century China." *Harvard Journal of Asiatic Studies* 60, no. 2 (2000): 413–443.

Hardacre, Helen. *Shintō and the State 1868-1988*. Princeton, NJ: Princeton University Press, 1989.

Hashimoto, Satoru. *Afterlives of Letters: The Transnational Origins of Modern Chinese, Japanese and Korean Literatures* (forthcoming).

Hay, Stephen N. *Asian Ideals of East and West: Tagore and His Critics in Japan, China, and India*. Cambridge, MA: Harvard University Press. 2013.

He Shuangqing. *Leaves of Prayer,* trans. Elsie Choy. Hong Kong: Chinese University Press, 2003.

Heinrich, Ari Larissa. *The Afterlife of Images: Translating the Pathological Body Between China and the West*. Durham, NC: Duke University Press, 2008.

Hevia, James. *English Lessons: The Pedagogy of Imperialism in Nineteenth Century China*. Durham, NC: Duke University Press, 2003.

Hill, Michael Gibbs. *Lin Shu, Inc.: Translation and the Making of Modern Chinese Culture*. Oxford: Oxford University Press, 2013.

Hofmeyr, Isabel. "Against the Global South." In *Global South and Literature*, ed. Russell West-Pavlov, 307–314. Cambridge: Cambridge University Press, 2018.

——. *The Portable Bunyan: A Transnational History of the Pilgrim's Progress.* Princeton, NJ: Princeton University Press, 2018.

Hon, Tze-ki. *Revolution as Restoration: Guocui xuebao and China's Path to Modernity, 1905-1911.* Leiden: Brill, 2013.

Hsia, Chih-Tsing. *A History of Modern Chinese Fiction.* New Haven, CT: Yale University Press, 1971.

Hu Xijin. Twitter Post, January 26, 2021, 8:16 a.m. Accessed February 7, 2021, https://twitter.com/HuXijin_GT/status/1354055650679033857.

Huang Yi. "Su Manshu yindu wenxue yi jie lun" 蘇曼殊印度文學譯結論 [On Su Manshu's translation and ntroduction of Indian Lilterature]. *Zhongguo bijiao wenxue* 中國比較文學 1, no. 66 (2007).

Huang Ying [A. Ying]. *Xiandai zhongguo nü zuojia* 現代中國女作家 [Women writers in modern China]. Shanghai: Beixin shuju chuban, 1931.

Hung, Chang-tai. *Going to the People: Chinese Intellectuals and Folk Literature, 1918-1937.* Cambridge, MA: Council on East Asian Studies, Harvard University, 1985.

Huters, Theodore. *Bringing the World Home: Appropriating the West in Late Qing and Early Republican China.* Honolulu: Hawai'i University Press, 2005.

Iovene, Paola. *Tales of Futures Past: Anticipation and the Ends of Literature in Contemporary China.* Stanford, CA: Stanford University Press, 2014.

Ip, Hung-yok. "Buddhism, Literature and Chinese Modernity: Su Manshu's Imaginings of Love (1911–1916)." In *Beyond the May Fourth Paradigm: In Search of Chinese Modernity,* ed. Kai-Wing Chow, Tze-ki Hon, Hung-Yok Ip, and Don C. Price. Plymouth, UK: Lexington Books, 2008.

Isaka, Riho. "Language and Dominance: The Debates over the Gujarati Language in the Late Nineteenth Century." *South Asia: Journal of South Asian Studies* 25, no. 1 (April 2002): 467–479.

Iser, Wolfgang. *The Act of Reading: A Theory of Aesthetic Response.* Baltimore: Johns Hopkins University Press, 1978.

Jhunjhunwala, Lakshmi Niwas. *The World Parliament of Religions, 1893.* Kolkata: Advaita Ashrama. 2010.

Ji Xianlin. "Deguo xuexi shenghuo huiyi" 德國學習生活回憶 [Memories of my student life in Germany]. In *Ji Xianlin quanji* [Collected works of Ji Xianlin]. Vol. 13, 406–407. Beijing: Waiyu jiaoxue yu yanjiu chubanshe, 2009.

——. *Guanyu baliwen fo bensheng gushi* 關於巴利文《佛本生故事》[On the Pāli Jataka]. *Shijie wenxue* 5 (1963): 61–77.

——. "Jinian yindu gudai weida de shiren jialituosuo." 紀念印度古代偉大的詩. *Renmin ribao,* May 26, 1956.

——. *Ji Xianlin quanji* [Collected works of Ji Xianlin], 30 vols. Beijing: Waiyu jiaoxue yu yanjiu chubanshe, 2009.

——. *Niupeng zaji* 牛棚雜憶 [Memories of the cowshed]. Beijing: Zhonggong zhongyang dang shi chubanshe, 2005.

——. "Tuhuoluoyu [Tocharian] de faxian yu kaoshi ji qi zai Zhong yin wenhua jiaoliu Zhong de zuoyong" 吐火羅語的發現與考釋及其在中印文化交流中的作用 [The discovery and philological study of Tocharian and its use in studying China-India exchange]. In *Ji Xianlin quanji* [Collected works of Ji Xianlin]. Vol. 13, 145–162. Beijing: Waiyu jiaoxue yu yanjiu chubanshe, 2009.

——. "Yindu wenxue zai Zhongguo" 印度文學在中國 [Indian literature in China]. In *Ji Xianlin quanji* [Collected works of Ji Xianlin]. Vol. 13. Beijing: Waiyu jiaoxue yu yanjiu chubanshe, 2009.

——. "Yindu wenxue zai Zhongguo" 印度文學在中國 [Indian literature in China]. In *Zhongguo xiju qiyuan* 中國戲劇起源 [The origins of Chinese drama] ed. Li Xiaobing et al., 188. Shanghai: Zhishi chubanshe, 1990.

——. *Tang shi* 糖史 [A history of sugar]. In *Ji Xianlin quanji* [Collected Works of Ji Xian-lin]. Vol. 13. Beijing: Waiyu jiaoxue yu yanjiu chubanshe, 2009.

Jiang, Chenxin. *The Cowshed: Memories of the Chinese Cultural Revolution.* New York: New York Review of Books, 2016.

Jiang, Jingkui, and Yan Jia. "The History of the Production of India-Related Knowl-edge in Post-1950 China." *History Compass* 16, no. 4 (2018): 1–12.

Jiang Kongyang. "Guanyu shehuizhuyi xianshizhuyi" 關於社會主義現實主義 [About Socialist Realism, 1958]. Translated and cited in Yang Lan, "'Socialist Realism versus 'Revolutionary Realism plus Revolutionary Romanticism.'" In *In the Party Spirit: Socialist Realism and Literary Practice in the Soviet Union, East Germany and China*, ed. Hilary Chung et al. (Amsterdam: Rodopi, 1996), 96.

Jiang Qian. "Translation and the Development of Science Fiction in Twentieth-Century China." *Science Fiction Studies* 40, no. 1 (2013).

Jin Kemu, trans. Bharata-muni "wulun" 舞論 [On Dance], Dandin, "Shi jing" 詩鏡 (Mirror of Poetry), Visvanatha "wen jing" 文鏡 (Mirror of literature) In *Gudian wenyi lilun congshu* 古典文藝理論叢書 no. 10. Beijing: Renmin chubanshe, 1965.

——. *Fanyu wenxue shi* 梵語文學史 [A history of Sanskrit literature]. Beijing: Renmin wenxue chubanshe, 1964.

Jones, Andrew F. *Developmental Fairy Tales: Evolutionary Thinking and Modern Chinese Cul-ture.* Cambridge, MA: Harvard University Press, 2011.

Jones, Donna V. *The Racial Discourse of Life Philosophy: Négritude, Vitalism and Modernity.* New York: Columbia University Press, 2010.

Jones, Sir William W. "Preface." In *Sacontala: or, The Fatal Ring.* London: Charleton Tucker, 1870.

——. "The Third Anniversary Discourse, Delivered February 2, 1786." *Asiatic Researches, or, Transactions of the Society Instituted in Bengal, for Inquiring into the His-tory and Antiquities, the Arts, Sciences, and Literature of Asia* 1 (1801): 422–423.

Joseph, Tony. *Early Indians: The Story of Our Ancestors and Where We Came From.* New Delhi: Juggernaut, 2018.

Josephson, Jason Ānanda. *The Invention of Religion in Japan.* Chicago: University of Chi-cago Press, 2012.

Kaplan, Amy. "Imperial Triangles: Mark Twain's Foreign Affairs." *Modern Fictions Studies* 43, no. 1 (1997): 237–248.

Karl, Rebecca E. "Creating Asia: China in the World at the Beginning of the Twenti-eth Century." *The American Historical Review* 103, no. 4 (1998): 1096–1118.

——. *Staging the World: Chinese Nationalism at the Turn of the Twentieth Century.* Durham, NC: Duke University Press, 2001.

Keane, Webb, *Christian Moderns: Freedom & Fetish in the Mission Encounter.* Berkeley: Uni-versity of California Press, 2004.

Kemple, Thomas M., and Renisa Mawani. "Global Public Life: The Sociological Imagination and its Imperial Shadows." *Theory, Culture & Society* 26, no. 7–8 (2009): 228–249.

Kern, Kathi. "Spiritual Border-Crossing in the US Women's Rights Movement." In *American Religious Liberalism*, ed. Leigh E. Schmidt and Sally M. Promey, 162–181. Bloomington: Indiana University Press, 2012.

Khan, Naveeda. *Muslim Becoming: Aspiration and Skepticism in Pakistan*. Durham, NC: Duke University Press, 2012.

Kieschnick, John, and Meir Shahar. *India in the Chinese Imagination: Myth, Religion and Thought*. Philadelphia: University of Pennsylvania Press, 2013.

King, Richard. *Milestones on a Golden Road: Writing for Chinese Socialism 1945–1980*. Vancouver: University of British Columbia Press, 2013.

——. *Orientalism and Religion*. New York: Routledge, 1999.

Ko, Dorothy. *Cinderella's Sisters: A Revisionist History of Footbinding*. Berkeley: University of California Press, 2005.

Kopf, David. *British Orientalism and the Bengal Renaissance: the Dynamics of Indian Modernization, 1773–1835*. Calcutta: Firma K. L. Mukhopadhyay, 1969.

Krämer, Hans Martin. "How 'Religion' Came To Be Translated as 'Shūkyō:' Shimaji Mokurai and the Appropriation of Religion in Early Meiji Japan." *Japan Review* 25 (2013): 89–111.

Kraus, Richard. "Let a Hundred Flowers Blossom, Let a Hundred Schools of Thought Contend." In *Words and Their Stories: Essays on the Language of the Chinese Revolution*, ed. Ban Wang, 249–253. Leiden: Brill, 2010.

Krishnan, Ananth. *The India China Newsletter* (blog). Accessed February 28, 2022, https://indiachina.substack.com.

Krishnaswamy, Revathi. "Nineteenth-Century Language Ideology: A Postcolonial Perspective." *Interventions* 7, no. 1 (2005): 43–71.

Krishnaswamy, Revathi, and John C. Hawley, eds. *The Postcolonial and the Global*. Minneapolis: University of Minnesota Press, 2008.

Lao She. *Luotuo xiangzi* 駱駝祥子 [Camel]. Beijing: Foreign Languages Press, 1997.

Lee, Christopher J. "Between a Moment and an Era: The Origins and Afterlives of Bandung." In *Making A World After Empire: The Bandung Moment and Its Political Afterlives*, ed. Christopher J. Lee, 1–44. Athens: Ohio University Press, 2010.

Lee, Haiyan. "Tears that Crumbled The Great Wall: The Archaeology of Feeling in the May Fourth Folklore Movement." *Journal of Asian Studies* 64, no. 1 (2005): 35–65.

——. *Revolution of the Heart: A Genealogy of Love in China, 1900–1950*. Stanford, CA: Stanford University Press, 2006.

Lee, Leo Ou-fan. *The Romantic Generation of Chinese Writers*. Cambridge, MA: Harvard University Press, 1973.

Legge, James. "Lesson 156." In *Graduated Reading: Comprising a Circle of Knowledge in 200 Lessons*. Hong Kong: London Missionary Society Press, 1864.

Leow, Rachel. "A Missing Peace: The Asia-Pacific Peace Conference in Beijing, 1952, and the Emotional Making of Third World Internationalism." *Journal of World History* 30, no. 1–2 (2019): 21–53.

——. *Taming Babel: Language in the Making of Malaya.* London: Cambridge University Press,

Levin, Michael. *J. S. Mill on Civilization and Barbarism.* New York: Routledge, 2004.

Liang Qichao. "Wen ye san jie zhi bie" 文野三節之別 [Distinctions between three groups of people from savage to civilized]. *Yinbingshi heji.* Vol. 2. Beijing: Zhonghua shuju, 1989.

Li Wei. *Weiwen shicao: Xiangei yingxiong de bianfangbudui* [Songs of Salutation: In dedication to the Hero Frontier Guards]. Chengdu: Chengdu junqu zhengzhibu wenhuabu yin, 1963.

——. "Zang bao zhiqian" 藏胞支前 [Tibetan brothers supporting the troops]. In *Weiwen shicao: Xiangei yingxiong de bianfangbudui* [Songs of salutation: In dedication to the Hero Frontier Guards]. Chengdu: Chengdu junqu zhengzhibu wenhuabu yin, 1963.

Li Xiaobing et al., eds. *Zhongguo xiju qiyuan* 中國戲劇起源 [The origins of Chinese drama]. Shanghai: Zhishi chubanshe, 1990.

Liang Qichao. "Lun fojiao yu qunzhi zhi guanxi" 論佛教與群治之關係 [On the relationship between Buddhism and the Government of the People]. In *Yinbing shi heji Vol. 2.* Beijing: Zhonghua shuju, 2003.

——. "Lun xiaoshuo yu qunzhi zhi guanxi" 論小說與群治之關係 [On the relationship between fiction and the Government of the People]. In *Yinbing shi heji Vol. 2.* Beijing: Zhonghua shuju, 2003.

——. "Yindu shiji yu fojiao zhi guanxi" 印度史跡與佛教之關係 [The connection between Indian relics and Buddhism]. In *Liang Qichao yu yindu wenhua, yindu wenxue* [Liang Qichao and Indian Culture and Literature], ed. Yu Kuizhan. *Wenhua wenxue* 1 (2003).

Lin, Xiaoqing Diana. "Creating Modern Metaphysics: Feng Youlan and Chinese Realism." *Modern China* 40, no. 1 (2014): 40–73.

Liu He. "Xuyan: quanqiu shi yanjiu de xin lujing" 序言：全球史研究的新路徑 [Introduction: A new direction in the study of global history]. In *Shijie zhixu yu wenming dengji: quanqiushi yanjiu de xin lujing* 世界秩序與文明等級 [World order and stages of civilization: A new direction in the study of global history]. Beijing: Shenghuo, dushu, xinzhi sanlian shudian, 2016.

Liu, Jane Qian. "The Making of Transcultural Lyricism in Su Manshu's Fiction." *Modern Chinese Literature and Culture* 28, no. 2 (2016): 43–89.

Liu Jianshu. "Zhongguo jieshou yindu fanju de lishi yanjiu: zhishi, sikao yu duihua, yi Shagongdaluo wei shijiao" 中國接受印度梵劇的歷史研究：知識，思考與對話以沙恭達羅為視角 [A study of the Chinese reception of Sanskrit drama: Knowledge, thought and dialog with a focus on Śakuntalā]. *Dongfang luntan* 4 (2017): 93–99.

Liu Lixia. "Guanyu hehe ben shengjing de chenggong fanyi ji qi dui zhongguo xin wenxue de yingxiang" 關於和合本聖經的成功翻譯及其對中國新文學的影響 [On the success of the Union Version translation and its impact on modern Chinese literature]. *Nanjing shifan daxue wenxueyuan xuebao* 3 (2005): 89–95.

Liu, Lydia H. *The Clash of Empires: The Invention of China in Modern World Making.* Cambridge, MA: Harvard University Press, 2005.

——. "The Gift of a Living Past." In *Ashis Nandy: A Life in Dissent*, ed. Ramin Jahanbegloo and Ananya Vajpeyi, 1–18. New Delhi: Oxford University Press, 2018.

——. "Life as Form: How Biomimesis Encountered Buddhism in Lu Xun." *Journal of Asian Studies* 68, no. 1 (2009): 21–54.

——. "Translingual Folklore and Folklorics in China." In *A Companion to Folklore*, ed. Regina F. Bendix and Galit Hasan-Rokem, 190–210. Malden, MA: Wiley Blackwell, 2012.

——. *Translingual Practice: Literature, National Culture, and Translated Modernity China, 1900-1937.* Stanford, CA: Stanford University Press, 1995.

Liu, Lydia H., Rebecca E. Karl, and Dorothy Ko. *The Birth of Chinese Feminism: Essential Texts in Transnational Theory.* New York: Columbia University Press, 2013.

Liu Xiaoqing. "Writing as Translating: Modern Chinese Women's Writing in the Early Twentieth Century." PhD dissertation. University of South Carolina, 2009.

Llamas, Regina. "Retribution, Revenge and the Ungrateful Scholar in Early Chinese Southern Drama." *Asia Major* 20, no. 2 (2007): 75–101.

Londré, Felicia Hardison. *World Theater: From the English Restoration to the Present.* New York: Continuum, 1999.

Lu Jin. *Xin shi de chuang zao yu jian shang* 新詩的創造與鑑賞 [On creation and appreciation of new poetry]. Chongqing: Chongqing chubanshe, 1982.

Lu Xun 魯迅. "Zai lun chongyi" 再論重譯 [On mediated translation, again]. *Shenbao ziyoutan* July 7, 1934.

——. *The New Year's Sacrifice* [*Zhu fu* 祝福]. In *The Complete Stories of Lu Xun*, trans. Yang Xianyi and Gladys Yang. Bloomington: Indiana University Press, 1981.

Macdonell, Arthur Anthony. *A History of Sanskrit Literature.* New York: D. Appleton, 1900.

Macy, John. *The Story of the World's Literature.* London: Peter Owen Limited, 1925.

Mahler, Anne Garland. *From the Tricontinental to the Global South: Race, Radicalism, and Transnational Solidarity.* Durham, NC: Duke University Press, 2018.

Majumdar, Jatindra Kumar. *Raja Rahmon Roy and Progressive Movements in India.* Calcutta: Art Press, 1941.

Malte-Brun, Conrad. *Universal Geography: Or A Description of All Parts of the World on A New Plan, Vol 1.* Philadelphia: Anthony Finley, 1827.

Mangalagiri, Adhira. "A Donkey Wisdom: Can Literature Help Us Respond to the China-India Border Clash?" *Economic & Political Weekly* 55, no. 34 (August 22, 2020). Accessed February 7, 2021, https://www.epw.in/journal/2020/34/commentary /donkeys-wisdom.html.

——. "Ellipses of Cultural Diplomacy: The 1957 Chinese Literary Sphere in Hindi." *Journal of World Literature* 4 (2019): 508–529.

——. "A Poetics of Writers' Conferences: Literary Relation in the Cold War World." *Comparative Literature Studies* 58, no. 3 (2021): 509–531.

——. "Slave of the Colonizer: The Indian Policeman in Chinese Literature." In *Beyond Pan-Asianism: Connecting China and India 1840s-1960s*, ed. Tansen Sen and Brian Tsui, 32–34. New Delhi: Oxford University Press. 2021.

——. *States of Disconnect: China-India Relation in the Twentieth Century.* Forthcoming by Columbia University Press.

Mani, B. Venkat. *Recoding World Literature: Libraries, Print Culture, and Germany's Pact with Books.* New York: Fordham University Press, 2017.

Mao Chen. "In and Out of Home: Bing Xin Recontextualized." In *Asian Literary Voices: From Marginal to Mainstream*, ed. Philip F. Williams. Amsterdam: Amsterdam University Press, 2010.

Mao Dun. "Bing Xin lun" 冰心論 [Comments on Bing Xin]. In *Bing Xin yanjiu ziliao* 冰心研究資料. Beijing: Beijing chubanshe, 1984.

——. *Chuncan* 春蠶 [Spring silkworms]. Beijing: Foreign Languages Press, 1956.

Masuzawa, Tomoko. *The Invention of World Religions: Or, How European Universalism Was Preserved in the Language of Pluralism*. Chicago: University of Chicago Press, 2005.

Maxey, Trent Elliott. *The "Greatest Problem": Religion and State Formation in Meiji Japan*. Cambridge, MA: Harvard University Asia Center, 2014.

McGetchin, Douglas T. *Indology, Indomania, and Orientalism: India's Rebirth in Modern Germany*. Madison, NJ: Fairleigh Dickinson University Press, 2009.

McGrath, Jason. "Cultural Revolution Model Opera Films and the Realist Tradition in Chinese Cinema." *The Opera Quarterly* 26, no. 2–3 (2010): 343–376.

McMahan, David L. *The Making of Buddhist Modernism*. New York: Oxford University Press, 2009.

Mignolo, Walter D. *The Darker Side of Western Modernity: Global Futures, Decolonial Options*. Durham, NC: Duke University Press, 2011.

Mignolo, Walter D., and Catherine E. Walsh. *On Decoloniality: Concepts, Analytics, Praxis*. Durham, NC: Duke University Press, 2018.

Mishra, Pankaj. *From the Ruins of Empire: The Revolt Against the West and the Remaking of Asia*. Harmondsworth, UK: Penguin, 2012.

Mohanty, Sharmistha. "Editorial Sutras." *Almost Island* (Monsoon 2009): 3.

Mokosso, Henry Efesoa. *American Evangelical Enterprise in Africa: The Case of the United Presbyterian Mission in Cameroon*. New York: Peter Lang Publishing, 2007.

Monier-Williams, Monier. *Sakoontala or the Lost Ring: An Indian Drama*. New York: Dodd, Mead and Company, 1885.

Mori Noriko, "Liang Qichao, Late-Qing Buddhism, and Modern Japan." In *The Role of Japan in Liang Qichao's Introduction of Modern Western Civilization to China*, ed. Joshua A. Fogel. Berkeley: University of California, 2004.

——. "Unfinished Revolution: A Paradox of Mourning Subjectivity in Su Manshu's *The Lone Swan*." *Frontiers of Literary Studies in China* 9, no. 1 (2015): 104–130.

Mosca, Matthew. *From Frontier Policy to Foreign Policy: The Question of India and the Transformation of Geopolitics in Qing China*. Stanford, CA: Stanford University Press, 2013.

Mu Mutian 穆木天. "Lun chongyi ji qita xia" 論重譯及其它(下) [On mediated translation and other matters, second part]. *Shenbao ziyoutan*, July 2, 1934.

Mufti, Aamir R. *Forget English! Orientalisms and World Literature*. Cambridge, MA: Harvard University Press, 2016.

Mukherjee, Meenakshi. "Mrs. Mullens and Mrs. Collins: Christianity's Gift to Indian Fiction." *The Journal of Commonwealth Literature* 16, no. 1 (1981): 65–75.

Müller, Max. *Introduction to the Science of Religion: Four Lectures Delivered at the Royal Institution in February and May 1870*. London: Longmans, Green, and Co., 1893.

——. *The Sacred Books of the East Vol 1: The Upanishads*. London: Routledge, 2013.

Muñiz, Iris Fernández. "Tracking Sources in Indirect Translation Archaeology: A Case Study on a 1917 Spanish Translation of Ibsen's *Et Dukkehjem* (1879)." In *New*

Horizons in Translation Research and Education, vol. 4, ed. T. Rautaoja et al., 115–132. Joensuu, Finland: University of Eastern Finland, 2016.

Murphy, Lawrence R. *The American University in Cairo: 1919-1987*. Cairo: American University in Cairo Press, 1987.

Murthy, Viren. *The Political Philosophy of Zhang Taiyan: The Resistance of Consciousness*. Leiden: Brill, 2011.

——. "Rethinking Pan-Asianism through Zhang Taiyan: India as Method." In *Beyond Pan-Asianism: Connecting China and India, 1840s-1960s*, ed. Tansen Sen and Brian Tsui, 94–128. New Delhi: Oxford University Press, 2021.

Naithani, Sadhana. "The Colonizer-Folklorist." *Journal of Folklore Research* 34, no. 1 (1997): 1–14.

——. *The Story-Time of the British Empire: Colonial and Postcolonial Folkloristics*. Jackson: University Press of Mississippi, 2010.

Nandy, Ashis. "Open Pasts, Open Futures," *Almost Island* (Monsoon 2009): 2. Accessed February 10, 2022, https://static1.squarespace.com/static/612b5c38a84af13ad 0a05fe2/t/6198e09d49dabd2b10dcf097/1637408925938/china.pdf.

Nedostup, Rebecca. *Superstitious Regimes: Religion and the Politics of Chinese Modernity*. Cambridge, MA: Harvard Asia Center: Harvard East Asian Monographs, 2009.

"New English and Chinese School Books." *The Chinese Recorder and Missionary Journal*, 1902.

Nielsen, Cynthia R. "Frantz Fanon and the Négritude Movement: How Strategic Essentialism Subverts Manichean Binaries." *Callaloo* 36, no. 2 (2013): 342–352.

"Notices of Recent Publications." *The Chinese Recorder and Missionary Journal*, 1875.

Numark, Mitch. "Translating Dharma: Scottish Missionary Orientalists and the Politics of Religious Understanding in Nineteenth Century Bombay." *Journal of Asian Studies* 70, no. 2 (2011): 471–500.

Okakura, Kakuzō. *The Ideals of the East: With Special Reference to the Art of Japan*, 2nd ed. New York: E. P. Dutton and Company, 1905.

Osterhammel, Jürgen. *The Transformation of the World: A Global History of the Nineteenth Century*. Princeton, NJ: Princeton University Press. 2014.

Ostler, Jeffrey, and Nancy Shoemaker. "Forum: Settler Colonialism in Early American History: Introduction," *William and Mary Quarterly* 76, no. 3 (2019): 361–368.

Ouyang Jianghe. "Huojin huayuan" 霍金花園 [Hopkins Garden], trans. Lucas Klein in *Almost Island* (Monsoon, 2019): 7.

Owen, Stephen, trans. *The Poetry of Du Fu*. Boston: De Gruyter, 2016.

——. "Omen of the World: Meaning in the Chinese Lyric." In *Chinese Aesthetics and Literature: A Reader*, ed. Corinne H. Dale, 78–79. Albany: State University of New York Press, 2004.

Pennington, Brian K. *Was Hinduism Invented? Britons, Indians, and the Colonial Construction of Religion*. New York: Oxford University Press, 2005.

Pollock, Sheldon, and Benjamin Elman. *What China and India Once Were: The Pasts That May Shape the Global Future*. New York: Columbia University Press, 2018.

Prashad, Vijay. *The Darker Nations: A People's History of the Third World*. New York: The New Press, 2008.

Qin, Amy. "Tagore Translation Deemed Racy is Pulled from Stores in China." *New York Times*, February 2, 2015.

Qu Qiubai, "Taigeer de guojia guannian yu dong fang" 泰戈爾的國家觀念與東方 [Tagore's view of the nation-state and the East]. In *Wu si qian hou dong xi wenhua wenti lun zhan wen xuan*, ed. Chen Song. Beijing: Zhongguo shehui kexue chubanshe, 1989.

Quijano, Aníbal. "Coloniality of Power, Eurocentrism and Latin America." *Nepantla: Views from South* 1, no. 3 (2000): 533–580.

Reich, David. *Who We Are and How We Got Here.* New York: Oxford University Press, 2018.

Renfrew, Colin. *Archaeology and Language: The Puzzle of Indo-European Origins.* Cambridge: Cambridge University Press, 1987.

"Review of Colportage in India During 1873; with Suggestions for Its Improvement." *The Chinese Recorder and Missionary Journal*, 1874.

Riedel, Bruce. *JFK's Forgotten Crisis: Tibet, the CIA, and the Sino-Indian War.* Washington, DC: Brookings Institution Press, 2015.

Rosa, Alexandra Assis, Hanna Pięta, and Rita Bueno Maia, eds. "Theoretical, Methodological and Terminological Issues Regarding Indirect Translation: An Overview." *Translation Studies* 10, no. 2 (2017).

Rule, Paul. "Goa-Macao-Beijing: The Jesuits and Portugal's China Connection." In *Vasco da Gama and the Linking of Europe and Asia*, ed. Anthony Disney and Emily Booth, 248–260. New Delhi: Oxford University Press, 2000.

Saaler, Sven, and Christopher W. A .Szpilman, eds. *Pan-Asianism: A Documentary History Volumes 1 and 2.* Lanham, MD: Rowman & Littlefield, 2011.

Said, Maire, and Edward Said, trans. "Philology and Weltliteratur by Erich Auerbach." *The Centennial Review* 13, no. 1 (1969).

Said, Edward. *Culture and Imperialism.* New York: Knopf, 1993.

Schleiermacher, Friedrich. "On the Different Methods of Translating." In *Theories of Translation: An Anthology of Essays from Dryden to Derrida*, ed. Rainer Schulte and John Biguenet, 36–54. Chicago: University of Chicago Press, 1992.

Schneider, Julia C. "A Non-Western Colonial Power? The Qing Empire in Postcolonial Discourse." *Journal of Asian History* 54, no. 2 (2020): 311–342.

Schwarcz, Vera. *The Chinese Enlightenment: Intellectuals and the Legacy of the May 4th Movement of 1919.* Berkeley: University of California Press, 1986.

Sen, Amartya. "Tagore and His India." In *The Argumentative Indian: Writings on Indian History, Culture and Identity.* London: Allen Lane, 2005.

Sen, Tansen. "The Belittling of Tagore by a Chinese Novelist." *Times of India*, January 22, 2016.

——. "China-India Studies: Emergence, Development, and State of the Field." *The Journal of Asian Studies* 80, no. 2 (2021): 363–387.

——. "The Impact of Zhen He's Expeditions on Indian Ocean Interactions." *Bulletin of the School of Oriental and African Studies* 79 no. 3 (2016): 609–636.

——. *India, China and the World: A Connected History.* Lanham, MD: Rowman & Littlefield, 2017.

——. "Introduction: Ji Xianlin and Sino-Indology." *China Report* 48, no. 1–2 (2012): 1–10.

Seth, Sanjay. "Nationalism, Modernity and the 'Woman Question' in India and China." *The Journal of Asian Studies* 72, no. 2 (2013): 273–297.

Sharf, Robert H. "The Zen of Japanese Nationalism." *History of Religion* 33, no. 1 (1993): 1–43.

——. *Coming to Terms with Chinese Buddhism*. Honolulu: University of Hawai'i Press, 2002.

Shen Yanbing. "Zuihou yiye" 最後一頁 [The final page]. *Xiaoshuo yuebao* 13, no. 2 (1922).

Shepard, William O. "Christianity and the New Orient." *Methodist Review*, September 1914.

Shih, Shu-Mei. *The Lure of the Modern: Writing Modernism in Semicolonial China, 1917–1937*. Berkeley: University of California Press, 2001.

Shoemaker, Nancy. "A Typology of Colonialism." *Perspectives on History* 57, no. 3 (October 2015): 2–15.

Singh, K. Natwar. *My China Diary 1956–88*. New Delhi: Rupa Publications, 2009.

Slater, David. "The Imperial Present and the Geopolitics of Power." *Geopolítica(s)* 1, no. 2 (2010): 191–205.

Smith, Craig A. "The Datong Schools and Late Qing Sino-Japanese Cooperation." *Twentieth-Century China* 42, no. 1 (2017): 3–25.

Song, Mingwei. *Young China: National Rejuvenation and the Bildungsroman, 1900–1959*. Cambridge, MA: Harvard University Asia Center, 2015.

Song Shaopeng. "Xi yang jing li de zhong guo nü xing" 西洋鏡裏的中國女性 [Chinese women in the Western mirror]. In *Shijie zhixu yu wenming dengji*, ed. Lydia H. Liu (Beijing: Sheng huo du shu xin zhi san lian shu dian, 2016), 309.

South Commission. *The Report of the South Commission: The Challenge to the South*. New York: Oxford University Press, 1990.

Spencer, Herbert. *Social Statics: The Conditions Essential to Human Happiness Specified, and the First of Them Developed*. New York: Robert Schalkenbach Foundation, 1954.

Spivak, Gayatri Chakravorty. "How do We Write, Now?" *PMLA* 133, no. 1 (2018): 166–170.

St. André, James. "Relay Translation." In *Routledge Encyclopedia of Translation Studies*, ed. Mona Baker and Gabriela Saldanha. New York: Routledge, 2019.

Stoler, Ann Laura. "Considerations on Imperial Comparisons." In *Empire Speaks Out: Languages of Rationalization and Self-Description in the Russian Empire*, ed. Ilya Gerasimov, Jan Kusber, and Alexander Semyonov, 33–55. Leiden: Brill, 2009.

——. *Haunted by Empire: Geographies of Intimacy in North American History*. Durham, NC: Duke University Press, 2006.

Stoler, Ann Laura, and Carole McGranahan. "Introduction: Refiguring Imperial Terrains." In *Imperial Formations* (School for Advanced Research Series), ed. Ann Laura Stoler, Carole McGranahan, and Peter C. Perdue. Oxford: James Currey, 2007.

Stoler Miller, Barbara, ed. *Theater of Memory: The Plays of Kālidāsa*. New York: Columbia University Press, 1984.

Su Manshu. "Fan wen dian zi xu" 《梵文典》自序; "Chu bu fan wen dian qishi" 《初步梵文典》啟事; "Fan wen dian qishi"《梵文典》啟事. In *Su Manshu wenji Vol. 1*, ed. Ma Yijun, 257–265. Guangzhou: Hua cheng chubanshe, 1991.

——. "Suoluo haibin dunji ji" 婆羅海濱遁跡記 [A record of seclusion on Sal Beach]. In *Su Manshu wenji*. Vol. 2, ed. Ma Yinzhu. Guangzhou: Hua cheng chubanshe, 1991.

——. "Xiaoshuo conghua" 小說叢話 [Notes on fiction] in *Xin xiaoshuo* 1, no. 11 (1904).

Sun Mei. "Zhongguo xiqu yuan yu yindu fanju shuo zai tantao" 中國戲曲源於印度梵劇説在探討 [Renewed discussion of the theory that Chinese drama originated in Sanskrit drama]. *Wenxue yichan* 2 (2006): 75–83.

Sun Yinxue. *Taigeer yu Zhongguo* 泰戈爾與中國 [Tagore and China]. Guilin: Guangxi shifan daxue chubanshe, 2005.

Tageldin, Shaden. *Disarming Words: Empire and the Seduction of Translation in Egypt.* Berkeley: University of California Press, 2011.

Tagore, Rabindranath. *Chitra.* New York: Macmillan, 1914.

——. *Creative Unity.* London: Macmillan, 1922.

——. *The Essential Tagore*, ed. Fakrul Alam and Radha Chakravarty. Cambridge, MA: Belknap Press, 2011.

——. *Gitanjali* [Song offerings]. London: Macmillan, 1913.

——. *Nationalism/Rabindranath Tagore & Manabendranath Roy.* Kolkata: Renaissance, 2004.

——. *Personality.* London: Macmillan, 1917.

——. "Shiren de zongjiao" [The poet's religion], trans. Yu Zhi. *Xiaoshuo yuebao* 9, no. 14 (1923): 2–3.

——. *Talks in China: Lectures Delivered in April and May 1924.* Calcutta: Visva Bharati, 1925.

Thampi, Madhavi. "Indian Soldiers, Policemen and Watchmen in China in the Nineteenth and Early Twentieth Centuries." *China Report* 35, no. 4 (1999): 404–408.

Thapar, Romila. Śakuntalā: *Texts, Readings, Histories.* New Delhi: Kali for Women, 2010.

Thiong'o, Ngũgĩ wa. *Decolonising the Mind: The Politics of Language in African Literature.* London: J. Currey, 1986.

Thornber, Karen. "Breaking Discipline, Integrating Literature: Africa-China Relationships Reconsidered." *Comparative Literature Studies* 53, no. 4 (2016): 694–721.

——. *Empire of Texts in Motion: Chinese, Korean and Taiwanese Transculturations of Japanese Literature.* Cambridge, MA: Harvard Asia Center, 2009.

Tihanov, Galin. *The Birth and Death of Literary Theory: Regimes of Relevance in Russia and Beyond.* Stanford, CA: Stanford University Press, 2019.

Toury, Gideon. "A Lesson from Indirect Translation." In *Descriptive Translation Studies and Beyond,* revised edition, 161–178. Amsterdam: John Benjamins, 1995.

——. *Descriptive Translation Studies and Beyond: Revised Edition.* Amsterdam: John Benjamins, 2012.

Towns, Ann. *Women and States: Norms and Hierarchies in International Societies.* Cambridge: Cambridge University Press, 2010.

Trautmann, Thomas R. *Aryans and British India.* Berkeley: University of California Press, 1997.

Tsu, Jing. "Getting Ideas About World Literature in China." *Comparative Literature Studies* 47, no. 3 (2010): 290–317.

——. *Failure, Nationalism and Literature: The Making of Modern Chinese Identity 1895-1937.* Stanford, CA: Stanford University Press, 2005.

Tsui, Brian. "Frugal Modernity: Livelihood and Consumption in Republican China." *Journal of Asian Studies* 74, no. 2 (2015): 391–409.

——. "When Culture Meets State Diplomacy: The Case of Cheena Bhavana." In *Beyond Pan-Asianism: Connecting China and India, 1840s-1960s,* ed. Tansen Sen and Brian Tsui, 236–255. New Delhi: Oxford University Press, 2021.

——. *China's Conservative Revolution: The Quest for a New Order, 1927-1949.* Cambridge: Cambridge University Press. 2018.

Tuck, Eve, and K. Wayne Yang. "Decolonization is Not a Metaphor." *Decolonization: Indigeneity, Education & Society* 1, no. 1 (2012): 1–40.

van der Veer, Peter. "Spirituality in Modern Society." *Social Research* 76, no. 4 (2009): 1097–1120.

——. *The Modern Spirit of Asia: The Spiritual and the Secular in China and India.* Princeton, NJ: Princeton University Press, 2014.

Van Fleit, Krista. *Literature the People Love: Reading Chinese Texts from the Early Maoist Period (1949-1966).* London: Palgrave Macmillan, 2013.

——. "'The Law Has No Conscience:' The Cultural Construction of Justice and the Reception of Awara in China." *Asian Cinema* 24, no. 2 (2013): 141–159.

Vanacker, Beatrijs and Tom Toremans. "Pseudotranslation and Metafictionality." *Interférences littéraires* 19 (2016): 23–38.

Vanhove, Pieter. "'A World to Win:' China, the Afro-Asian Writers' Bureau, and the Reinvention of World Literature." *Critical Asian Studies* 51, no. 2 (2019): 144–165.

Venuti, Lawrence. *The Translator's Invisibility: A History of Translation.* New York: Routledge, 2008.

Viswanathan, Gauri. *Masks of Conquest: Literary Study & British Rule in India.* New York: Columbia University Press, 2015.

Volland, Nicolai. *Socialist Cosmopolitanism: The Chinese Literary Universe 1945-1965.* New York: Columbia University Press, 2017.

Wagner, Rudolph G. "China and India Pre-1939." In *Routledge Handbook of China-India Relations,* ed. Kanti Bajpai et al., 47–48. New York: Taylor and Francis, 2020.

Wan Shigo, and Liu He, eds. *Tianyi heng bao* 天義衡報 [Natural justice, equity]. Vol. 1. Beijing: Zhongguo renmin daxue chubanshe, 2016.

Wang Benchao. "Shengjing yu zhongguo xiandai wenxue de wenti jiangou" 聖經與中國現代文學的文體建構 [The Bible and modern Chinese literature's stylistic development]. *Guizhou shehui wenxue* 1 (2001): 49–56.

Wang Guowei. "Song Yuan xiqu shi," chaps. 1 and 16. Accessed November 25, 2021, https://ctext.org/wiki.pl?if=gb&res=228945&remap=gb.

Wang Tongzhao. "Taigeer de sixiang yu qi shige de biaoxiang" 泰戈爾的思想與其詩歌的表象 [The thought and poetics of Tagore] *Xiaoshuo yuebao* 14, no. 9 (1923).

Wang Xiangyuan. *Fanxin foying: Zhongguo zuojia yu yindu wenhua* 梵心佛影：中國作家與印度文化 [The noble mind and the shadow of Buddha: Chinese writers and Indian culture]. Beijing: Beijing shifan daxue chubanshe, 2007.

Wang Xianming, and Shu Wen. "Jindai Zhongguoren dui Lusuo de jieshi" 近代中國人對盧梭 的解釋 [Modern Chinese understandings of Rousseau]. *Jindaishi yanjiu* 2 (1995): 16–22.

Wanguo gongbao 萬國公報 [A review of the times] 77, (1895): 66.

Washbourne, Kelly. "Nonlinear Narratives: Paths of Indirect and Relay Translation." *Meta* 58, no. 3 (2013): 607–625.

West China Missionary News (1908). Chunking: West China Missions Advisory Board.

West China Missionary News 9, no. 7 (1907). Chunking: West China Missions Advisory Board.

West-Pavlov, Russell. "Toward the Global South: Concept or Chimera, Paradigm or Panacea?" *Global South and Literature.* Cambridge: Cambridge University Press, 2018.

West, Philip. *Yenching University and Sino-Western Relations.* Cambridge, MA: Harvard University Press, 1976.

Weston, Timothy. *The Power of Position: Beijing University, Intellectuals, and Chinese Political Culture.* Berkeley: University of California Press, 2004.

Wilcox, Emily. "Performing Bandung: China's Dance Diplomacy with India, Indonesia, and Burma, 1953–1962." *Intra-Asian Cultural Studies* 18, no. 4 (2017): 518–539.

Williams, John R. *The Buddha in the Machine: Art, Technology and the Meeting of East and West.* New Haven, CT: Yale University Press, 2014.

Williams, Samuel Wells. *The Middle Kingdom: A Survey of the Chinese Empire and Its Inhabitants.* New York: J. Wiley, 1861.

Wilson, A. Leslie. *A Mythical Image: The Idea of India in German Romanticism.* Durham, NC: Duke University Press, 1964.

Wolfe, Patrick. "Settler Colonialism and the Elimination of the Native." *Journal of Genocide Research* 8, no. 4 (2006): 387–409.

Wolfgang von Goethe, Johann. *Conversations of Goethe with Johann Peter Eckermann,* trans. John Oxenford. Boston: Da-Capo Press, 1998.

Wong, Lawrence Wang-chi. "Lions and Tigers in Groups: The Crescent Moon School in Modern Chinese Literary History." In *Literary Societies of Republican China,* ed. Kirk A. Denton and Michel Hockx, 279–312. Lanham, MD: Lexington Books, 2008.

Wright, Richard. *The Color Curtain: A Report on the Bandung Conference.* Mississippi: University of Mississippi-Jackson, 1956.

Wu Shengqing. *Modern Archaics: Continuity and Innovation in the Chinese Lyric Tradition.* Cambridge, MA: Harvard University Asia Center, 2013.

Wu Xue. Shagongdaluo 沙恭達羅. *Renmin huabao* 7 (1957): 20–22.

Xi Liu. "Kang Youwei's Journey to India: Chinese Discourse on India During the Late Qing and Republican Periods." *China Report* 48, no. 1–2 (2012): 171–185.

——. "The Merchant's Wife," trans. William Nienhauser. In *Columbia Anthology of Modern Chinese Literature,* ed. Howard Goldblatt and Joseph Lau. New York: Columbia University Press, 1995.

Xu Dishan. "Bu po yi de lao fu ren" 補破衣的老婦人 [The old lady mending clothes]. In *Kong shan ling yu: Xu Dishan suibi.* Beijing: Beijing daxue chubanshe, 2006.

——. "Fanju tili ji qi zai hanju shang de diandian didi" 梵劇體例及其在漢劇上的點點滴滴 [The stylistic rules of Sanskrit drama and their gradual diffusion into Chinese drama]. *Xiaoshuo yuebao* 17 (1927): 1–36.

——. *Fuji mixin di yanjiu* 扶箕迷信底研究 [A study of spirit writing superstition]. Taipei, Taiwan: Shangwu yinshuguan, 1945 [1941].

——. "Jin sanbai nian lai Yindu wenxue gaiguan" 近三百年來印度文學概觀 [A general survey of Indian literature of the last three hundred years]. *Tianjin yi shi bao* 12, (1929).

——. *Mengjiala minjian gushi* 孟加拉民間故事 [Folk-tales of Bengal]. Shanghai: Shangwu yinshu guan, 1929.

——. *San wen jingdian quanji* 散文精典全集 [Completed collection of prose]. Jilin: Shidai wenyi chubanshe, 2003.

——. "Yuguan" 玉官. In *Modern Chinese Stories and Novellas, 1919-1949*, trans. Cecile Chu-chin Sun, ed. C. T. Hsia, Leo Ou-fan Lee, and Joseph S. M. Lau. New York: Columbia University Press, 1981.

——. "Shang ren fu" 商人婦 [The merchant's wife] in *Xu Dishan ling yi xiao shuo* 許地山靈異小說. Shanghai: Shanghai wenyi chubanshe, 1996.

——. "A Study of Certain Chinese Texts relating to Manichaeism," Master's thesis, Columbia University, 1924.

——. *Yindu wenxue* 印度文學 [Indian literature]. Beijing: Shangwu yinshuguan, 1930.

——. "Zhongguo wenxue suo shou de Yindu Yilan wenxue de yingxiang" 中國文學所受的印度義蘭文學的影響 [On the impact of Indian and Persian literatures on Chinese literature]. *Xiaoshuo yuebao* 16, no. 7 (1925).

——. "Zongjiao de shengzhang yu miewang" 宗教的生長與滅亡 [The rise and fall of religions]. *Dongfang zazhi* 19, no. 10 (1922): 27–42.

Xu Zhimo 徐志摩. "Art and Life." In *Xu Zhimo quanji bu bian* 徐志摩全集補編 [The complete works of Xu Zhimo supplemented]. Xianggang: Shangwu yinshuguan, 1993.

——. "Tai shan ri chu" 泰山日出 [Sunrise over Mount Tai]. *Xiaoshuo yuebao* 14, no. 9 (1923): 1–2.

Xu Zhuzhen. "Wo souji mixin minge hou de yidian ganxiang" 我搜集迷信民歌後的一點感想 [My thoughts after collecting superstitious folksongs]. *Geyao zhoukan* 34 (1924): 2.

Xue Keqiao. "Xu Dishan de xue shu cheng jiu yu yindu wenhua de lianxi" 許地山的學術成就與印度文化的聯繫 [The relation between Indian culture and Xu Dishan's scholarly achievements]. *Wen shi zhe*, no. 4 (2003).

——. *Zhongguo yu nanya wenhua jiaoliu zhi* 中國與南亞文化交流志 [Cultural Exchanges between China and South Asia]. Beijing: Zhongguo da baikequanshu chubanshe, 2018.

Yan Jia. "Cultural Bandung or Writerly Cold War? Revisiting the 1956 Asian Writers' Conference from an India-China Perspective." In *The Cultural Cold War and the Global South: Sites of Contest and Communitas*, ed. Kerry Bystrom. New York: Routledge, 2021.

——. "Trans-popular Aesthetics: the Reception of Hindi Popular Fiction in 1980s China." *Journal of World Literature* 4 (2019): 530–551.

Yang Jianlong. *Kuangye de husheng: Zhongguo xiandai zuojia yu jidujiao wenhua* 曠野的呼聲：中國現代作家與基督教文化 [A Cry in the Wilderness: Modern Chinese Writers and Christian Culture]. Shanghai: Shanghai jiaoyu chubanshe, 1998.

Yang Lan. "'Socialist Realism' versus 'Revolutionary Realism plus Revolutionary Romanticism.'" In *The Party Spirit: Socialist Realism and Literary Practice in the Soviet Union, East Germany and China*, ed. Hilary Chung et al. Atlanta: Rodopi, 1996.

Yang Mengya. "Taigeer fanghua yu ershi jishi zhongguo wentan." 泰戈爾訪華與二十幾中國文壇 [Tagore's visit to China and the Chinese Literary Circle in the 1920s]. *Zhongzhou xuekan* 154, no. 4 (2006): 212–216.

Yao Dadui. *Xiandai de xiansheng: wan qing hanyu jidujiao wenxue* 現代的先聲：晚清漢語基督教文學 [The harbinger of modernity: Late Qing Chinese Christian literature]. Guangzhou: Zhongshan daxue chubanshe, 2016.

Yao Yuanmei. "Nanya guancha: Yindu bianjieguan ji 'lang wai po' zuofa" 南亞觀察：印度邊界觀及'狼外婆'做法 [South-Asia survey: India's concept of borders and the practice of 'The Wolf in Sheep's Skin'], *Pengpai xinwen*, October 7, 2020, accessed February 11 2022, https://www.thepaper.cn/newsDetail_forward_9458212; and https://www.hindustantimes.com/india-news/why-is-sikh-soldier-a-bogeyman-for-chinese-army-at-ladakh/story-4FuLsEa991pKKEuafxmKcL.html.

"Yazhou dianyingzhou zai Beijing deng di jieshu: ge guo dianying daibiao guankan 'Shagongdaluo'" 亞洲電影周'在北京等地結束 各國電影代表觀看'沙恭達羅' [Asia Film Week has concluded in Beijing and elsewhere: Delegates of all countries watched *Shagongdaluo*] *Renmin ribao*, August 9, 1957.

Yeats, W. B. "Introduction." In *Gitanjali*. London: Macmillan, 1912.

Yeh, Catherine Vance. *The Chinese Political Novel: Migration of a World Genre*. Cambridge, MA: Harvard University Asia Center, 2015.

Ying, Lei. "Lu Xun, the Critical Buddhist: A Monstrous Ekayāna." *The Journal of Chinese Literature and Culture* 3, no. 2 (2016): 400–428.

Yoon, Duncan M. "Bandung Nostalgia and the Global South." In *Global South and Literature*, ed. Russel West-Pavlov, 23–33. Cambridge: Cambridge University Press, 2018.

——. "'Our Forces Have Redoubled:' World Literature Postcolonialism, and the Afro-Asian Writers' Bureau." *Cambridge Journal of Postcolonial Literary Inquiry* 2, no. 2 (2015): 233–252.

Young, Robert J. C. *Postcolonialism: An Historical Introduction*. Oxford: Blackwell, 2001.

Yu, Shiao-ling. "Politics and Theater in the PRC: Fifty Years of Teahouse on the Chinese Stage." *Asian Theater Journal* 30, no. 1 (2013): 90–121.

Yuan Hongming. "Bianzuan 'yeman shenghuo shi' zhengqiu tonggong de xiaoxi" 編纂野蠻生活史 [Information regarding soliciting skilled collaborators for the compilation of a history of barbarian life]. *Minsu* 1, no. 3 (1932): 28.

Zachs, Fruma. "Toward a Proto-Nationalist Concept of Syria? Revisiting the American Presbyterian Missionaries in the Nineteenth-Century Levant." *Die Welt des Islams* 41, no. 2 (2001): 145–173.

Zeng Pu. *Nie hai hua* 孽海花 [A flower in the sea of retribution]. Shanghai: Zhen mei shan shudian, 1941.

Zeng Qiong. "Tagore's Influence on the Chinese Writer Bing Xin." In *Tagore and China*, ed. Tan Chung, Amiya Dev, Wang Bangwei, and Wei Liming, 255–272. New Delhi: Sage Publications India. 2011.

Zetzsche, Jost Oliver. *The Bible in China: The History of the Union Version or the Culmination of Protestant Missionary Bible Translation in China*. London: Routledge, 1999.

Zhang Guanglin. *Zhongguo mingjia lun Taigeer* 中國名家論泰戈爾 [Famous Chinese writers on Tagore]. Beijing: Zhongguo uaqiao chubanshe, 1994.

Zhang Fuji. "Shagongdaluo" pailian chang shang de yi duan duihua" "沙恭達羅" 排練場上的一段對話 [A conversation during the stage rehearsals of Śakuntalā] *Renmin ribao*, May 13, 1957.

Zhang Ke. "Through the 'Indian Lens:' Observations and Self-Reflections in Late Qing Chinese Travel Writing on India." In *Beyond Pan-Asianism: Connecting China and*

India, 1840s-1960, ed. Tansen Sen and Brian Tsui, 131–154. New Delhi: Oxford University Press. 2021.

Zheng Zhenduo 鄭振鐸. *Chatuben zhongguo wenxue shi* 插圖本中國文學史 [An illustrated history of Chinese literature]. Beijing: Wenxue guji kan xing she, 1959.

——. "Huanying Taigeer" 歡迎泰戈爾. [Welcome Tagore]. *Xiaoshuo yuebao* 4, no. 9 (1923).

——. "Wenxue dagang" 文學大綱. [Outline of literature]. In *Zheng Zhenduo quan ji* 鄭振鐸全集 [Collected works of Zheng Zhenduo]. Shijiazhangshi: Hua shan wenyi chubanshe, 1998.

——. "Xiwen de qilai" 西文的起來 [The Rise of Western Culture]. In *Zhongguo xiju qiyuan* 中國戲劇起源 [The origins of Chinese drama], ed. Li Xiaobing et al., 123. Shanghai: Zhishi chubanshe, 1990.

Zhong Yurou. *Chinese Grammatology: Script Revolution and Literary Modernity 1916-1958.* New York: Columbia University Press, 2019.

Zhou Huaizong, "Feng Tang chong yi Taigeer shi ji bei ping shi dui Taigeer de 'xiedu'" 馮唐重譯泰戈爾詩集被評是對泰戈爾的褻瀆 [Feng Tang's retranslation of Tagore criticized as "blasphemy"]. *Beijing chenbao*, November 25, 2015.

Zhou Yang. "Wenxue de zhenshixing" 文學的真實性 [The truthfulness of literature], 1933.

Zhou Zuoren 周作人. "Ren de wenxue" 人的文學 [Literature of humans]. *Xin Qingnian* 5, no. 6 (1918): 575–584.

——. "Zhong guo minge de jiazhi" 中國民歌的價值 [The value of Chinese folksongs]. *Geyao zhoukan* 4, no. 6 (1923).

Index

Aandhiyan (Indian film, 1952), 130
Achebe, Chinua, 2
Africa, 11, 36, 125, 128, 173n52
Afro-Asian alliance movement, 7, 174n53
Afro-Asian Writers' Bureau, 207
allegory, 51
Allen, Young J., 35–36, 99, 181n49
Almost Island (journal), 164
Amano, Ikuho, 185n84
Amrith, Sunil, 178n8
Anagol, Padma, 36
anarchism, 8, 19, 39; Chinese anarchists in Tokyo, 43; Rousseau as influence on, 54
anatomy, 30, 31, 32
Anderson, Marston, 198n61
anthropology, 28, 103, 105
anti-imperialism, 2, 3, 10, 43–44, 60
Anti-Rightist Campaign [Fan you yundong] (1957–1959), 149
Apter, Emily, 17
Arabic language, 14, 95, 98
"Art and Life" (Xu, 1923), 191n47
Aryan migration theory, 57, 58, 186n97
Asia, 128, 173n52; discourse of redemptive Asia, 11; as "mother of

spiritual humanity," 10; as remedy for Western spiritual bankruptcy, 10
"Asianness" episteme, 20, 62, 173n50, 192n69
Asian Writers Conference (Tashkent, 1958), 131
Asia Solidarity Society (Yazhou heqin hui), 43–44, 48, 184n66, 190n35
Asiatic Society, 15, 134
Assamese language, 13, 131
Avestan language, 104
Awara (Indian film, 1951), 130, 131
Aydin, Cemil, 62

Bai Juyi, 151
Bain, Francis William, 194n5
Bai Shan, 154, 155
Ba Jin, 195n14
Baker, Charles, 180n28
Bandung Conference (1955), 7, 128, 190n35
"Baugmaree" (Dutt), 45
Bay of Bengal, 26
Beebee, Thomas O., 185n84
Bei Dao, 158, 165
Belgium, 15
Bellamy, Edward, 30